Holt California Mathematics

Course 1
Know-It Notebook™

HOLT, RINEHART AND WINSTON

A Harcourt Education Company

Orlando • **Austin** • New York • San Diego • London

ISBN-13: 978-0-03-094532-8
ISBN-10: 0-03-094532-1

7 8 9 10 1421 12 11 10
4500235591

Contents

iii

Holt Mathematics

Holt Mathematics

USING THE *KNOW-IT NOTEBOOK*™

This *Know-It Notebook* will help you take notes, organize your thinking, and study for quizzes and tests. There are *Know-It Notes*™ pages for every lesson in your textbook. These notes will help you identify important mathematical information that you will need later. Then at the end of every chapter, a fun *Foldnotes* activity will help you remember key terms.

Know-It Notes

Lesson Objectives

A good note-taking practice is to know the objective the content covers.

Vocabulary

Another good note-taking practice is to keep a list of the new vocabulary.

- Use the page references or the glossary in your textbook to find each definition.
- Write each definition on the lines provided.

Additional Examples

Your textbook includes examples for each math concept taught. Additional examples in the *Know-It Notebook* help you take notes so you remember how to solve different types of problems.

- Take notes as your teacher discusses each example.
- Write notes in the blank boxes to help you remember key concepts.
- Write final answers in the shaded boxes.

Check It Out!

Complete the Check It Out! problems that follow some lessons. Use these to make sure you understand the math concepts covered in the lesson.

- Write each answer in the space provided.
- Check your answers with your teacher or another student.
- Ask your teacher to help you understand any problem that you answered incorrectly.

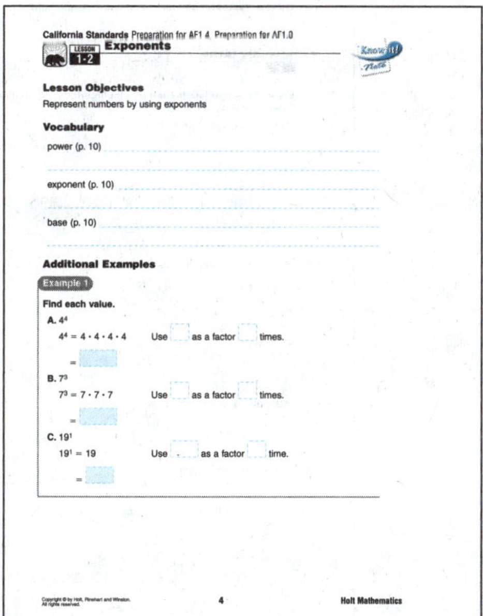

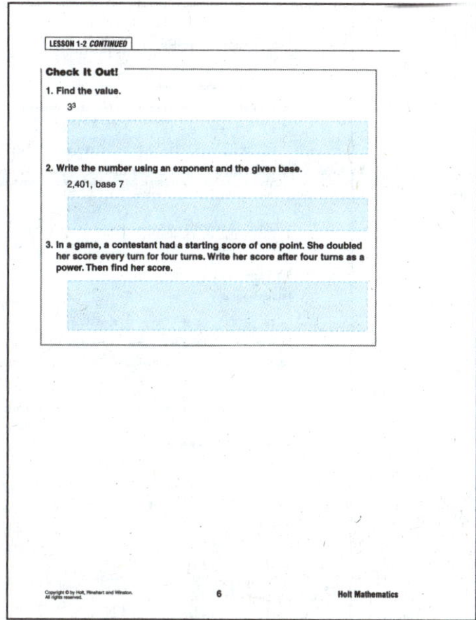

v

Holt Mathematics

Chapter Review

Complete Chapter Review problems that follow each chapter. This is a good review before you take the chapter test.

- Write each answer in the space provided.
- Check your answers with your teacher or another student.
- Ask your teacher to help you understand any problem that you answered incorrectly.

Big Ideas

The Big Ideas have you summarize the important chapter concepts in your own words. You must think about and understand ideas to put them in your own words. This will also help you remember them.

- Write each answer in the space provided.
- Check your answers with your teacher or another student.
- Ask your teacher to help you understand any question that you answered incorrectly.

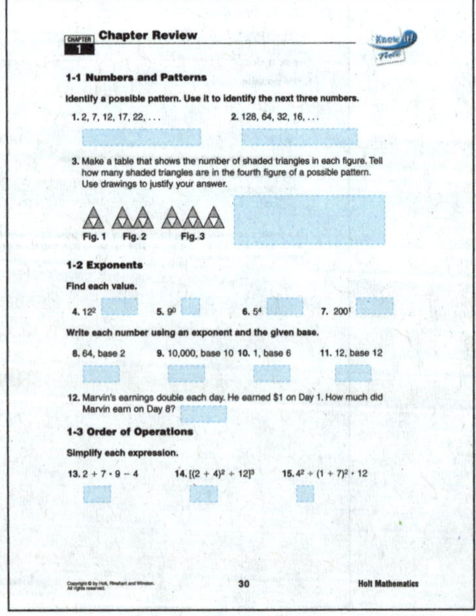

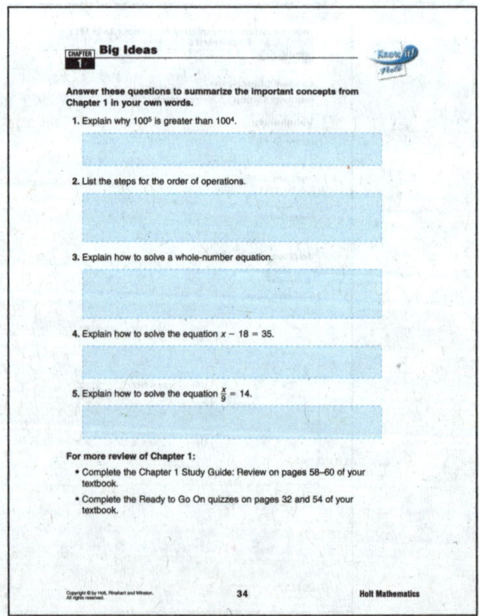

Holt Mathematics

NOTE TAKING STRATEGIES

Taking good notes is very important in many of your classes and will be even more important when you take college classes. This notebook was designed to help you get started. Here are some other steps that can help you take good notes.

Getting Ready

1. Use a loose-leaf notebook. You can add pages to this where and when you want to. It will help keep you organized.

During the Lecture

2. If you are taking notes during a lecture, write the big ideas. Use abbreviations to save time. Do not worry about spelling or writing every word. Use headings to show changes in the topics discussed. Use numbering or bullets to organize supporting ideas under each topic heading. Leave space before each new heading so that you can fill in more information later.

After the Lecture

3. As soon as possible after the lecture, read through your notes and add any information that will help you understand them when you review later. You should also summarize the information into key words or key phrases. This will help your comprehension and will help you process the information. These key words and key phrases will be your memory cues when you are reviewing for or taking a test. At this time you may also want to write questions to help clarify the meaning of the ideas and facts.

4. Read your notes out loud. As you do this, state the ideas in your own words and do as much as you can by memory. This will help you remember and will also help with your thinking process. This activity will help you understand the information.

5. Reflect upon the information you have learned. Ask yourself how new information relates to information you already know. Ask how this relates to your personal experience. Ask how you can apply this information and why it is important.

Before the Test

6. Review your notes. Don't wait until the night before the test to review. Do frequent reviews. Don't just read through your notes. Put the information in your notes into your own words. If you do this you will be able to connect the new material with material you already know, and you will be better prepared for tests. You will have less test anxiety and better recall.

7. Summarize your notes. This should be in your own words and should only include the main points you need to remember. This will help you internalize the information.

Holt Mathematics

Numbers and Patterns

LESSON 1-1

Lesson Objectives

Identify and extend patterns

Additional Examples

Example 1

Identify a possible pattern. Use it to write the next three numbers.

A. 3, 12, 48, ▪, ▪, ▪, . . .

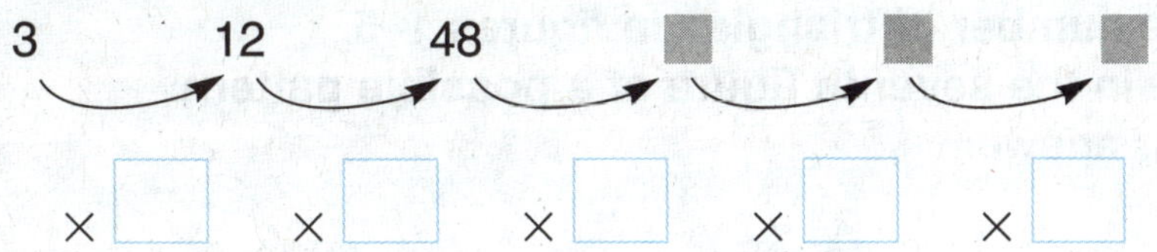

A pattern is to   to get to the next number.

$48 \times 4 =$ $192 \times 4 =$ $768 \times 4 =$

The next three numbers will be   .

B. 7, 12, 17, ▪, ▪, ▪, . . .

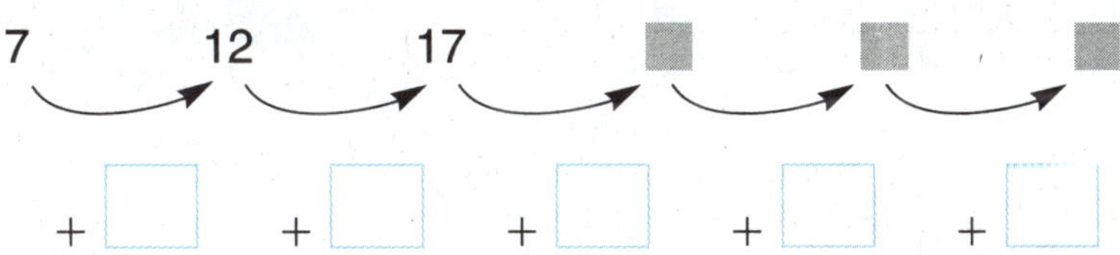

A pattern is to   to get to the next number.

$17 + 5 =$ $22 + 5 =$ $27 + 5 =$

The next three numbers will be   .

Holt Mathematics

Example 2

Identify a possible pattern. Use it to draw the next three figures.

The pattern is

The next three figures will be

Example 3

Make a table that shows the number of triangles in figures 1–5.
Tell how many triangles are in the seventh figure of a possible pattern.
Use drawings to justify your answer.

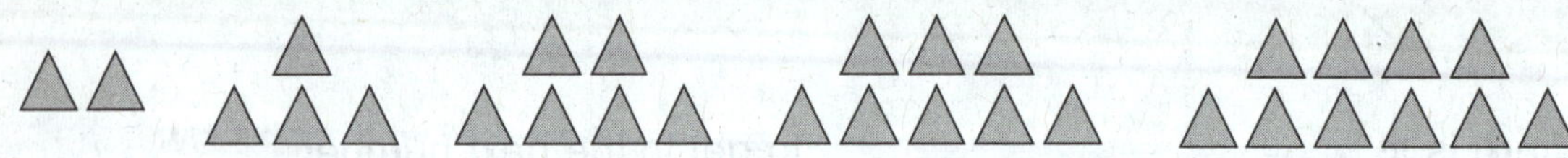

Figure 1   Figure 2   Figure 3   Figure 4   Figure 5

Make a table that shows the number of triangles in each figure.

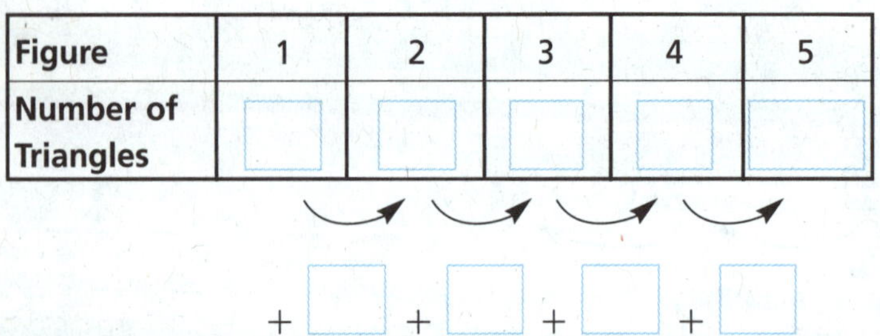

Figure	1	2	3	4	5
Number of Triangles					

$+ \square + \square + \square + \square$

The pattern is to $\square$ triangles each time.

Figure 6 has $10 + 2 = \square$ triangles.   Figure 7 has $12 + 2 = \square$ triangles.

Figure 6   Figure 7

Figure 7 will have $\square$ triangles.

2

Holt Mathematics

Check It Out!

1. Identify a possible pattern. Use it to write the next three numbers.

45, 41, 37, ▉, ▉, ▉, . . .

2. Identify a possible pattern. Use it to draw the next three figures.

3. Make a table that shows the number of squares in figures 1–5. Tell how many squares are in the seventh figure of a possible pattern. Use drawings to justify your answer.

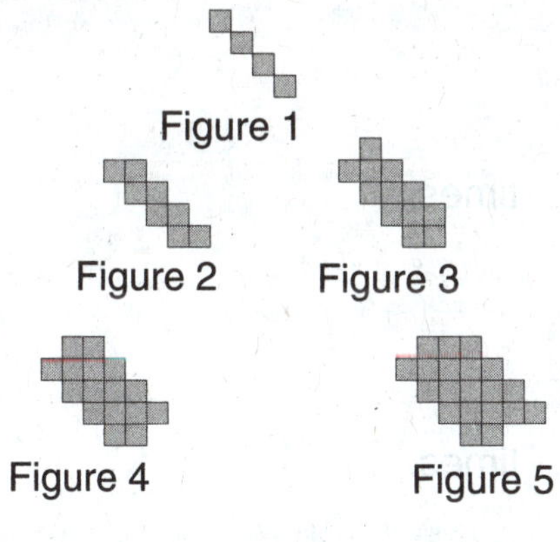

Figure 1

Figure 2   Figure 3

Figure 4   Figure 5

Holt Mathematics

Exponents

LESSON 1-2

Lesson Objectives

Represent numbers by using exponents

Vocabulary

power (p. 10) _______________________________

exponent (p. 10) _______________________________

base (p. 10) _______________________________

Additional Examples

Example 1

Find each value.

A. 4^4

$\quad 4^4 = 4 \cdot 4 \cdot 4 \cdot 4$  Use ☐ as a factor ☐ times.

$\quad = $ ☐

B. 7^3

$\quad 7^3 = 7 \cdot 7 \cdot 7$  Use ☐ as a factor ☐ times.

$\quad = $ ☐

C. 19^1

$\quad 19^1 = 19$ Use ☐ as a factor ☐ time.

$\quad = $ ☐

Holt Mathematics

Example 2

Write each number using an exponent and the given base.

A. 625, base 5

$625 = 5 \cdot 5 \cdot 5 \cdot 5$ ☐ is used as a factor ☐ times.

= ☐

B. 64, base 2

$64 = 2 \cdot 2 \cdot 2 \cdot 2 \cdot 2 \cdot 2$ ☐ is used as a factor ☐ times.

= ☐

Example 3

On Monday, Erik tells 3 people a secret. The next day each of them tells 3 more people. If this pattern continues, how many people will learn the secret on Friday?

On Monday, ☐ people know the secret.

On Tuesday, ☐ times as many people learned as those who learned it on Monday.

On Wednesday, ☐ times as many people learned as those who learned it on Tuesday.

On Thursday, ☐ times as many people learned as those who learned it on Wednesday.

On Friday, 3 times as many people learned as those who learned it on

☐.

Each day the number of people is ☐ times greater.

$3 \cdot 3 \cdot 3 \cdot 3 \cdot 3 =$ ☐ = ☐

On Friday, ☐ people will learn the secret.

5

Holt Mathematics

Check It Out!

1. Find the value.

3^3

2. Write the number using an exponent and the given base.

2,401, base 7

3. In a game, a contestant had a starting score of one point. She doubled her score every turn for four turns. Write her score after four turns as a power. Then find her score.

Holt Mathematics

LESSON 1-3
Order of Operations

Lesson Objectives

Use the order of operations to simplify numerical expressions

Vocabulary

numerical expression (p. 14) _______________________________

____

order of operations (p. 14) _______________________________

____

____

Additional Examples

Example 1

Simplify each expression. Use the order of operations to justify your work.

A. $3 + 15 \div 5$

$3 + 15 \div 5$ Divide.

$3 + \boxed{}$ Add.

B. $44 - 14 \div 2 \cdot 4 + 6$

$44 - 14 \div 2 \cdot 4 + 6$ $\boxed{}$ and $\boxed{}$ from left to right.

$44 - \boxed{} \cdot 4 + 6$

$44 - \boxed{} + 6$ $\boxed{}$ and $\boxed{}$ from left to right.

$\boxed{} + 6$

Holt Mathematics

Example 2

Simplify each expression.

A. $42 - (3 \cdot 4) \div 6$

$42 - (3 \cdot 4) \div 6$ Perform the operation inside the ______.

$42 - \boxed{} \div 6$ Divide.

$42 - \boxed{}$ Subtract.

$\boxed{}$

B. $[(26 - 4 \cdot 5) + 6]^2$

$[(26 - 4 \cdot 5) + 6]^2$ The parentheses are inside the brackets, so perform the operations inside the ______ first.

$[(26 - \boxed{}) + 6]^2$

$[\boxed{} + \boxed{}]^2$

$\boxed{}^2$

$\boxed{}$

Example 3

Sandy runs 4 miles per day. She ran 5 days during the first week of the month. She ran only 3 days each week for the next 3 weeks. Simplify the expression $(5 + 3 \cdot 3) \cdot 4$ to find how many miles she ran last month.

$(5 + 3 \cdot 3) \cdot 4$ Perform the operations inside the ______ first.

$(5 + \boxed{}) \cdot 4$ Add.

$\boxed{} \cdot 4$ Multiply.

$\boxed{}$

Sandy ran $\boxed{}$ miles last month.

Holt Mathematics

Check It Out!

1. Simplify the expression. Use the order of operations to justify your work.

   $2 + 3^2 \cdot 4$

2. Simplify the expression.

   $[(32 - 4 \cdot 4) + 2]^2$

3. Jill is learning vocabulary words for a test. On the first day, she learned 30 words. She is learning 4 new words a day for 3 days each week. Evaluate the expression $3 \cdot 4 \cdot 7 + 30$ to find out how many words she will know at the end of seven weeks.

Holt Mathematics

Properties of Numbers

LESSON 1-4

Lesson Objectives

Identify properties of numbers and use them to simplify numerical expressions

Vocabulary

Commutative Property (p. 20) _______________________________

____

Associative Property (p. 20) _______________________________

____

Identity Property (p. 20) _________________________________

____

Distributive Property (p. 21) ______________________________

____

Additional Examples

Example 1

Tell which property is represented.

A. $(2 \cdot 6) \cdot 1 = 2 \cdot (6 \cdot 1)$

$(2 \cdot 6) \cdot 1 = 2 \cdot (6 \cdot 1)$ The numbers are ____________.

B. $3 + 0 = 3$

$3 + 0 = 3$ One of the addends is ____.

C. $7 + 9 = 9 + 7$

$7 + 9 = 9 + 7$ The order of the variables is ____________.

Holt Mathematics

Example 2

Simplify each expression. Justify each step.

A. $21 + 16 + 9$

$21 + 16 + 9 = \boxed{} + 9 + \boxed{}$ $\boxed{}$ Property

$ = 16 + (9 + 21)$ $\boxed{}$ Property

$ = 16 + \boxed{}$ Add.

$ = \boxed{}$

B. $20 \cdot 9 \cdot 5$

$20 \cdot 9 \cdot 5 = 20 \cdot \boxed{} \cdot \boxed{}$ $\boxed{}$ Property

$ = 20 \cdot (5 \cdot 9)$ $\boxed{}$ Property

$ = 20 \cdot \boxed{}$ Multiply.

$ = \boxed{}$

Example 3

Use the Distributive Property to find 6(54).

Method 1: $6(54) = 6(\boxed{} + \boxed{})$ Rewrite 54 as $\boxed{} + \boxed{}$.

$ = (6 \cdot \boxed{}) + (6 \cdot \boxed{})$ Use the $\boxed{}$ Property.

$ = \boxed{} + \boxed{}$ Multiply.

$ = \boxed{}$ Add.

Holt Mathematics

Use the Distributive Property to find 6(54).

Method 2: 6(54) = 6(☐ − ☐)   Rewrite 54 as ☐ − ☐.

= (6 · ☐) − (6 · ☐)   Use the ☐
Property.

= ☐ − ☐   Multiply.

= ☐   Subtract.

Check It Out!

1. Tell which property is represented.

(5 · 1) · 2 = 5 · (1 · 2)

2. Simplify the expression.

17 + 14 + 3

3. Use the Distributive Property to find 8(19).

Holt Mathematics

Evaluating Algebraic Expressions

LESSON 1-5

Lesson Objectives

Evaluate algebraic expressions

Vocabulary

variable (p. 24) ______________________________________

constant (p. 24) ______________________________________

algebraic expression (p. 24) ______________________________________

evaluate (p. 24) ______________________________________

Additional Examples

Example 1

The expression $b + 9$ represents Chad's age when his brother is b years old. Evaluate the expression for each value of b, and then tell what the value of the expression means.

A. $b = 5$ $b \quad + 9$

☐ $+ 9$ Substitute ☐ for b.

☐   Add.

When his brother is ☐, Chad is ☐.

B. $b = 2$ $b \quad + 9$

☐ $+ 9$ Substitute ☐ for b.

☐   Add.

When his brother is ☐, Chad is ☐.

Holt Mathematics

Example 2

Evaluate each expression for the given value of the variable.

A. $4x - 3$ for $x = 2$

$4(\boxed{}) - 3$ Substitute $\boxed{}$ for x.

        Multiply.

$\boxed{} - 3$ Subtract.

$\boxed{}$

B. $s \div 5 + s$, for $s = 15$

$\boxed{} \div 5 + \boxed{}$ Substitute 15 for $\boxed{}$.

        Divide.

$\boxed{} + 15$ Add.

$\boxed{}$

Example 3

Evaluate $\dfrac{6}{a} + 4b - c$, for $a = 3$, $b = 2$, and $c = 7$.

$\dfrac{6}{a} + 4b - c$

$\boxed{} + 4(\boxed{}) - \boxed{}$ Substitute $\boxed{}$ for a, $\boxed{}$ for b, and $\boxed{}$ for c.

     Divide and multiply from $\boxed{}$ to $\boxed{}$.

$\boxed{} + \boxed{} - \boxed{}$ Add and subtract from $\boxed{}$ to $\boxed{}$.

$\boxed{}$

Holt Mathematics

Check It Out!

1. The expression $y + 7$ represents Sidney's age when her brother is y years old. Evaluate the expression for each value of y, and then tell what the value of the expression means.

    $y = 8$

2. Evaluate the expression for the given value of the variable.

    $4y^2 + 2y$ for $y = 3$

3. Evaluate $\dfrac{8}{w} - x + 2z$ for $w = 2$, $x = 3$, and $z = 4$.

Holt Mathematics

Writing Algebraic Expressions

LESSON 1-6

Lesson Objectives

Translate words into numbers, variables, and operations

Additional Examples

Example 1

Write each phrase as an algebraic expression.

A. the quotient of a number and 4

quotient means "[   ]"

[   ]

B. w increased by 5

increased by means "[   ]"

[   ]

C. the difference of 3 times a number and 7

difference of means "[   ]"

times means "[   ]"

[   ] · [   ] − 7

[   ]

D. the quotient of 4 and a number, increased by 10

$$\frac{[\ \ ]}{n} + [\ \ ]$$

[   ]

Holt Mathematics

Example 2

A. Mr. Campbell drives at 55 mi/h. Write an expression for how far he can drive in h hours. Then evaluate the expression for $h = 3$, and tell what the value of the expression means.

You need to put [ ] parts together. This involves multiplication.

55mi/h $\cdot$ h hours = [ ]   Write the expression.

55 $\cdot$ [ ]   Substitute 3 for h.

[ ]   Multiply.

Mr. Campbell can drive [ ] miles in [ ] hours if he drives at 55 miles per hour.

B. On a test, multiple-choice questions are worth 1 point, short-answer questions are worth 2 points, and essay questions are worth 10 points. Write an algebraic expression for Maritza's total points if she answers m multiple-choice, s short-answer, and e essay questions correctly. Then evaluate the expression for $m = 48$, $s = 8$, and $e = 3$, and tell what the expression means.

Multiply to put [ ] parts together:

Points for multiple-choice questions: [ ]

Points for short-answer questions: [ ]

Points for essay questions: [ ]

Total points: [ ]   Write the expression.

[ ] + [ ] + [ ]   Substitute 48 for m, 8 for s, and 3 for e.

[ ] + [ ] + [ ]   Multiply from left to right.

[ ]   Add.

Maritza earned [ ] points on the test.

Holt Mathematics

Check It Out!

1. Write the phrase as an algebraic expression.

4 times the difference of y and 8

2. Julie Ann works on an assembly line building computers. She can assemble 8 units an hour. Write an expression for the number of units she can produce in h hours. Then evaluate the expression for $h = 5$, and tell what the value of the expression means.

Holt Mathematics

LESSON 1-7 — Equations and Their Solutions

Lesson Objectives

Determine whether a number is a solution of an equation

Vocabulary

equation (p. 34) ____

____

solution (p. 34) ____

____

Additional Examples

Example 1

Determine whether the given value of each variable is a solution.

A. $b - 447 = 1{,}203$ for $b = 1{,}650$

$$b - 447 = 1{,}203$$

$$1{,}650 - 447 \overset{?}{=} 1{,}203 \qquad \boxed{}\; 1{,}650 \text{ for } b.$$

$$1{,}203 \overset{?}{=} 1{,}203 \qquad \boxed{}.$$

Because $\boxed{} = \boxed{}$,

$1{,}650$ is a solution to $b - 447 = 1{,}203$.

B. $27x = 1{,}485$ for $x = 54$

$$27x = 1{,}485$$

$$27 \cdot 54 \overset{?}{=} 1{,}485 \qquad \boxed{}\; 54 \text{ for } x.$$

$$1{,}458 \overset{?}{=} 1{,}485 \qquad \boxed{}.$$

Because $\boxed{} \neq \boxed{}$,

54 is not a solution to $27x = 1{,}485$.

Holt Mathematics

Example 2

Paulo says that the park is 19 yards long. Jamie says that the park is 664 inches long. Determine if these two measurements are equal.

One yard has 36 inches.

$36 \cdot y = i$

$36 \cdot y = 664$ Substitute [ ] for i.

$36 \cdot 19 \overset{?}{=} 664$ Substitute [ ] for y.

$684 \overset{?}{=} 664$ [ ].

Because [ ] $\neq$ [ ], 19 yards is not equal to 664 inches.

Check It Out!

1. Determine whether the given value of the variable is a solution.

$u + 56 = 139$ for $u = 73$

2. Anna says that the table is 7 feet long. John says that the table is 84 inches long. Determine if these two measurements are equal.

Holt Mathematics

LESSON 1-8 Solving Equations by Subtracting

Lesson Objectives

Solve whole-number equations by subtracting

Vocabulary

inverse operations (p. 40) ____

____

Additional Examples

Example 1

Solve each equation. Check your answers.

A. $x + 87 = 152$

$x + 87 = 152$ 87 is added to x.

$\underline{-87 \quad -87}$ [   ] 87 from both sides to

undo the [   ].

$x \quad = $ [   ]

Check $x + 87 = 152$

$65 + 87 \overset{?}{=} 152$ Substitute [   ] for x in the equation.

$152 \overset{?}{=} 152 \checkmark$ [   ] is the solution.

B. $72 = 18 + y$

$72 = \quad 18 + y$ 18 is added to y.

$\underline{-18 \quad -18}$ [   ] 18 from both sides to

undo the [   ].

[   ] $= \quad y$

Check $72 = 18 + y$

$72 \overset{?}{=} 18 + 54$ Substitute [   ] for y in the equation.

$72 \overset{?}{=} 72 \checkmark$ [   ] is the solution.

Holt Mathematics

Example 2

Johnstown, Cooperstown, and Springfield are located in that order in a straight line along a highway. It is 12 miles from Johnstown to Cooperstown and 95 miles from Johnstown to Springfield. Find the distance *d* between Cooperstown and Springfield.

distance between Johnstown and Springfield		distance between Johnstown and Cooperstown		distance between Cooperstown and Springfield
95	=	12	+	d

$$95 = 12 + d \qquad \text{12 is added to } d.$$

$$-12 \quad -12 \qquad \boxed{} \text{ 12 from both sides to undo}$$

$$\text{the } \boxed{}.$$

$$\boxed{} = d$$

It is $\boxed{}$ miles from Cooperstown to Springfield.

Check It Out!

1. Solve the equation. Check your answer.

$$u + 43 = 78$$

2. Patterson, Jacobsville, and East Valley are located in that order in a straight line along a highway. It is 17 miles from Patterson to Jacobsville and 35 miles from Patterson to East Valley. Find the distance *d* between Jacobsville and East Valley.

Holt Mathematics

Solving Equations by Adding

LESSON 1-9

Lesson Objectives

Solve whole-number equations by adding

Additional Examples

Example 1

Solve each equation. Check your answer.

A. $y - 23 = 39$

$$y - 23 = \quad 39 \qquad \text{23 is subtracted from } y.$$

$$+\ 23 \quad +\ 23 \qquad \boxed{}\ \text{23 to both sides to undo the}$$

$$\boxed{}.$$

$$y \quad = \boxed{}$$

Check $y - 23 = 39$

$$62 - 23 \overset{?}{=} 39 \qquad \text{Substitute } \boxed{} \text{ for } y \text{ in the equation.}$$

$$39 \overset{?}{=} 39\ \checkmark \qquad \boxed{} \text{ is the solution.}$$

B. $78 = s - 15$

$$78 = s - 15 \qquad \text{15 is subtracted from } s.$$

$$+\ 15 \qquad +\ 15 \qquad \boxed{}\ \text{15 to both sides to undo the}$$

$$\boxed{}.$$

$$\boxed{} = s$$

Check $78 = s - 15$

$$78 \overset{?}{=} 93 - 15 \qquad \text{Substitute } \boxed{} \text{ for } s \text{ in the equation.}$$

$$78 \overset{?}{=} 78\ \checkmark \qquad \boxed{} \text{ is the solution.}$$

Holt Mathematics

Solve the equation. Check your answer.

C. $z - 3 = 12$

$z - 3 = 12$ 3 is subtracted from z.

$\underline{+\ 3} \quad \underline{+\ 3}$ [ ] 3 to both sides to undo the

[ ].

$z \quad = \quad$ [ ]

Check $z - 3 = 12$

$15 - 3 \stackrel{?}{=} 12$ Substitute [ ] for z in the equation.

$12 \stackrel{?}{=} 12$ ✓   [ ] is the solution.

Check It Out!

1. Solve the equation. Check your answer.

$57 = c - 13$

Holt Mathematics

LESSON 1-10 Solving Equations by Dividing

Lesson Objectives

Solve whole-number equations by dividing

Additional Examples

Example 1

Solve each equation. Check your answers.

A. $5p = 75$

$5p = 75$ *p* is multiplied by 5.

$\dfrac{5p}{5} = \dfrac{75}{5}$ [____] both sides by 5 to undo the

[________].

$p =$ [____]

Check $5p = 75$

$5(15) \stackrel{?}{=} 75$ Substitute [____] for *p* in the equation.

$75 \stackrel{?}{=} 75 \checkmark$ [____] is the solution.

B. $16 = 8r$

$16 = 8r$ *r* is multiplied by 8.

$\dfrac{16}{8} = \dfrac{8r}{8}$ [____] both sides by 8 to undo the

[________].

[____] $= r$

Check $16 = 8r$

$16 \stackrel{?}{=} 8(2)$ Substitute [____] for *r* in the equation.

$16 \stackrel{?}{=} 16 \checkmark$ [____] is the solution.

Holt Mathematics

Example 2

PROBLEM SOLVING APPLICATION

The area of a rectangle is 56 square inches. Its length is 8 inches. What is its width?

1. Understand the Problem

The answer will be the ______ of the rectangle in inches.

List the important information:

- The area of the rectangle is ______ square inches.

- The length of the rectangle is ______ inches.

Draw a diagram to represent this information.

2. Make a Plan

You can write and solve an equation using the formula for area. To find the area of a rectangle, multiply its length by its width.

$$A = lw$$
$$56 = 8w$$

w

l

3. Solve

$56 = 8w$ w is multiplied by 8.

$$\frac{56}{8} = \frac{8w}{8}$$ ______ both sides by 8 to undo the

______ .

______ $= w$

So the width of the rectangle is ______ inches.

Holt Mathematics

4. Look Back

Arrange 56 identical squares in a rectangle. The length is 8, so line up the squares in rows of 8. You can make 7 rows of 8, so the width of the rectangle is 7.

Check It Out!

1. Solve the equation. Check your answer.

$8a = 72$

2. The area of a rectangle is 48 square inches. Its width is 8 inches. What is its length?

Holt Mathematics

LESSON 1-11

Solving Equations by Multiplying

Lesson Objectives

Solve whole-number equations by multiplying

Additional Examples

Example 1

Solve each equation. Check your answers.

A. $\dfrac{x}{7} = 5$

$\dfrac{x}{7} = 5$ x is divided by 7.

$7 \cdot \dfrac{x}{7} = 7 \cdot 5$ ⬚ both sides by 7 to undo the ⬚.

$x = $ ⬚

Check $\dfrac{x}{7} = 5$

$\dfrac{35}{7} \stackrel{?}{=} 5$ Substitute ⬚ for x in the equation.

$5 \stackrel{?}{=} 5$ ✓   ⬚ is the solution.

B. $13 = \dfrac{p}{6}$

$13 = \dfrac{p}{6}$ p is divided by 6.

$6 \cdot 13 = 6 \cdot \dfrac{p}{6}$ ⬚ both sides by 6 to undo the ⬚.

⬚ $= p$

Check $13 = \dfrac{p}{6}$

$13 \stackrel{?}{=} \dfrac{78}{6}$ Substitute ⬚ for p in the equation.

$13 \stackrel{?}{=} 13$ ✓   ⬚ is the solution.

Holt Mathematics

Example 2

At Elk Meadows Park an aspen tree is one-third the height of a pine tree.

height of aspen $= \dfrac{\text{height of pine}}{3}$

The aspen tree is 14 feet tall. How tall is the pine tree?

Let h represent the height of the pine tree.

$$14 = \frac{h}{3}$$ Substitute 14 for height of aspen. h is divided by 3.

$$3 \cdot 14 = 3 \cdot \frac{h}{3}$$ [____________] both sides by 3 to undo the [____________].

[____________] $= h$

The pine tree is [____] feet tall.

Check It Out!

1. Solve the equation. Check your answer.

$$72 = \frac{p}{4}$$

2. Jamie weighs one-half as much as her father.

Jamie's weight $= \dfrac{\text{father's weight}}{2}$

Jamie weighs 95 pounds. How many pounds does her father weigh?

Holt Mathematics

1-1 Numbers and Patterns

Identify a possible pattern. Use it to identify the next three numbers.

1. 2, 7, 12, 17, 22, . . .

2. 128, 64, 32, 16, . . .

3. Make a table that shows the number of shaded triangles in each figure. Tell how many shaded triangles are in the fourth figure of a possible pattern. Use drawings to justify your answer.

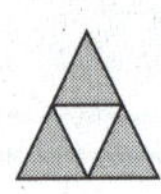 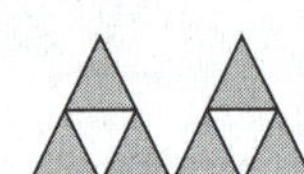 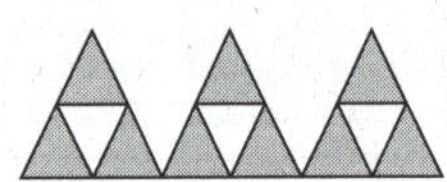

Fig. 1   Fig. 2   Fig. 3

1-2 Exponents

Find each value.

4. 12^2

5. 9^0

6. 5^4

7. 200^1

Write each number using an exponent and the given base.

8. 64, base 2

9. 10,000, base 10

10. 1, base 6

11. 12, base 12

12. Marvin's earnings double each day. He earned \$1 on Day 1. How much did Marvin earn on Day 8?

1-3 Order of Operations

Simplify each expression.

13. $2 + 7 \cdot 9 - 4$

14. $[(2 + 4)^2 \div 12]^3$

15. $4^2 \div (1 + 7)^2 \cdot 12$

Holt Mathematics

1-4 Properties of Numbers

Tell which property is represented.

16. $2 \cdot (4 \cdot 3) = (2 \cdot 4) \cdot 3$ **17.** $7 + 5 = 5 + 7$ **18.** $5 \cdot 1 = 5$

Use the Distributive Property to find each product.

19. $5(11 + 7) =$ **20.** $(19 + 3)2 =$

1-5 Evaluating Algebraic Expressions

Evaluate $n + 8$ for each value of n.

21. $n = 4$ **22.** $n = 0$ **23.** $n = 10$ **24.** $n = 17$

Evaluate each expression for the given value of the variable.

25. $10x + 9$ for $x = 3$ **26.** $14y - 6$ for $y = 5$

27. $2c^2 + 4c$ for $c = 4$ **28.** $z \div 8 + z$ for $z = 40$

Evaluate each expression for the given values of the variables.

29. $\dfrac{15}{y} + 6z$ for $y = 3$ and $z = 7$ **30.** $12p - 4q + 9$ for $p = 2$ and $q = 1$

Holt Mathematics

1-6 Writing Algebraic Expressions

Write each phrase as an algebraic expression.

31. 12 less than a number

32. the sum of 6 and a number

33. 5 times a number

34. 4 divided into a number

35. The Fruit Factory sold q bananas for $0.45 each. Write an algebraic expression for the amount sold. Then evaluate the expression for $q = 6$, and tell what the value of the expression means.

1-7 Equations and Their Solutions

Determine whether the given value of each variable is a solution.

36. $46 + t = 63$
for $t = 27$

37. $7u = 42$
for $u = 6$

38. $d - 26 = 12$
for $d = 38$

39. Ty bought 7 pens and should get $2.25 back in change. The cashier gave him 10 quarters. Determine if Ty was given the correct amount of change. Explain.

1-8 Solving Equations by Subtracting

Solve each equation. Check your answers.

40. $h + 34 = 87$

41. $79 = 61 + v$

42. $46 = d + 12$

43. A high school library has fiction and non-fiction books. There are 2,730 fiction books. The library has 7,680 books altogether. Write and solve an equation to find the number of non-fiction books in the high school library.

44. The drama club sold 596 tickets to the play. There were 387 people at the play on Friday. How many people were at the play on Saturday? Write and solve an equation to find the number of people at the play on Saturday.

Holt Mathematics

1-9 Solving Equations by Adding

Solve each equation. Check your answers.

45. $r - 17 = 7$

46. $180 = 220 - k$

47. $74 - l = 59$

48. A football field is 100 yards long. A football team is on their own 34-yard line. Write and solve an equation to find the number of yards the team must go to score a touchdown.

1-10 Solving Equations by Dividing

Solve each equation. Check your answers.

49. $7j = 28$

50. $125 = 5f$

51. $77 = 7w$

52. Corban bought 4 CDs for $60. Each CD cost the same amount. Write and solve an equation to find the amount Corban spent per CD.

1-11 Solving Equations by Multiplying

Solve each equation. Check your answers.

53. $10 = \dfrac{t}{6}$

54. $\dfrac{x}{5} = 8$

55. $6 = \dfrac{p}{8}$

56. Franz bought $\dfrac{1}{3}$ as many cups of raisins as cups of nuts.

$$\text{cups of raisins} = \frac{\text{cups of nuts}}{3}$$

Franz bought 4 cups of raisins. How many cups of nuts did Franz buy?

Holt Mathematics

Big Ideas

Answer these questions to summarize the important concepts from Chapter 1 in your own words.

1. Explain why 100^5 is greater than 100^4.

2. List the steps for the order of operations.

3. Explain how to solve a whole-number equation.

4. Explain how to solve the equation $x - 18 = 35$.

5. Explain how to solve the equation $\frac{x}{9} = 14$.

For more review of Chapter 1:

- Complete the Chapter 1 Study Guide: Review on pages 58–60 of your textbook.
- Complete the Ready to Go On quizzes on pages 32 and 54 of your textbook.

Holt Mathematics

LESSON 2-1

Introduction to Integers

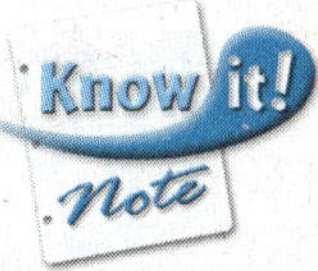

Lesson Objectives

Compare and order integers and determine absolute value

Vocabulary

opposite (p. 70) _______________________________

____

integer (p. 70) ________________________________

____

absolute value (p. 71) _________________________

____

Additional Examples

Example 1

Graph the integer −7 and its opposite on a number line.

The opposite of −7 is ☐.

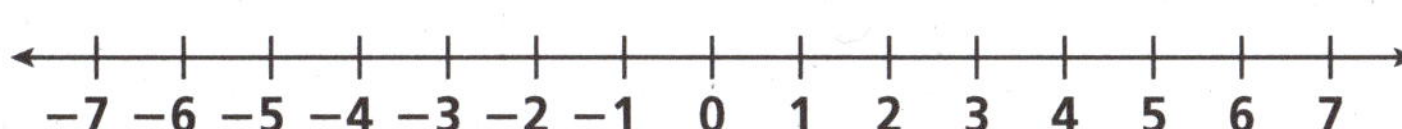

Example 2

Compare the integers. Use < or >.

A. 4 ☐ −4

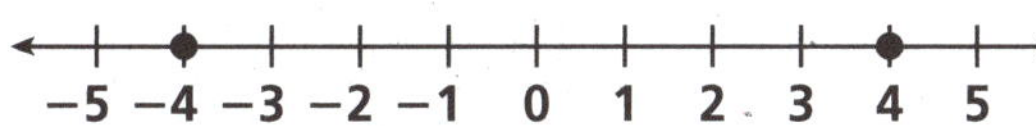

4 is farther to the ☐ than −4, so 4 ☐ −4.

B. −15 ☐ −9

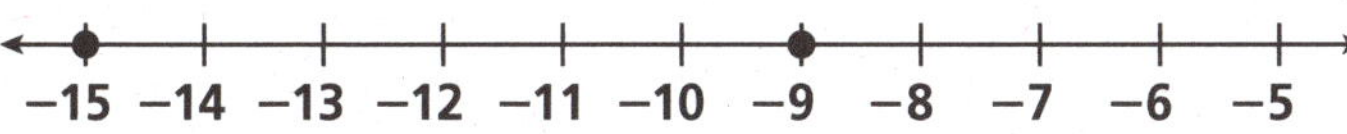

−9 is farther to the ☐ than −15, so −15 ☐ −9.

Holt Mathematics

Example 3

Use a number line to order the integers from least to greatest.

−3, 6, −5, 2, 0, −8

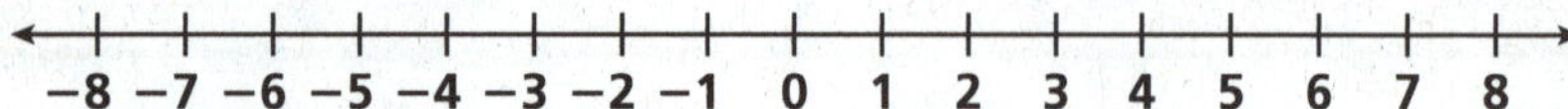

Example 4

Use a number line to find each absolute value.

A. $|8|$

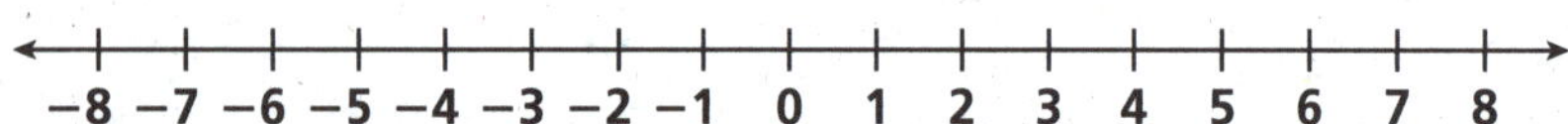

8 is 8 units from 0, so $|8|$ = ____.

B. $|-12|$

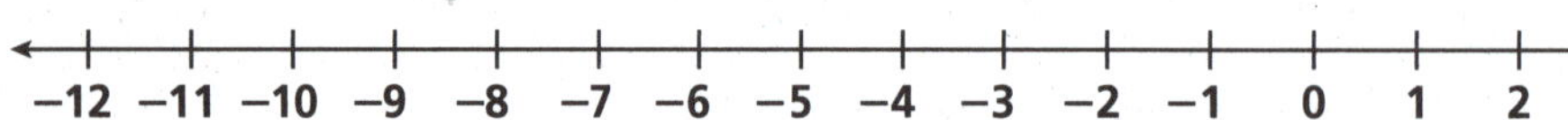

−12 is 12 units from 0, so $|-12|$ = ____.

Check It Out!

1. Graph the integer −5 and its opposite on a number line.

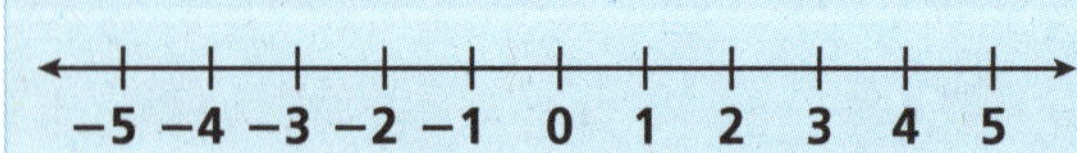

2. Compare the integers. Use < or >.

−4 ▮ −11

Holt Mathematics

3. Use a number line to order the integers from least of greatest.

−5, 4, −3, 2, −1, −2

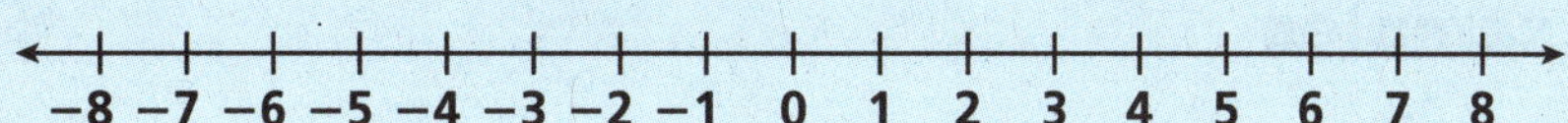

4. Use a number line to find the absolute value.

|3|

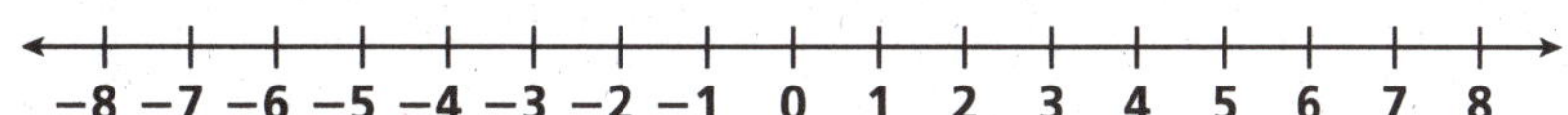

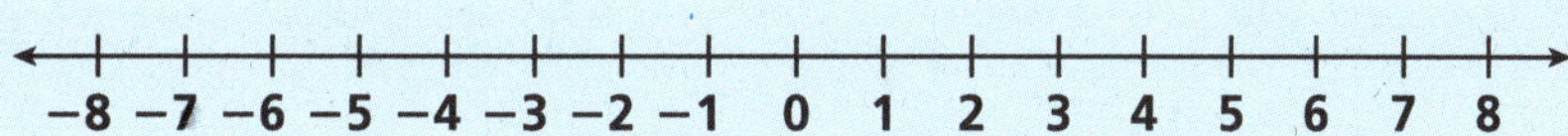

37

Holt Mathematics

LESSON 2-2

Adding Integers

Lesson Objectives

Add integers

Additional Examples

Example 1

Use a number line to find each sum.

A. $-7 + (-4)$

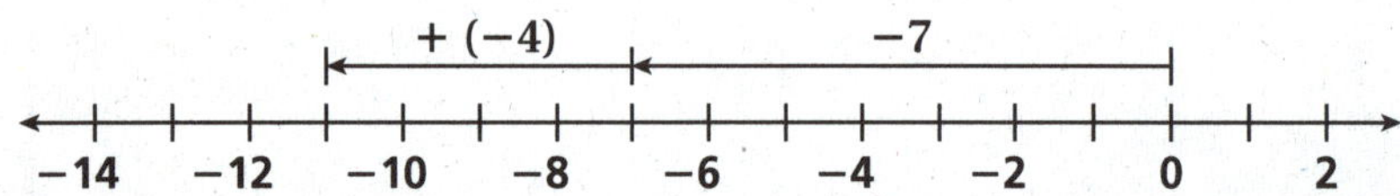

Start at 0. Move left ☐ units. Then move left ☐ more units.

$-7 + (-4) =$ ☐

B. $-12 + 19$

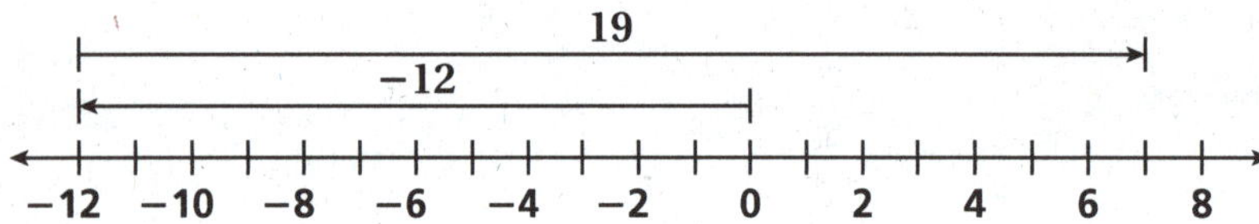

Start at ☐. Move ☐ 12 units. Then move ☐

19 units.

$-12 + 19 =$ ☐

Example 2

Find each sum.

A. $-4 + 8$ The signs are ☐.

Find the difference of the ☐ values.

Think: $8 - 4 = 4$.

Use the sign of the integer with the ☐ absolute

value (positive).

Holt Mathematics

Find each sum.

B. $23 + (-35)$ The ⬚ are different.

$23 + (-35)$ Find the ⬚ of the absolute values.

Think: ⬚ $-$ ⬚ $= 12$.

Use the ⬚ of the integer with the greater absolute value (⬚).

Example 3

Evaluate $x + y$ for $x = -42$, $y = 71$.

$x + y$ Substitute ⬚ for x and ⬚ for y.

⬚ $+$ ⬚   The signs are ⬚ .

Think: ⬚ $-$ ⬚ $= 29$.

Use the sign of the integer with the greater absolute ⬚ (positive).

Holt Mathematics

Example 4

The jazz band's income from a bake sale was $286. Expenses were $21. Use integer addition to find the band's total profit or loss.

$286 + (-21)$ Use negative for the ____________.

$286 - 21$ Find the ____________ of the absolute values.

____________   The ____________ is positive.

The band's profit was $____________.

Check It Out!

1. Use a number line to find the sum.

$-4 + (-5)$

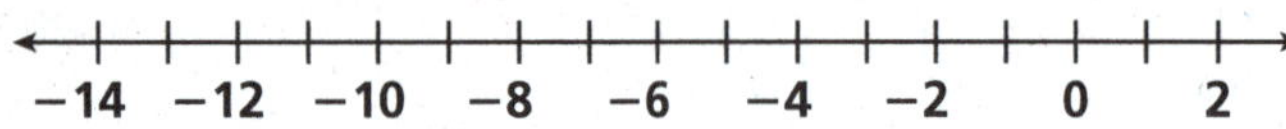

2. Find the sum.

$-13 + (-24)$

3. Evaluate $x + y$ for $x = -24$, $y = 17$.

4. The French Club was raising money for a trip to Washington D. C. Their carwash raised $730. They had expenses of $52. Use integer addition to find the club's total profit or loss.

Holt Mathematics

California Standards NS2.3, AF1.2

Subtracting Integers

LESSON 2-3

Lesson Objectives

Subtract integers

Additional Examples

Example 1

Use a number line to find each difference.

A. $4 - 1$

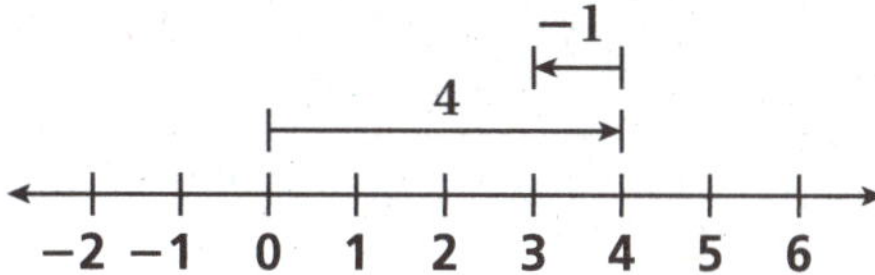

-2 -1 0 1 2 3 4 5 6

Start at 0. Move right ☐ units. To subtract ☐, move to the left ☐ unit.

$4 - 1 =$ ☐

B. $-3 - 1$

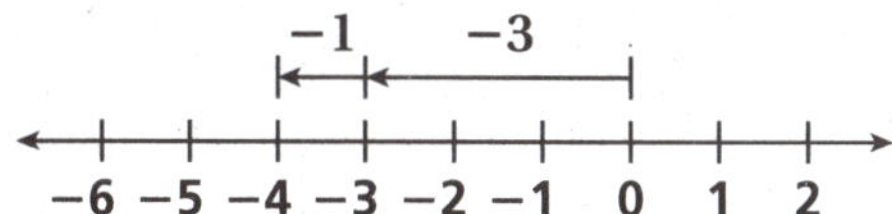

-6 -5 -4 -3 -2 -1 0 1 2

☐ at 0. Move ☐ 3 units. To subtract 1, move to

the ☐ 1 unit.

$-3 - 1 =$ ☐

Example 2

Find the difference.

$5 - (-2)$

$5 + 2$ ⸻ Add the ☐ of -2.

☐

Holt Mathematics

Example 3

Evaluate $x - y$ for each set of values.

A. $x = -3$ and $y = 2$

$x - y$

$-3 - 2 = \boxed{} + (\boxed{})$ $\boxed{}$ for x and y.

$= \boxed{}$ Add the opposite of $\boxed{}$.

B. $x = 4$ and $y = -6$

$x - y$

$4 - (-6) = \boxed{} + \boxed{}$ Substitute for $\boxed{}$ and $\boxed{}$.

$= \boxed{}$ Add the $\boxed{}$ of -6.

Example 4

Find the difference between 32°F and −10°F.

$\boxed{} - (\boxed{})$

$32 \boxed{} 10 = \boxed{}$ Add the opposite of $\boxed{}$.

The difference in temperatures is $\boxed{}$ °F.

Check It Out!

1. Use a number line to find the difference.

$-4 - (-2)$

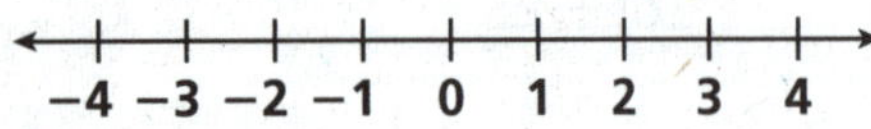

Holt Mathematics

2. Find the difference.

$$-2 - (-6)$$

3. Evaluate $x - y$ **for** $x = -4$ **and** $y = 5$.

4. Find the difference between 8°F and −5°F.

Holt Mathematics

LESSON 2-4

Multiplying and Dividing Integers

Lesson Objectives

Multiply and divide integers

Additional Examples

Example 1

Use a number line to find each product.

A. $-7 \cdot 2$

$-7 \cdot 2 = 2 \cdot (-7)$

$= \boxed{}$

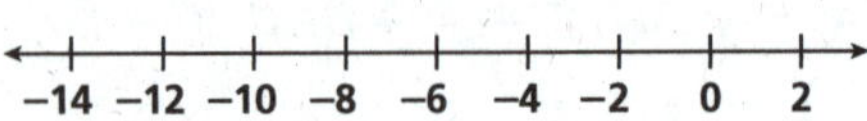

Use the Commutative Property.

Think: Start at 0.

Add -7 $\boxed{}$ times.

B. $-8 \cdot 3$

$-8 \cdot 3 = 3 \cdot (-8)$

$= \boxed{}$

Use the Commutative Property.

Think: Start at 0.

Add -8 $\boxed{}$ times.

Example 2

Find each product.

A. $-6 \cdot (-5)$

$-6 \cdot (-5) = \boxed{}$ Both signs are $\boxed{}$, so the product

is $\boxed{}$.

B. $-4 \cdot 7$

$-4 \cdot 7 = \boxed{}$ The signs are $\boxed{}$, so the

product is $\boxed{}$.

Holt Mathematics

Example 3

Find each quotient.

A. $35 \div (-5)$

$35 \div (-5)$

The ⬚ are different, so the ⬚ is negative.

B. $-48 \div 6$

$-48 \div 6$

⬚

The signs are ⬚, so the quotient is ⬚.

Example 4

At 7:00, the temperature was 14°F. As a cold front approached, the temperature dropped 6°F per hour over the next 4 hours. What was the temperature at 11:00?

$14 -$ ⬚ · ⬚   Multiply ⬚ by ⬚ to find the total number of degrees, then subtract it from the original temperature of 14°F. Subtract the total number of degrees to find out what the temperature was at 11:00.

$14 -$ ⬚

⬚

The temperature at 11:00 was ⬚ °F.

Holt Mathematics

Check It Out!

1. Use a number line to find the product.

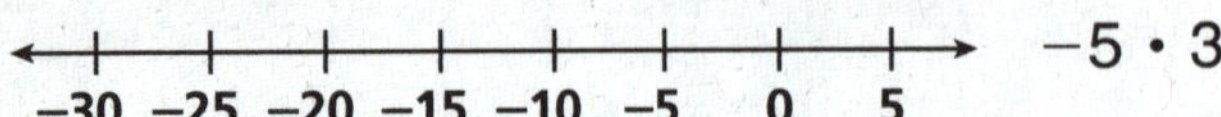

$-5 \cdot 3$

2. Find the product.

$-2 \cdot (-8)$

3. Find the quotient.

$-25 \div (-5)$

4. At 4:00, the train was 20 miles from the station. The train traveled 18 miles away from the station per hour over the next 6 hours. How far was the train from the station at 10:00?

Holt Mathematics

LESSON 2-5

Solving Equations Containing Integers

Lesson Objectives

Solve one-step equations with integers

Vocabulary

additive inverse (p. 94) _______________________________

____

Additional Examples

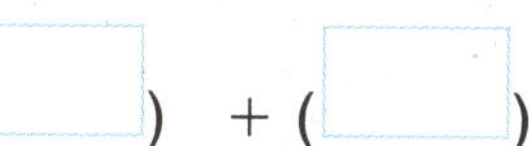

Example 1

Solve each equation.

A.　　　$-6 + x = -7$

$\underline{+\ \boxed{}}$　　　$\underline{+\ \boxed{}}$　　　Add $\boxed{}$ to both sides.

$x = \boxed{}$

B.　　$p + 5 = -3$

$\underline{+\ (\boxed{})}$　$+\ (\boxed{})$　　Add $\boxed{}$ to both sides.

$p = \boxed{}$

C.　　$y - 9 = -40$

$\underline{+\ \boxed{}}$　　　$+\ \boxed{}$　　　Add $\boxed{}$ to both sides.

$y = \boxed{}$

Example 2

Solve each equation. Check each answer.

$\dfrac{b}{-5} = 6$

$\dfrac{b}{-5} = 6$　　　　　Multiply both sides by $\boxed{}$.

$\left(\boxed{}\right)\dfrac{b}{-5} = \left(\boxed{}\right)6$

$b = \boxed{}$

Holt Mathematics

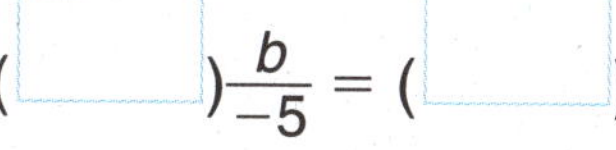

Example 3

In 2003, a manufacturer made a profit of $300 million. This amount was $100 million more than the profit in 2002. What was the profit in 2002?

Let p represent the profit in 2002 (in millions of dollars).

Profit in 2003 is $⬚ million more than profit in 2002.

$$\boxed{} = \boxed{} + p$$

$$300 = 100 + p$$

$$\frac{-\boxed{}}{} \quad \frac{-\boxed{}}{}$$

$$\boxed{} = p$$

The profit in 2002 was $⬚ million.

Check It Out!

1. Solve the equation. Check the answer.

$$y - 7 = -34$$

2. Solve the equation. Check the answer.

$$\frac{c}{4} = -24$$

3. This year the class bake sale made a profit of $243. This was an increase of $125 over last year. How much did they make last year?

Holt Mathematics

The Coordinate Plane

LESSON 2-6

Lesson Objectives

Locate and graph points on a coordinate plane

Vocabulary

coordinate plane (p. 100)

axes (p. 100)

x-axis (p. 100)

y-axis (p. 100)

quadrants (p. 100)

origin (p. 100)

coordinates (p. 100)

x-coordinate (p. 100)

y-coordinate (p. 100)

Holt Mathematics

Additional Examples

Example 1

Name the quadrant where each point is located.

A. *X* Quadrant

B. *Y* Quadrant

C. *S* Quadrant

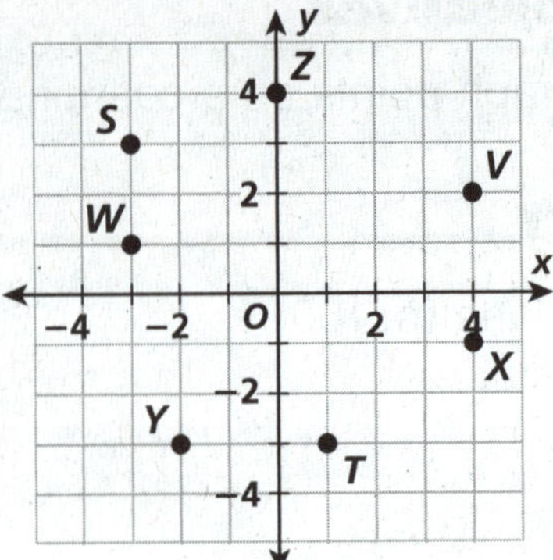

Example 2

Give the coordinates of each point.

A. *X*

From the origin, *X* is ☐ units

right, and ☐ unit down. (☐)

B. *Y*

From the origin, *Y* is ☐ units

left, and ☐ units down. (☐)

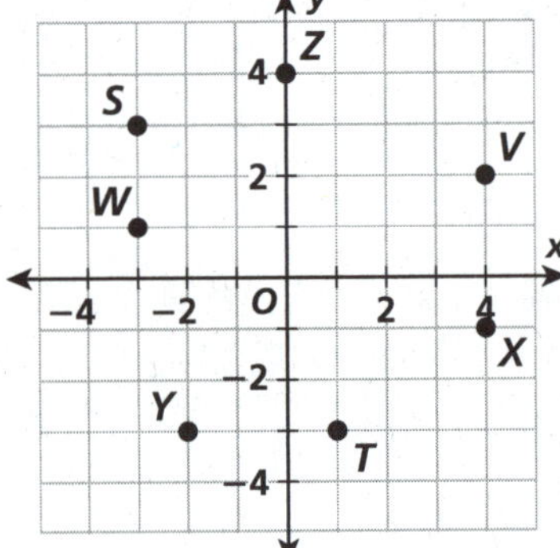

Example 3

Graph each point on a coordinate plane.

A. *V*(4, 2)

From the origin, move ☐ units

☐, and ☐ units ☐.

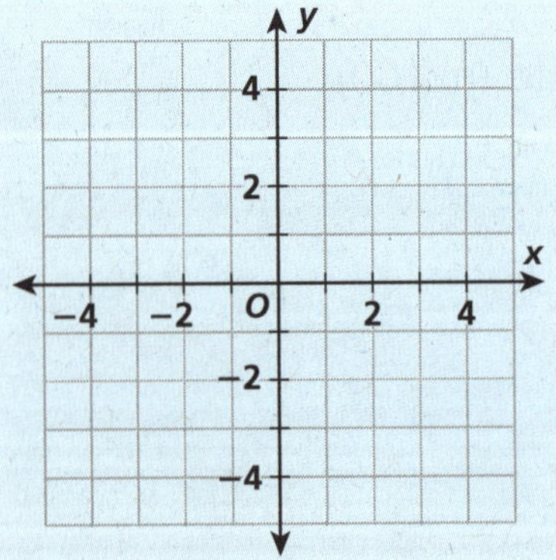

50

Holt Mathematics

B. $W(-3, 1)$

From the origin, move ☐ units ☐, and ☐ unit ☐.

C. $Z(0, 4)$

From the origin, move ☐ units up.

D. $T(1, -3)$

From the origin, move ☐ unit right, and ☐ units down.

Check It Out!

1. Name the quadrant where point *Z* is located.

2. Give the coordinates of point *W*.

3. Graph $M(-3, -3)$.

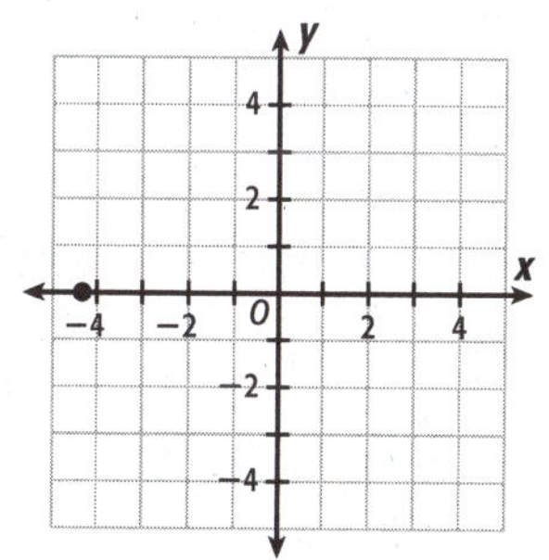

Holt Mathematics

Equations in Two Variables

LESSON 2-7

Lesson Objectives

Use data in a table to write an equation in two variables and use the equation to find a missing value

Additional Examples

Example 1

Write an equation in two variables that gives the values in the table. Use your equation to find the value of y for the indicated value of x.

x	3	4	5	6	7	10
y	12	16	20	24	28	

y is ☐ times x. — Compare x and y to find a pattern.

$y =$ ☐ — Use the pattern to write an equation.

$y = 4($ ☐ $)$ — Substitute ☐ for x.

$y =$ ☐ — Use your equation to find y when $x =$ ☐ .

Example 2

Write an equation for the relationship. Tell what each variable you use represents.

The height of a painting is 7 times its width.

$h =$ ☐ of painting — Choose ☐ for the equation.

$w =$ ☐ of painting

☐ — Write an equation.

Holt Mathematics

Example 3

PROBLEM SOLVING APPLICATION

The school choir tracked the number of tickets sold and the total amount of money received. They sold each ticket for the same price. They received $80 for 20 tickets, $88 for 22 tickets, and $108 for 27 tickets. Write an equation for the relationship.

1. **Understand the Problem**

   The answer will be an equation that describes the relationship between the number of [______] sold and the money [______].

2. **Make a Plan**

   You can make a table to display the data.

3. **Solve**

   Let t be the number of [______]. Let m be the amount of [______] received.

t	20	22	27
m	80	88	108

    m is equal to [___] times t.   Compare t and m.

   [______]   Write an equation.

4. **Look Back**

   Substitute the t and m values in the table to check that they are solutions of the equation $m = 4t$.

   $m = 4t$ (20, 80) $m = 4t$ (22, 88) $m = 4t$ (27, 108)

   $80 \stackrel{?}{=} 4 \cdot 20$ $88 \stackrel{?}{=} 4 \cdot 22$ $108 \stackrel{?}{=} 4 \cdot 27$

   $80 \stackrel{?}{=} 80$ ✓ $88 \stackrel{?}{=} 88$ ✓ $108 \stackrel{?}{=} 108$ ✓

Holt Mathematics

Check It Out!

Write an equation in two variables that gives the values in the table. Use the equation to find the value of *y* for the indicated value of *x*.

1.

x	3	4	5	6	7	10
y	5	6	7	8	9	

2. **Write an equation for the relationship. Tell what each variable you use represents.**

   The height of a mirror is 4 times its width.

3. **The school theater tracked the number of tickets sold and the total amount of money received. They sold each ticket for the same price. They received $45 for 15 tickets, $63 for 21 tickets, and $90 for 30 tickets. Write an equation for the relationship.**

Holt Mathematics

LESSON 2-8

Graphing Equations

Lesson Objectives

Use ordered pairs to graph linear equations

Vocabulary

linear equation (p. 108) ______________________________

Additional Examples

Example 1

Use the given *x*-values to write solutions of the equation as ordered pairs.

$y = 4x + 2$; $x = 1, 2, 3$

Make a table by using the given values for x to find values for y.

Write these solutions as _____________ pairs.

x	$4x + 2$	y

(x, y)

Example 2

Determine whether the ordered pair is a solution to the given equation.

$(3, 21)$; $y - 7x$

$y = 7x$ Write the equation.

$\boxed{} \overset{?}{=} 7(\boxed{})$ Substitute $\boxed{}$ for x and 21 for $\boxed{}$.

$21 \overset{?}{=} 21$ ✓

So ($\boxed{}$) is a solution to $y = 7x$.

Holt Mathematics

Example 3

Use the graph of the linear equation to find the value of *y* for the given value of *x*.

x = 4

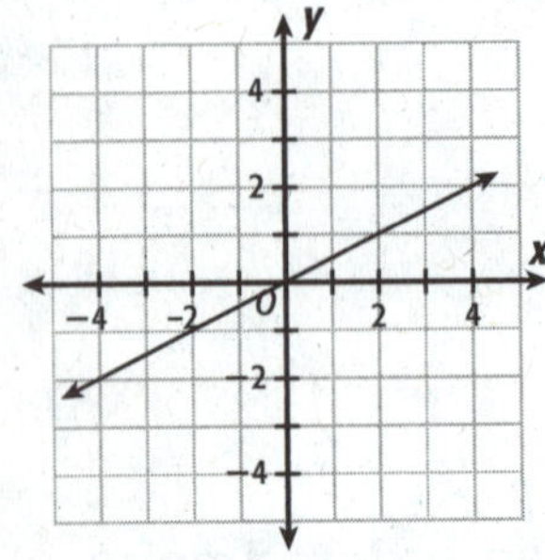

Start at the origin and move ⬚ units

⬚ .

Move ⬚ until you reach the graph. Move left

to find the *y*-value on the ⬚ .

When *x* = 4, *y* = ⬚ . The ordered pair is

(⬚).

Example 4

Graph the equation *y* = −*x* − 2.

Make a table. Substitute different values for *x*.

Write the solutions as ordered pairs.

x	−*x* − 2	*y*	*(x, y)*
⬚	⬚	⬚	⬚
⬚	⬚	⬚	⬚
⬚	⬚	⬚	⬚

Graph the ⬚ pairs on a ⬚ plane.

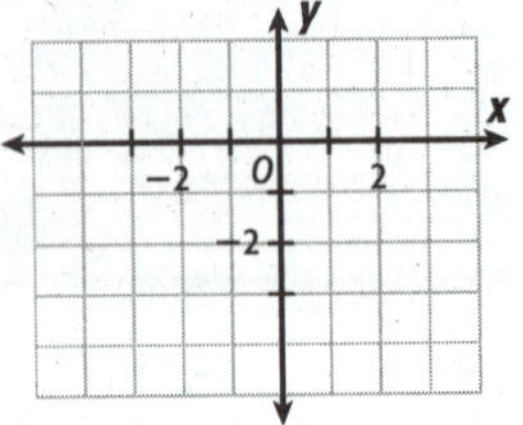

Draw a line through the points to represent

⬚ the values of ⬚ you could have

chosen and the ⬚ values of *y*.

Holt Mathematics

Check It Out!

1. Use the given *x*-values to write solutions of the equation $y = 3x + 2$ as ordered pairs. $x = 2, 3, 4, 5$.

2. Determine whether the ordered pair is a solution of the given equation. $(4, 20)$; $y = 5x$

3. Use the graph of the linear equation to find the value of *y* for the given value of *x*.

   $x = 2$

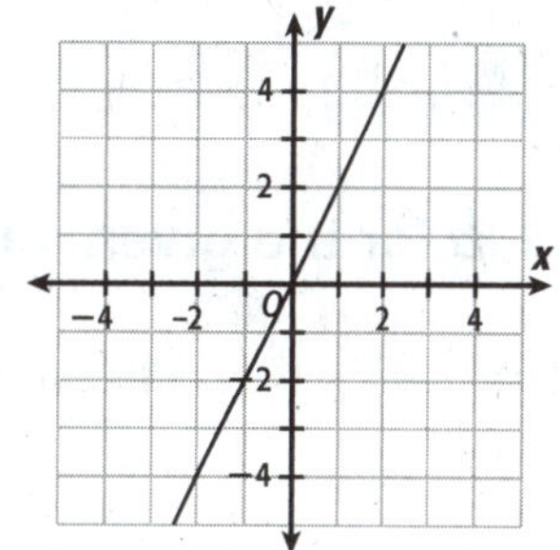

4. Graph the equation $y = -x - 4$.

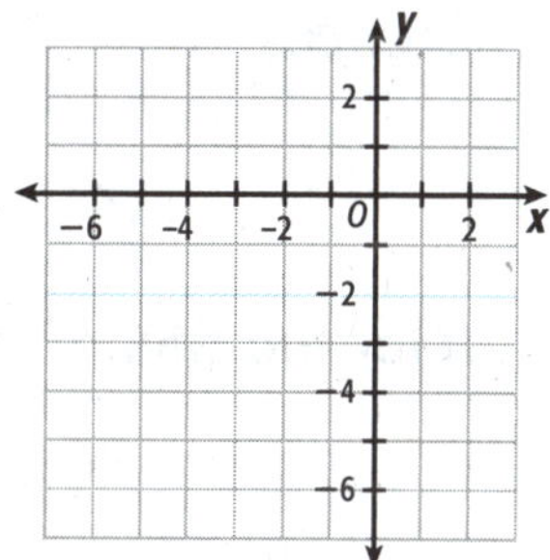

Holt Mathematics

2-1 Introduction to Integers

Compare the integers. Use < or >.

1. 4 ☐ −6

2. −2 ☐ 2

3. −14 ☐ −9

Use a number line to find each absolute value.

4. $|-6|$

5. $|3|$

6. $|-9|$

2-2 Adding Integers

Find each sum.

7. −8 + 6

8. 13 + (−3)

9. −7 + (−4)

Evaluate $a + b$ **for the given values.**

10. $a = 8, b = -17$

11. $a = -44, b = 49$

12. $a = -5, b = -14$

2-3 Subtracting Integers

Find each difference.

13. 7 − 11

14. −9 − (−15)

15. −7 − 6

Evaluate $a - b$ **for the given values.**

16. $a = 8, b = -3$

17. $a = -4, b = 11$

18. $a = 3, b = 8$

2-4 Multiplying and Dividing Integers

Find each product.

19. 6 · (−3)

20. −4 · 8

21. −8 · (−5)

Find each quotient.

22. 45 ÷ (−9)

23. −24 ÷ 4

24. −39 ÷ (−3)

Holt Mathematics

2-5 Solving Equations Containing Integers

Solve. Check your answer.

25. $8h = -48$ **26.** $-15 + k = 35$ **27.** $27 - x = -42$

28. This year, 84 students performed at the Spring Choral Concert. There were 4 groups with an equal number of students that performed. How many students were in each group?

2-6 The Coordinate Plane

Name the quadrant where each ordered pair is located.

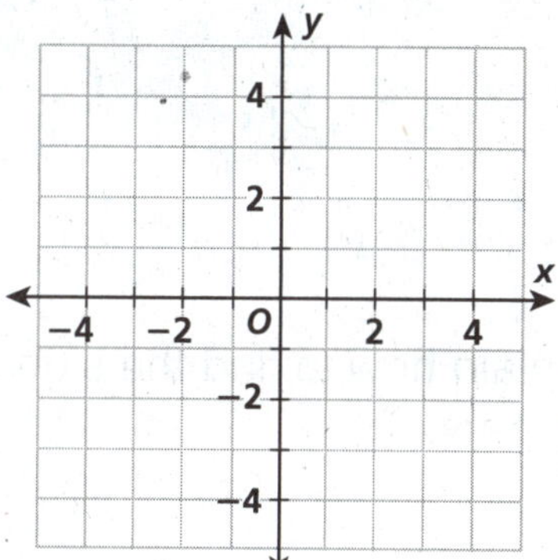

29. $(-3, 5)$

30. $(4, -2)$

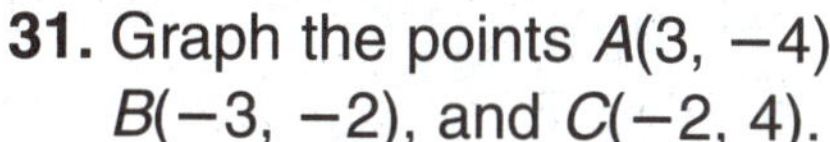

31. Graph the points $A(3, -4)$, $B(-3, -2)$, and $C(-2, 4)$.

2-7 Equations in Two Variables

Write an equation in two variables that gives the values in each table, and then find the missing terms.

32.

x	1	2	3	6	10
y	3	7	11	23	

33.

x	35	20	10	0	-15
y	-7	-4		0	3

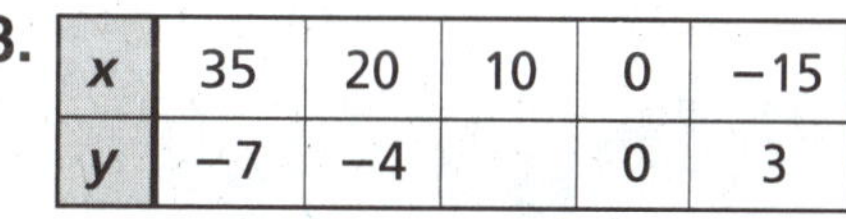

2-8 Graphing Equations

Complete the table, and then use the table to graph the equation.

34. $y = 3x + 1$

x	-1	0	1	2
y				

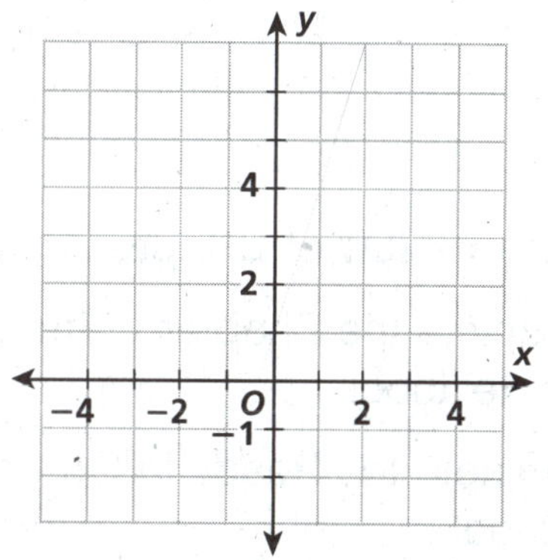

Holt Mathematics

Answer these question to summarize the important concepts from Chapter 2 in your own words.

1. Explain why -5 and 5 have the same absolute value.

2. Explain how to find the sign of the answer when subtracting integers.

3. Explain how to find the sign of the answer when multiplying or dividing integers.

4. Explain how to solve the equation $5 + x = 12$.

5. Explain how to graph the point $(-7, 9)$.

For more review of Chapter 2:

- Complete the Chapter 2 Study Guide and Review on pages 118–120 of your textbook.

- Complete the Ready to Go On quizzes on pages 98 and 114 of your textbook.

Holt Mathematics

LESSON 3-1

Prime Factorization

Lesson Objectives

Find the prime factorizations of composite numbers

Vocabulary

prime number (p. 128) _______________________________

____

composite number (p. 128) _______________________________

____

prime factorization (p. 128) _______________________________

____

Additional Examples

Example 1

Tell whether each number is prime or composite.

A. 11

The positive factors of 11 are ☐ and ☐.

So 11 is ☐.

B. 16

The positive factors of 16 are ☐, ☐, ☐, ☐, and ☐.

So 16 is ☐.

Holt Mathematics

Example 2

Write the prime factorization of each number.

A. 24

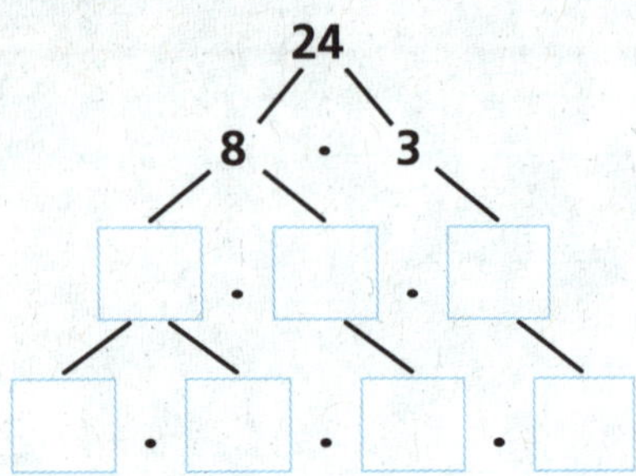

Write ☐ as the product of two positive factors. Continue factoring until all factors are ☐.

The prime factorization of 24 is ☐. Using exponents, you can write this as ☐.

B. 150

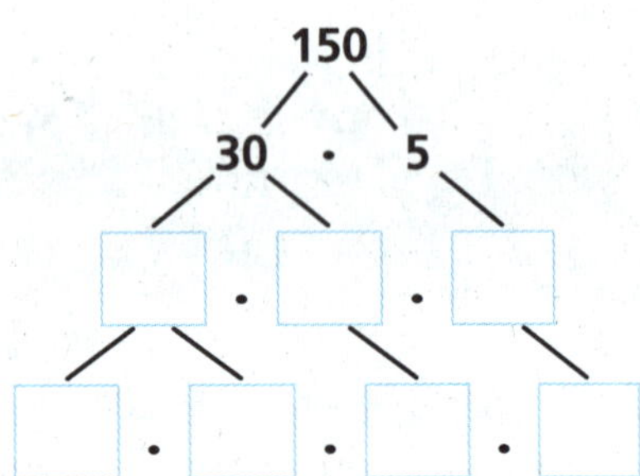

Write ☐ as the product of two positive factors. Continue factoring until all factors are ☐.

The prime factorization of 150 is ☐, or ☐.

Holt Mathematics

Example 3

Write the prime factorization of each number.

A. 476

```
 2 | 476
 2 | 238
 7 | 119
17 |  17
        1
```

Divide 476 by 2. Write the quotient below 476.

Keep dividing by a ⬚ factor.

Stop when the quotient is ⬚.

The prime factorization of 476 is ⬚, or ⬚.

B. 275

```
 5 | 275
 5 |  55
11 |  11
        1
```

Divide 275 by 5. Write the quotient below 275.

Keep dividing by a ⬚ factor.

Stop when the quotient is ⬚.

The prime factorization of 275 is ⬚, or ⬚.

Check It Out!

1. Tell whether the number is prime or composite.

14

2. Write the prime factorization of the number.

90

3. Write the prime factorization of the number.

325

Holt Mathematics

Greatest Common Divisor

LESSON 3-2

Lesson Objectives

Find the greatest common divisor of two or more whole numbers

Vocabulary

greatest common divisor (GCD) (p. 132) _______________________________

____

Additional Examples

Example 1

Find the greatest common divisor (GCD) of 12, 36, and 54.

12: 1, 2, 3, 4, 6, 12

36: 1, 2, 3, 4, 6, 9, 12, 18, 36

54: 1, 2, 3, 6, 9, 18, 27, 54

List all of the ______________ of each number.

Circle the ______________ factor that is in all the lists.

The GCD is ☐.

Example 2

Find the greatest common divisor (GCD).

A. 40, 56

$40 = 2 \cdot 2 \cdot 2 \cdot 5$

$56 = 2 \cdot 2 \cdot 2 \cdot 7$

$2 \cdot 2 \cdot 2 = $ ☐

The GCD is ☐.

Write the ______________ factorization of each number and circle the ______________ prime factors.

______________ the common prime factors.

Holt Mathematics

Find the greatest common divisor (GCD).

B. 252, 180, 96, 60

$252 = 2 \cdot 2 \cdot 3 \cdot 3 \cdot 7$

$180 = 2 \cdot 2 \cdot 3 \cdot 3 \cdot 5$

$96 = 2 \cdot 2 \cdot 2 \cdot 2 \cdot 2 \cdot 3$

$60 = 2 \cdot 2 \cdot 3 \cdot 5$

Write the prime [　　　] of each number and circle the common [　　　] factors.

[　] · [　] · [　] = 12

Multiply the common prime [　　　].

The GCD is [　　　].

Example 3

PROBLEM SOLVING APPLICATION

You have 120 red beads, 100 white beads, and 45 blue beads. You want to use all the beads to make identical bracelets that have red, white, and blue beads on each. What is the greatest number of bracelets you can make?

1. **Understand the Problem**

   Rewrite the question as a statement.

   - Find the [　　　] number of bracelets you can make.

   List the important information:

   - There are [　　] red beads, [　　] white beads, and [　　] blue beads.

   - Each bracelet must have the [　　] number of red, white, and blue beads.

   The answer will be the [　　] of 120, 100, and 45.

2. **Make a Plan**

   You can list the prime factors of 120, 100, and 45 to find the GCD.

Holt Mathematics

3. Solve

$120 = \square \cdot \square \cdot \square \cdot \square \cdot \square$

$100 = \square \cdot \square \cdot \square \cdot \square$

$45 = \square \cdot \square \cdot \square$

Circle the prime $\square$ that are common to $\square$, $\square$, and $\square$.

The GCD of 120, 100, and 45 is $\square$.

You can make $\square$ bracelets.

4. Look Back

If you make 5 bracelets, each one will have $\square$ red beads, $\square$ white beads, and $\square$ blue beads, with nothing left over.

Check It Out!

1. Find the greatest common divisor (GCD) of 14, 28, and 63.

2. Find the greatest common divisor (GCD).

360, 250, 170, 40

3. Nathan has made fishing flies that he plans to give away as gift sets. He has 24 wet flies and 18 dry flies. Using all of the flies, how many sets can he make?

Holt Mathematics

LESSON 3-3

Least Common Multiple

Lesson Objectives

Find the least common multiple of two or more whole numbers

Vocabulary

multiple (p. 136) ____

____

least common multiple (LCM) (p. 136) _______________________________

____

Additional Examples

Example 1

Find the least common multiple (LCM).

A. 2, 7

   2: 2, 4, 6, 8, 10, 12, 14   List some [   ] of each number.

   7: 7, 14, 21, 28, 35   Find the [   ] value that is in both lists.

   The LCM is [   ].

B. 3, 6, 9

   3: 3, 6, 9, 12, 15, 18, 21   List some [   ] of each number.

   6: 6, 12, 18, 24, 30   Find the [   ] value that is in all the lists.

   9: 9, 18, 27, 36, 45

   The LCM is [   ].

Holt Mathematics

Example 2

Find the least common multiple (LCM).

A. 60, 130

$60 = 2 \cdot 2 \cdot 3 \cdot 5$ Write the [ ] factorization of each number.

$130 = 2 \cdot 5 \cdot 13$ Circle the [ ] prime factors.

[ ] , [ ] , [ ] , [ ] , [ ] List the [ ] factors, using the circled factors only once.

[ ] · [ ] · [ ] · [ ] [ ] the factors in the list.

The LCM is [ ].

B. 14, 35, 49

$14 = 2 \cdot 7$ Write the prime [ ] of each number.

$35 = 5 \cdot 7$

$49 = 7 \cdot 7$ Circle the common prime [ ].

[ ] , [ ] , [ ] , [ ] List the prime [ ], using the circled factors only once.

[ ] · [ ] · [ ] · [ ] Multiply the [ ] in the list.

The LCM is [ ].

Holt Mathematics

Example 3

Mr. Washington will set up the band chairs all in rows of 6 or all in rows of 8. What is the least number of chairs he will set up?

Find the LCM of ☐ and ☐.

$6 = ☐ \cdot ☐$

$8 = ☐ \cdot ☐ \cdot ☐$

The LCM is ☐ $\cdot$ ☐ $\cdot$ ☐ $\cdot$ ☐ $=$ ☐.

He will set up at least ☐ chairs.

Check it Out!

1. Find the least common multiple (LCM).

2, 6, 4

2. Find the least common multiple (LCM).

18, 36, 54

3. Two satellites are put into orbit over the same location at the same time. One orbits the earth every 24 hours, while the second completes an orbit every 18 hours. How much time will elapse before they are once again over the same location at the same time?

Holt Mathematics

LESSON 3-4 Equivalent Fractions and Mixed Numbers

Lesson Objectives

Identify, write, and convert between equivalent fractions and mixed numbers

Vocabulary

equivalent fractions (p. 142) _______________________________

____

improper fraction (p. 143) _______________________________

____

mixed number (p. 143) _______________________________

____

Additional Examples

Example 1

Find two fractions equivalent to $\frac{5}{7}$.

$$\frac{5}{7} = \frac{5 \cdot \square}{7 \cdot \square} = \boxed{}$$ Multiply the numerator and denominator by $\square$.

$$\frac{5}{7} = \frac{5 \cdot \square}{7 \cdot \square} = \boxed{}$$ Multiply the numerator and denominator by $\square$.

Example 2

Write the fraction $\frac{18}{24}$ in simplest form.

Find the GCD of $\square$ and $\square$.

$18 = 2 \cdot 3 \cdot 3$ The GCD is $\square = 2 \cdot 3$.

$24 = 2 \cdot 2 \cdot 2 \cdot 3$

$$\frac{18}{24} = \frac{18 \div \square}{24 \div \square} = \boxed{}$$ Divide the numerator and denominator

by $\square$.

Holt Mathematics

Example 3

Determine whether the fractions in each pair are equivalent.

A. $\frac{4}{6}$ and $\frac{28}{42}$

$\frac{4}{6} = \frac{4 \div \boxed{}}{6 \div \boxed{}} = \boxed{}$ Simplify both fractions and compare.

$\frac{28}{42} = \frac{28 \div \boxed{}}{42 \div \boxed{}} = \boxed{}$

$\frac{4}{6}$ and $\frac{28}{42}$ are $\boxed{}$ because both are equal to $\frac{2}{3}$.

B. $\frac{6}{10}$ and $\frac{20}{25}$

$\frac{6}{10} = \frac{6 \div \boxed{}}{10 \div \boxed{}} = \boxed{}$ Simplify both fractions and compare.

$\frac{20}{25} = \frac{20 \div \boxed{}}{25 \div \boxed{}} = \boxed{}$

$\frac{6}{10}$ and $\frac{20}{25}$ are $\boxed{}$ because their simplest forms are

not equal.

Holt Mathematics

Example 4

A. Write $\frac{13}{5}$ as a mixed number.

First divide the ____________ by the ____________.

$\frac{13}{5}$ = ____________   Use the ____________ and

____________ to write the mixed number.

B. Write $7\frac{2}{3}$ as an improper fraction.

First multiply the ____________ and ____________ number,

and then add the ____________.

$7\frac{2}{3} = \dfrac{3 \cdot \boxed{} + \boxed{}}{3} = \boxed{}$ Use the result to write the improper fraction.

Check It Out!

1. Find two fractions equivalent to $\frac{6}{12}$.

2. Write the fraction $\frac{15}{45}$ in simplest form.

3. Determine whether the fractions in each pair are equivalent.

$\frac{3}{9}$ and $\frac{6}{18}$

4. Write $\frac{15}{6}$ as a mixed number.

Holt Mathematics

LESSON 3-5

Equivalent Fractions and Decimals

Lesson Objectives

Write fractions as decimals, and vice versa, and determine whether a decimal is terminating or repeating

Vocabulary

terminating decimal (p. 146) _______________________________________

____

repeating decimal (p. 146) ____

____

Additional Examples

Example 1

Write each fraction as a decimal. Round to the nearest hundredth, if necessary.

A. $\frac{1}{4}$

$$
\begin{array}{r}
4\overline{)1.00} \\
-8 \\
\hline
20 \\
-20 \\
\hline
0
\end{array}
$$

$\frac{1}{4} = $ ____

B. $\frac{9}{5}$

$$
\begin{array}{r}
5\overline{)9.0} \\
-5 \\
\hline
4\,0 \\
-4\,0 \\
\hline
0
\end{array}
$$

$\frac{9}{5} = $ ____

C. $\frac{5}{3}$

$$
\begin{array}{r}
3\overline{)5.00} \\
-3 \\
\hline
2\,0 \\
-1\,8 \\
\hline
2\,0 \\
-1\,8 \\
\hline
2
\end{array}
$$

$\frac{5}{3} \approx $ ____

Example 2

Write each fraction as a decimal.

A. $\frac{4}{5}$

$\frac{4}{5} \times \dfrac{\boxed{}}{\boxed{}} = \dfrac{\boxed{}}{\boxed{}} = \boxed{}$

Multiply to get a power of ____ in the denominator.

Holt Mathematics

B. $\dfrac{37}{50}$

$$\dfrac{37}{50} \times \dfrac{\boxed{}}{\boxed{}} = \dfrac{\boxed{}}{\boxed{}}$$

Multiply to get a power of $\boxed{}$ in the denominator.

$$= \boxed{}$$

Example 3

Write each decimal as a fraction in simplest form.

A. 0.018

$$0.018 = \dfrac{18}{1{,}000} = \dfrac{18 \div 2}{1{,}000 \div 2} = \boxed{}$$

8 is in the $\boxed{}$ place.

B. 1.55

$$1.55 = \dfrac{155}{100} = \dfrac{155 \div 5}{100 \div 5} = \boxed{} \text{ or } \boxed{}$$

5 is in the $\boxed{}$ place.

Example 4

A football player completed 1,546 of the 3,875 passes he attempted. Find his completion rate. Write your answer as a decimal rounded to the nearest thousandth.

$$3875 \overline{)1546.0000} \quad 0.3989\ldots$$

Divide the $\boxed{}$ by the denominator.

$$\dfrac{1546}{3875} \approx \boxed{}$$

His completion rate is $\boxed{}$.

Holt Mathematics

Check It Out!

1. Write the fraction as a decimal. Round to the nearest hundredth, if necessary.

$$\frac{6}{5}$$

2. Write the fraction as a decimal.

$$\frac{18}{25}$$

3. Write the decimal as a fraction in simplest form.

1.30

4. Johnny Unitas, a former professional quarterback, completed 2,830 of the 5,186 passes he attempted. Find his completion rate. Write your answer as a decimal rounded to the nearest thousandth.

Holt Mathematics

LESSON 3-6

Comparing and Ordering Rational Numbers

Lesson Objectives

Compare and order fractions and decimals

Vocabulary

rational number (p. 151) _______________________________________

____

Additional Examples

Example 1

Compare the fractions. Write < or >.

A. $\dfrac{7}{9}$ ■ $\dfrac{5}{8}$

The LCM of the [   ] 9 and 8 is 72.

$\dfrac{7}{9} = \dfrac{7 \cdot \boxed{}}{9 \cdot \boxed{}} = \boxed{}$ Write [   ] fractions with 72 as the denominator.

$\dfrac{5}{8} = \dfrac{5 \cdot \boxed{}}{8 \cdot \boxed{}} = \boxed{}$

[   ] > [   ] , and so $\dfrac{7}{9}$ ■ $\dfrac{5}{8}$.   Compare the numerators.

B. $-\dfrac{2}{5}$ ■ $-\dfrac{3}{7}$

Both fractions can be written with a [   ] of 35.

$-\dfrac{2}{5} = \dfrac{-2 \cdot \boxed{}}{5 \cdot \boxed{}} = \boxed{}$ Write equivalent fractions with 35 as the [   ].

$-\dfrac{3}{7} = \dfrac{-3 \cdot \boxed{}}{7 \cdot \boxed{}} = \boxed{}$ Put the negative signs in the numerators.

$-$[   ] $> -$[   ] , and so $-\dfrac{2}{5}$ ■ $-\dfrac{3}{7}$.

Holt Mathematics

Example 2

Compare the decimals. Write < or >.

A. 0.427  0.425

0.427   Line up the ⬚ points.

The tenths and hundredths are the ⬚.

0.425   Compare the ⬚: 7 ⬚ 5.

Since 0.007 ⬚ 0.005, 0.427 ⬚ 0.425.

B. $0.7\overline{3}$ 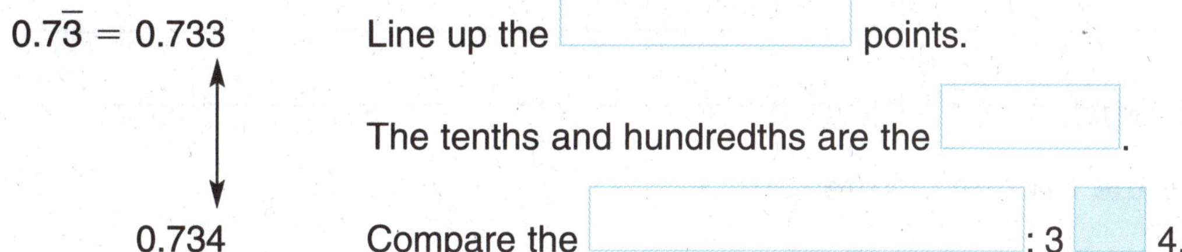 0.734   ⬚ is a repeating decimal.

$0.7\overline{3} = 0.733$ Line up the ⬚ points.

The tenths and hundredths are the ⬚.

0.734   Compare the ⬚: 3 ⬚ 4.

Since 0.003 ⬚ 0.004, $0.7\overline{3}$ ⬚ 0.734.

Holt Mathematics

Example 3

Order the numbers from least to greatest.

$\frac{4}{5}$, 0.93, and 0.9

Write as decimals with the same number of places.

$\frac{4}{5}$ = 0.80   0.93 = ⬚   0.9 = ⬚

Graph the numbers on a number line.

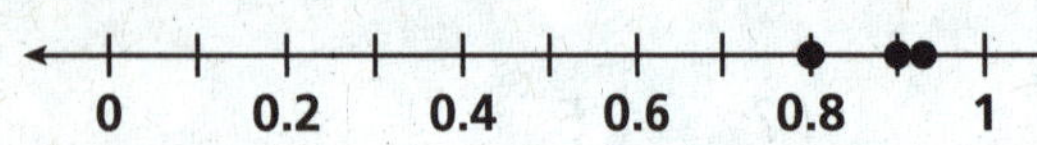

0.80 < 0.90 < 0.93   Compare the decimals.

From ⬚ to ⬚ , the numbers are ⬚ .

Check It Out!

1. Compare the fractions. Write < or >.

$\frac{5}{6}$ ⬚ $\frac{7}{8}$

$\frac{5}{6}$ ⬚ $\frac{7}{8}$

2. Compare the decimals. Write < or >.

0.535 ⬚ 0.538

0.535 ⬚ 0.538

3. Order the numbers from least to greatest.

$\frac{3}{5}$, 0.84, and 0.7

Holt Mathematics

Chapter Review

3-1 Prime Factorization

Tell whether each number is prime or composite.

1. 23 **2.** 35 **3.** 46

Write the prime factorization of each number.

4. 75 **5.** 48 **6.** 63

3-2 Greatest Common Divisor

Find the greatest common divisor (GCD).

7. 35, 49 **8.** 36, 48, 60 **9.** 54, 18, 72, 36

10. A Sports Club is preparing welcome gifts. There are 65 golf balls, 39 baseballs, and 26 tennis balls. What is the greatest number of gifts the Sports Club can prepare using all of the golf balls, baseballs, and tennis balls?

3-3 Least Common Multiple

Find the least common multiple (LCM).

11. 8, 10 **12.** 3, 8, 9 **13.** 2, 3, 4, 6

14. Charlie and Heather swam laps in the pool. Charlie completed one lap in 3 minutes and Heather completed one lap in 7 minutes. If they started swimming laps at the same time, in how many minutes will they finish a lap together?

3-4 Equivalent Fractions and Mixed Numbers

Write each fraction as an improper fraction or a mixed number.

15. $2\frac{13}{14}$ **16.** $\frac{17}{6}$ **17.** $\frac{15}{11}$ **18.** $3\frac{2}{7}$

Determine whether the fractions in each pair are equivalent.

19. $\frac{3}{7}$ and $\frac{4}{9}$ **20.** $\frac{9}{6}$ and $\frac{12}{8}$ **21.** $\frac{4}{5}$ and $\frac{12}{15}$

Holt Mathematics

3-5 Equivalent Fractions and Decimals

Write each fraction as a decimal.

22. $\frac{2}{5}$

23. $\frac{7}{20}$

24. $\frac{37}{50}$

25. $\frac{5}{8}$

Write each decimal as a fraction in simplest form.

26. 0.075

27. −1.15

28. 0.38

29. −2.8

3-6 Comparing and Ordering Rational Numbers

Compare the fractions. Write < or >.

30. $\frac{3}{5}$ ▉ $\frac{2}{3}$

31. $-\frac{6}{5}$ ▉ $-\frac{5}{6}$

32. $-\frac{4}{7}$ ▉ $-\frac{5}{9}$

Compare the decimals. Write < or >.

33. 0.378 ▉ 0.375

34. −0.19 ▉ −0.919

35. −5.9 ▉ 5.09

Holt Mathematics

Big Ideas

Answer these question to summarize the important concepts from Chapter 3 in your own words.

1. Explain how to find the GCD of two or more whole numbers.

2. Explain how to tell if two fractions are equivalent.

3. Explain how to write 0.25 as a fraction.

4. Explain how to compare fractions.

5. Explain why $0.\overline{7}$ is a rational number.

For more review of Chapter 3:

- Complete the Chapter 3 Study Guide and Review on pages 158–160 of your textbook.

- Complete the Ready to Go On quizzes on pages 140 and 154 of your textbook.

Holt Mathematics

Estimating with Fractions

LESSON 4-1

Lesson Objectives

Estimate sums, differences, products, and quotients of fractions and mixed numbers

Additional Examples

Example 1

A blue whale can grow to $33\frac{3}{5}$ m long, while the great white shark may be as long as $4\frac{1}{2}$ m. Estimate how much longer the blue whale is than the great white shark.

$$33\frac{3}{5} - 4\frac{1}{2}$$

$33\frac{3}{5} \longrightarrow \boxed{}$ $4\frac{1}{2} \longrightarrow \boxed{}$ $\boxed{}$ each mixed number.

$\boxed{} - \boxed{} = \boxed{}$ Subtract.

The blue whale is about $\boxed{}$ m longer than the great white shark.

Example 2

Estimate each sum or difference.

A. $\dfrac{7}{9} - \dfrac{2}{5}$

$\dfrac{7}{9} \longrightarrow 1$ $\dfrac{2}{5} \longrightarrow \dfrac{1}{2}$ $\boxed{}$ each fraction.

$\boxed{} - \boxed{} = \boxed{}$ Subtract.

B. $4\dfrac{5}{9} + 3\dfrac{1}{8}$

$4\dfrac{5}{9} \longrightarrow 4\dfrac{1}{2}$ $3\dfrac{1}{8} \longrightarrow 3$ Round each mixed $\boxed{}$.

$\boxed{} + \boxed{} = \boxed{}$ Add.

C. $2\dfrac{1}{8} - \dfrac{1}{12}$

$2\dfrac{1}{8} \longrightarrow 2$ $\dfrac{1}{12} \longrightarrow 0$ $\boxed{}$ each number.

$\boxed{} - \boxed{} = \boxed{}$ Add.

Holt Mathematics

Example 3

Estimate each product or quotient.

A. $3\frac{2}{9} \cdot 6\frac{5}{6}$

$3\frac{2}{9} \longrightarrow$ ☐ $6\frac{5}{6} \longrightarrow$ ☐   ☐ each mixed number to the nearest ☐ .

☐ • ☐ = ☐   Multiply.

B. $13\frac{4}{5} \div 2\frac{1}{4}$

$13\frac{4}{5} \longrightarrow$ ☐ $2\frac{1}{4} \longrightarrow$ ☐   ☐ each mixed number to the nearest ☐ .

☐ ÷ ☐ = ☐   Divide.

Check It Out!

1. A Cocker Spaniel may grow to weigh about $11\frac{1}{2}$ kilograms while the Chihuahua will not weigh more than $2\frac{7}{8}$ kilograms. Estimate how much more a Cocker Spaniel weighs than a Chihuahua.

2. Estimate the sum.

$4\frac{2}{9} - \frac{8}{15}$

3. Estimate the quotient.

$11\frac{7}{8} \div 3\frac{1}{3}$

Holt Mathematics

LESSON 4-2

Adding and Subtracting Fractions

Lesson Objectives

Add and subtract fractions

Additional Examples

Example 1

Add or subtract. Write each answer in simplest form.

A. $\frac{5}{8} + \frac{1}{8}$

$\frac{5}{8} + \frac{1}{8} = \frac{\boxed{} + \boxed{}}{8}$ Add the ___________ and keep the ___________.

$= \boxed{} = \boxed{}$ Simplify.

B. $\frac{9}{11} - \frac{4}{11}$

$\frac{9}{11} - \frac{4}{11} = \frac{\boxed{} - \boxed{}}{11}$ Subtract the ___________ and keep the ___________.

$= \boxed{}$ The answer is in the simplest form.

Example 2

Add or subtract. Write each answer in simplest form.

$\frac{3}{4} - \frac{2}{3}$

$\frac{3}{4} - \frac{2}{3} = \frac{3 \cdot 3}{4 \cdot 3} - \frac{2 \cdot 4}{3 \cdot 4}$ Multiply the ___________.

$= \boxed{} - \boxed{}$ Write ___________ fractions using the ___________ denominator.

$= \boxed{}$ Subtract.

Holt Mathematics

Example 3

In one Earth year, Jupiter completes about $\frac{1}{12}$ of its orbit around the Sun, while Mars completes about $\frac{1}{2}$ of its orbit. How much more of its orbit does Mars complete than Jupiter?

$$\frac{1}{2} - \frac{1}{12} = \boxed{} - \frac{1}{12}$$ The LCM of the denominators is $\boxed{}$.

$$= \boxed{} - \frac{1}{12}$$ Write $\boxed{}$ fractions

using the common $\boxed{}$.

$$= \boxed{}$$ Subtract.

Mars completes $\boxed{}$ more of its orbit than Jupiter does.

Check It Out!

1. Add. Write the answer in simplest form.

$$\frac{5}{6} + \frac{1}{6}$$

2. Subtract. Write the answer in simplest form.

$$\frac{3}{5} - \frac{1}{2}$$

3. It takes Michelle $\frac{5}{12}$ hour to drive to work. It takes Luke $\frac{1}{2}$ hour to drive to work. How much longer does it take Luke to drive to work?

Holt Mathematics

LESSON 4-3 Adding and Subtracting Mixed Numbers

Lesson Objectives

Add and subtract mixed numbers

Additional Examples

Example 1

Add. Write each answer in simplest form.

A. $9\frac{2}{3} + 12\frac{2}{3}$

$9\frac{2}{3} + 12\frac{2}{3} = \boxed{} + \dfrac{\boxed{}}{3}$ Add the $\boxed{}$, and then

add the $\boxed{}$.

$= \boxed{} + \boxed{}$ Rewrite the improper fraction as a

$\boxed{}$ number.

$= \boxed{}$ Add.

B. $5\frac{1}{8} + 3\frac{5}{6}$

$5\frac{1}{8} + 3\frac{5}{6} = 5\boxed{} + 3\boxed{}$ Find a $\boxed{}$ denominator.

$= \boxed{} + \boxed{}$ $\boxed{}$ the integers, and then $\boxed{}$

the fractions.

$= \boxed{}$ Add.

Example 2

Subtract. Write each answer in simplest form.

A. $4\frac{2}{3} - 2\frac{1}{3}$

$4\frac{2}{3} - 2\frac{1}{3} = \boxed{} + \dfrac{\boxed{}}{3}$ $\boxed{}$ the integers, and then

$\boxed{}$ the fractions.

$= \boxed{}$ Add.

Holt Mathematics

Subtract. Write each answer in simplest form.

B. $12\frac{8}{9} - 8\frac{2}{3}$

$12\frac{8}{9} - 8\frac{2}{3} = 12\boxed{} - 8\boxed{}$ Find a common denominator.

$\phantom{12\frac{8}{9} - 8\frac{2}{3}} = \boxed{} + \dfrac{\boxed{}}{9}$ Subtract the $\boxed{}$, and then

subtract the $\boxed{}$.

$\phantom{12\frac{8}{9} - 8\frac{2}{3}} = \boxed{}$ Add.

Example 3

Kevin is $48\frac{3}{8}$ inches tall. His brother Keith is $5\frac{5}{8}$ inches taller. How tall is Keith?

$48\frac{3}{8} + 5\frac{5}{8} = \boxed{} + \dfrac{\boxed{}}{8}$ $\boxed{}$ the integers, and then $\boxed{}$ the fractions.

$\phantom{48\frac{3}{8} + 5\frac{5}{8}} = \boxed{} + \boxed{}$ Rewrite $\frac{8}{8}$ as $\boxed{}$.

Keith is $\boxed{}$ inches tall.   Add.

Check It Out!

1. Add. Write the answer in simplest form.

$7\frac{4}{5} + 10\frac{2}{5}$

2. Subtract. Write the answer in simplest form.

$14\frac{1}{4} - 10\frac{3}{4}$

3. Alvin weighs $72\frac{2}{3}$ lbs. His baby brother weighs $15\frac{1}{3}$ lbs. How much do they weigh together?

Holt Mathematics

 **LESSON 4-4** 

Multiplying Fractions and Mixed Numbers

Lesson Objectives

Multiply fractions and mixed numbers

Additional Examples

Example 1

In 2001, the car toll on the George Washington Bridge was \$6.00. In 1995, the toll was $\frac{2}{3}$ of that toll. What was the toll in 1995?

$$6 \cdot \boxed{} = \boxed{} + \boxed{} + \boxed{} + \boxed{} + \boxed{} + \boxed{}$$

$$= \boxed{}$$

$$= \boxed{} \qquad \text{Simplify.}$$

$$= \$\boxed{} \qquad \text{Write the fraction as a decimal.}$$

The George Washington Bridge toll for a car was \$ \boxed{} in 1995.

Example 2

Multiply. Write each answer in simplest form.

A. $12 \cdot \frac{3}{4}$

$$12 \cdot \frac{3}{4} = \boxed{} \cdot \frac{3}{4} \qquad \text{Write 12 as a } \boxed{}.$$

$$= \frac{\overset{3}{\cancel{12}} \cdot 3}{1 \cdot \underset{1}{\cancel{4}}} \qquad \boxed{} \text{ a numerator and}$$

denominator by their GCD, 4.

$$= \boxed{} = \boxed{} \qquad \text{Multiply numerators.}$$

Multiply denominators.

B. $\frac{3}{5} \cdot \frac{1}{4}$

$$\frac{3}{5} \cdot \frac{1}{4} = \frac{3 \cdot 1}{5 \cdot 4} \qquad \boxed{} \text{ numerators.}$$

$$= \boxed{} \qquad \boxed{} \text{ denominators.}$$

Holt Mathematics

Example 3

Multiply. Write each answer in simplest form.

A. $\frac{2}{5} \cdot 1\frac{2}{3}$

$\frac{2}{5} \cdot 1\frac{2}{3} = \frac{2}{5} \cdot \boxed{}$ Write the $\boxed{}$ number as an

improper $\boxed{}$.

$= \frac{2}{\cancel{5}} \cdot \frac{\cancel{5}}{3}$ Divide a numerator and denominator by their GCD, 5.

$= \boxed{}$ $\boxed{}$ numerators. $\boxed{}$ denominators.

B. $4\frac{1}{5} \cdot 2\frac{1}{7}$

$4\frac{1}{5} \cdot 2\frac{1}{7} = \boxed{} \cdot \boxed{}$ Write the mixed $\boxed{}$ as

$\boxed{}$ fractions.

$= \frac{^3\cancel{21} \cdot \cancel{15}^3}{_1\cancel{5} \cdot \cancel{7}_1}$ Divide a numerator and denominator by their GCD, 7.

$= \boxed{}$ or $\boxed{}$ Multiply $\boxed{}$. Multiply $\boxed{}$.

Check It Out!

1. In 2002, the fee to park in a parking garage was $4. In 2000, the fee was $\frac{3}{4}$ of the fee in 2002. What was the fee in 2000?

2. Multiply. Write the answer in simplest form.

$\frac{3}{7} \cdot \frac{1}{8}$

3. Multiply. Write the answer in simplest form.

$\frac{3}{5} \cdot 2\frac{1}{3}$

Holt Mathematics

LESSON 4-5 — Dividing Fractions and Mixed Numbers

Lesson Objectives

Divide fractions and mixed numbers

Vocabulary

reciprocal (p. 192) _______________________________________

____

multiplicative inverse (p. 192) _______________________

____

Additional Examples

Example 1

Divide. Write each answer in simplest form.

A. $\dfrac{3}{7} \div \dfrac{2}{5}$

$$\dfrac{3}{7} \div \dfrac{2}{5} = \dfrac{3}{7} \cdot \boxed{}$$ Multiply by the $\boxed{}$ of $\dfrac{2}{5}$.

$$= \dfrac{3 \cdot 5}{7 \cdot 2}$$

$$= \boxed{} \text{ or } \boxed{}$$

B. $\dfrac{3}{8} \div 12$

$$\dfrac{3}{8} \div 12 = \dfrac{3}{8} \cdot \boxed{}$$

$$= \dfrac{\overset{1}{\cancel{3}}}{8} \cdot \dfrac{1}{\underset{4}{\cancel{12}}}$$ Multiply by the $\boxed{}$ of 12.

$$= \boxed{}$$ Simplify.

Holt Mathematics

Example 2

Divide. Write each answer in simplest form.

A. $5\frac{2}{3} \div 1\frac{1}{4}$

$5\frac{2}{3} \div 1\frac{1}{4} = \boxed{} \div \boxed{}$ Write mixed $\boxed{}$ as improper $\boxed{}$.

$= \dfrac{17}{3} \cdot \boxed{}$ Multiply by the $\boxed{}$ of $\dfrac{5}{4}$.

$= \boxed{}$ or $\boxed{}$

B. $\dfrac{3}{4} \div 2\frac{1}{2}$

$\dfrac{3}{4} \div 2\frac{1}{2} = \dfrac{3}{4} \div \boxed{}$ Write $2\frac{1}{2}$ as an $\boxed{}$ fraction.

$= \dfrac{3}{4} \cdot \boxed{}$

$= \dfrac{3 \cdot \overset{1}{\cancel{2}}}{\underset{2}{\cancel{4}} \cdot 5}$ Multiply by the $\boxed{}$ of $\dfrac{5}{2}$.

$= \boxed{}$ Simplify.

Holt Mathematics

Example 3

The life span of a golden dollar coin is 30 years, while paper currency lasts an average of $1\frac{1}{2}$ years. How many times longer will the golden dollar stay in circulation?

$30 \div 1\frac{1}{2} = \frac{30}{1} \div \frac{3}{2}$ Write both numbers as [ ] fractions.

$= \frac{30}{1} \cdot$ [ ] Multiply by the [ ] of $\frac{3}{2}$.

$= \frac{{}^{10}\cancel{30} \cdot 2}{1 \cdot \cancel{3}_1}$ Simplify.

$=$ [ ] or [ ]

The golden dollar will stay in circulation about [ ] times longer than paper currency.

Check It Out!

1. Divide. Write the answer in simplest form.

$\frac{3}{5} \div \frac{1}{2}$

2. Divide. Write the answer in simplest form.

$\frac{3}{5} \div 1\frac{2}{5}$

3. The average life of a queen ant is approximately 3 years. The life span of a worker ant is $\frac{3}{7}$ year. How many times longer will the queen ant live?

Holt Mathematics

LESSON 4-6 Solving Equations Containing Fractions

Lesson Objectives

Solve one-step equations that contain fractions

Additional Examples

Example 1

Solve. Write each answer in simplest form.

A. $x - \dfrac{3}{7} = \dfrac{5}{7}$

$$x - \dfrac{3}{7} = \dfrac{5}{7}$$
Since $\dfrac{3}{7}$ is ⬚ from x,

$$x - \dfrac{3}{7} + \boxed{} = \dfrac{5}{7} + \boxed{}$$
add ⬚ to both sides.

$$x = \boxed{} = \boxed{}$$
Simplify.

B. $\dfrac{3}{8} + t = \dfrac{5}{12}$

$$\dfrac{3}{8} + t = \dfrac{5}{12}$$
Since $\dfrac{3}{8}$ is ⬚ to t,

$$\dfrac{3}{8} + t - \boxed{} = \dfrac{5}{12} - \boxed{}$$
subtract ⬚ from both sides.

$$t = \boxed{} - \boxed{}$$
Find a common ⬚.

$$t = \boxed{}$$
Subtract.

Example 2

Solve. Write each answer in simplest form.

A. $\dfrac{3}{8}x = \dfrac{1}{4}$

$$\dfrac{3}{8}x = \dfrac{1}{4}$$

$$\dfrac{8}{3} \cdot \dfrac{3}{8}x = \dfrac{1}{\overset{}{\underset{1}{4}}} \cdot \dfrac{\overset{2}{8}}{3}$$
Multiply by the ⬚ of $\dfrac{3}{8}$.

$$x = \boxed{}$$
Then simplify.

Holt Mathematics

B. $4y = \dfrac{8}{9}$

$$4y = \dfrac{8}{9}$$

$$4y \cdot \dfrac{1}{4} = \dfrac{\overset{2}{8}}{9} \cdot \dfrac{1}{\underset{1}{4}} \qquad \text{Multiply by the reciprocal of } \boxed{}.$$

$$y = \boxed{} \qquad \text{Then simplify.}$$

Example 3

The amount of copper in brass is $\dfrac{3}{4}$ of the total weight. If a sample contains $4\dfrac{1}{5}$ ounces of copper, what is the total weight of the sample?

Let w represent the total weight of the sample.

$$\dfrac{3}{4}w = 4\dfrac{1}{5} \qquad \text{Write an equation.}$$

$$\dfrac{3}{4}w \cdot \boxed{} = 4\dfrac{1}{5} \cdot \boxed{} \qquad \text{Multiply by the } \boxed{}$$
$$\text{of } \dfrac{3}{4}.$$

$$w = \dfrac{\overset{7}{21}}{5} \cdot \dfrac{4}{\underset{1}{3}} \qquad \text{Write } 4\dfrac{1}{5} \text{ as an } \boxed{}$$ 
$$\text{fraction.}$$

$$w = \boxed{} \text{ or } \boxed{} \qquad \text{Then simplify.}$$

The sample weighs $\boxed{}$ ounces.

Holt Mathematics

Check It Out!

1. Solve. Write the answer in simplest form.

$$x - \frac{3}{8} = \frac{7}{8}$$

2. Solve. Write the answer in simplest form.

$$3y = \frac{6}{7}$$

3. The amount of copper in zinc is $\frac{1}{4}$ of the total weight. If a sample contains $5\frac{1}{3}$ ounces of copper, what is the total weight of the sample.

Holt Mathematics

LESSON 4-7
Adding, Subtracting, and Multiplying Decimals

Lesson Objectives

Add, subtract, and multiply decimals

Additional Examples

Example 1

Add or subtract. Estimate to check whether each answer is reasonable.

A. $4.55 + 11.3$

$$\begin{array}{r} 4.55 \\ +\ 11.30 \\ \hline \end{array}$$

Line up the [ ] points.

Use [ ] as a placeholder.

Add.

Estimate

$5 + 11 =$ [ ]   [ ] is a reasonable answer.

B. $28 - 15.911$

$$\begin{array}{r} {\scriptstyle 7\ 9\ 910} \\ 28.000 \\ -\ 15.911 \\ \hline \end{array}$$

Use zeros as placeholders.
Line up the decimal points.

Subtract.

Estimate

[ ] − [ ] = 12   [ ] is a reasonable answer.

Example 2

Multiply. Estimate to check whether each answer is reasonable.

A. $2.4 \cdot 2$

$$\begin{array}{r} 2.4 \\ \times\ \ 2 \\ \hline \end{array}$$

1 decimal place
0 decimal place

$1 + 0 = 1$ decimal place.

Estimate

$2 \cdot 2 = 4$ [ ] is a reasonable answer.

Holt Mathematics

Multiply. Estimate to check whether each answer is reasonable.

B. $-3.84 \cdot 0.9$

$$
\begin{array}{rl}
-3.84 & \text{2 decimal places} \\
\times\ \ 0.9 & \text{1 decimal place} \\
\hline
 &
\end{array}
$$

$2 + 1 = 3$ decimal places.

Estimate

$-4 \cdot 1 = -4$ _______ is a __________ answer.

Example 3

To find your weight on another planet, multiply the relative gravitational pull of the planet and your weight. The relative gravitational pull on Mars is 0.38. What would a person who weighs 85 pounds on Earth weigh on Mars?

$$
\begin{array}{r}
85 \\
\times\ 0.38 \\
\hline
680 \\
+\ 2550 \\
\hline

\end{array}
$$

□ decimal places

□ decimal places

□ + □ = □ decimal places

The person would weigh _______ pounds on Mars.

Holt Mathematics

Check It Out!

1. Add. Estimate to check whether the answer is reasonable.

   $6.78 + 13.2$

2. Multiply. Estimate to check whether the answer is reasonable.

   $3.2 \cdot 1.6$

3. Jet fuel weighs approximately 6.2 pounds per gallon. If a plane was serviced with 1,012 gallons of fuel, how many pounds of fuel were used?

Holt Mathematics

Dividing Decimals

LESSON 4-8

Lesson Objectives

Divide decimals and integers by decimals

Additional Examples

Example 1

Divide.

A. $8.28 \div 4.6$

$8.28 \div 4.6 = 82.8 \div 46$ ⁀ ⁀   Multiply both numbers by ☐ to make the divisor an integer.

```
      ☐
46)82.8
    46
    36 8
  − 36 8
       0
```

Divide as with whole numbers.

B. $18.48 \div (-1.75)$

$18.48 \div (-1.75) = 1,848 \div 175$ Multiply both numbers by ☐ to make the divisor an integer.

```
        ☐
175)1848.00
   − 175
      98 0
    − 87 5
      10 50
    − 10 50
          0
```

Use ☐ as placeholders.
Divide as with whole numbers.

$18.48 \div (-1.75) = $ ☐   The signs are ☐ .

Holt Mathematics

Example 2

Divide. Estimate to check whether each answer is reasonable.

A. $4 \div 1.25$

$4.00 \div 1.25 = 400 \div 125$ [____] both numbers by 100 to make the divisor an integer.

$$125)\overline{400.0}$$
$$-375$$
$$25\ 0$$
$$-25\ 0$$
$$0$$

Use zero as a [____]. Divide as with whole numbers.

Estimate

$4 \div 1 = 4$ The answer is [____].

B. $-24 \div (-2.5)$

$-24.0 \div (-2.5) = -240 \div (-25)$ Multiply both numbers by [____] to make the divisor an integer.

$$25)\overline{240.0}$$
$$-225$$
$$15\ 0$$
$$-15\ 0$$
$$0$$

Divide as with whole numbers.

$-24 \div (-2.5) =$ [____]   The signs are [____].

Estimate

$-24 \div (-3) = 8$ The answer is [____].

Holt Mathematics

Example 3

Eric paid $229.25 to rent a car. The fee to rent the car was $32.75 per day. For how long did Eric rent the car?

$$229.25 \div 32.75 = 22{,}925 \div 3{,}275$$

Multiply both numbers by ☐ to make the divisor an integer.

$$3{,}275\overline{)22{,}925}$$
$$-\ 22{,}925$$
$$0$$

Divide as with whole numbers.

Eric rented the car for ☐ days.

Check It Out!

1. Divide.

   $6.45 \div 0.5$

2. Divide. Estimate to check whether the answer is reasonable.

   $-22 \div (-2.5)$

3. Jace took a trip in which he drove 350 miles. During the trip his truck used 12.5 gallons of gas. What was his truck's gas mileage?

Holt Mathematics

LESSON 4-9

Metric Measurements

Lesson Objectives

Identify, convert, and compare metric units

Additional Examples

Example 1

Choose the most appropriate metric unit for each measurement. Justify your answer.

A. The amount of water a runner drinks each day

⬜ – the amount of water a runner drinks is similar to the amount of water in several large ⬜.

B. The length of a boat

⬜ – the length of a boat is similar to the width of several ⬜.

C. The mass of a car

⬜ – the mass of a car is similar to the mass of several ⬜.

Example 2

Convert each measure.

A. 530 cL to liters

530 cL = (530 ÷ ⬜) L   100 cL = 1 L, so divide by ⬜.

= ⬜ L   Move the decimal point ⬜ places

to the ⬜.

Holt Mathematics

Convert each measure.

B. 1,070 g to milligrams

1,070 g = (1,070 × ______) mg   1 g = 1,000 mg, so multiply by ______ .

= ______ mg   Move the decimal point ______ places

to the ______ .

Example 3

Elizabeth buys one pumpkin that has a mass of 3 kg and another that has a mass of 2,150 g. Which pumpkin has the greater mass? Use estimation to explain why your answer makes sense.

Convert 2,150 g to kilograms.

2,150 g = (2,150 ÷ ______) kg   1,000 g = 1 kg, so divide by ______ .

= ______ g   Move the decimal point ______ places

to the ______ .

The ______ pumpkin has the greater mass.

Check

2,150 g is about ______ g or 2 kg   Round 2,150 to the nearest ______ .

3 kg > 2 kg, so the answer makes sense.

Holt Mathematics

Check It Out!

1. **Choose the most appropriate metric unit for the measurement. Justify your answer.**

   The amount of liquid in 10 teardrops

2. **Convert the measure.**

   580 g to centigrams

3. **Tyesha purchases a bag of potatoes that has a mass of 2.5 kg and another bag that has a mass of 3,850 g. Which bag has the greater mass? Use estimation to explain why your answer makes sense.**

104

Holt Mathematics

LESSON 4-10 Solving Equations Containing Decimals

Lesson Objectives

Solve one-step equations that contain decimals

Additional Examples

Example 1

Solve.

A. $n - 2.75 = 8.3$

$$n - 2.75 = 8.30$$

$$+\boxed{} \quad +\boxed{}$$

$$n = \boxed{}$$

Since 2.75 is subtracted from $\boxed{}$, add 2.75 to $\boxed{}$.

B. $a + 32.66 = 42$

$$a + 32.66 = 42.00$$

$$-\boxed{} \quad -\boxed{}$$

$$a = \boxed{}$$

Since 32.66 is $\boxed{}$ to a, $\boxed{}$ 32.66 from both sides.

Example 2

Solve.

A. $\dfrac{x}{4.8} = 5.4$

$$\dfrac{x}{4.8} = 5.4$$

$$\dfrac{x}{4.8} \cdot \boxed{} = 5.4 \cdot \boxed{}$$

$$x = \boxed{}$$

Since $\boxed{}$ is divided by 4.8, multiply $\boxed{}$ by 4.8.

Holt Mathematics

Solve.

B. $9 = 3.6d$

$$9 = 3.6d$$

Since d is ☐ by 3.6,

☐ both sides by 3.6.

$$\frac{9}{\boxed{}} = \frac{3.6d}{\boxed{}}$$

$\boxed{} = d$

Think: $9 \div 3.6 = 90 \div 36$

$\boxed{} = d$

Example 3

PROBLEM SOLVING APPLICATION

A board-game box is 2.5 inches tall. A toy store has shelving space measuring 15 inches vertically in which to store the boxes. How many boxes can be stacked in the space?

1. **Understand the Problem**

   Rewrite the question as a statement.

   Find the number of boxes that can be placed on the shelf.

   List the important information:

   • Each board-game box is ☐ inches tall.

   • The store has shelving space measuring ☐ inches.

2. **Make a Plan**

   The total height of the boxes is equal to the height of one box ☐ the number of boxes. Since you know how tall the shelf is, you can write an equation with b being the number of boxes.

   $\boxed{} b = 15$

Holt Mathematics

3. Solve

$$2.5b = 15$$

Since ☐ is multiplied by 2.5,

$$\frac{2.5b}{\boxed{}} = \frac{15}{\boxed{}}$$

divide ☐ by 2.5.

$$b = \boxed{}$$

☐ boxes can be stacked in the space.

4. Look Back

You can round 2.5 to ☐ and estimate how many boxes will fit on the shelf.

$$15 \div \boxed{} = 5$$

So ☐ boxes is a reasonable answer.

Check It Out!

1. Solve.

$$a + 27.51 = 36$$

2. Solve.

$$9 = 2.5d$$

3. A canned good is 4.5 inches tall. A grocery store has shelving measuring 18 inches vertically in which to store the cans. How many cans can be stacked in the space?

Holt Mathematics

Chapter Review

4-1 Estimating with Fractions

Estimate each sum, difference, product, or quotient.

1. $4\frac{3}{5} - 2\frac{5}{12}$

2. $15\frac{1}{3} + 2\frac{8}{9} - 9\frac{5}{11}$

3. $4\frac{1}{5} \cdot 7\frac{7}{9}$

4. $23\frac{6}{7} \div (-1\frac{1}{12})$

4-2 Adding and Subtracting Fractions

Add or subtract. Write each answer in simplest form.

5. $-\frac{1}{4} + \frac{3}{8} + \frac{5}{12}$

6. $\frac{5}{6} - \frac{3}{15} - \frac{2}{5}$

7. Kevin ran for $\frac{3}{4}$ hour, swam for $\frac{1}{2}$ hour, and bicycled for $\frac{5}{6}$ hour. How long did Kevin run, swim, and bike altogether?

4-3 Adding and Subtracting Mixed Numbers

Compare. Write <, >, or =.

8. $10\frac{1}{4} - 4\frac{3}{4}$ ▪ $12\frac{3}{5} - 6\frac{9}{10}$

9. $16\frac{7}{8} + 4\frac{3}{4}$ ▪ $25\frac{1}{8} - 3\frac{1}{2}$

10. Maggie hiked $7\frac{5}{8}$ miles at Turkey Run State Park, and $12\frac{3}{10}$ miles at Starved Rock State Park. How many more miles did Maggie hike at Starved Rock than Turkey State Park?

4-4 Multiplying Fractions and Mixed Numbers

Multiply. Write each answer in simplest form.

11. $6 \cdot \frac{5}{9}$

12. $\frac{7}{8} \cdot \frac{2}{3}$

13. $1\frac{4}{5} \cdot 8\frac{5}{6}$

14. Caitlin drove at a speed of 65 miles per hour for $6\frac{3}{4}$ hours. How many miles did she travel?

Holt Mathematics

4-5 Dividing Fractions and Mixed Numbers

Divide. Write each answer in simplest form.

15. $\frac{4}{5} \div 6\frac{2}{3}$

16. $2\frac{7}{8} \div 1\frac{1}{12}$

17. $\frac{5}{9} \div 2\frac{2}{9}$

18. $3\frac{1}{3} \div \frac{3}{10}$

19. Tommy and his three brothers worked for $177\frac{3}{5}$ hours. What was the average number of hours each brother worked?

4-6 Solving Equations Containing Fractions

Solve. Write each answer in simplest form.

20. $\frac{5}{7}x = \frac{5}{8}$

21. $w + \frac{3}{4} = \frac{11}{12}$

22. $-\frac{17}{55} + d = \frac{28}{55}$

23. $2\frac{5}{18}p = 5\frac{4}{9}$

24. Mark spends $\frac{1}{3}$ of his day sleeping and $\frac{1}{4}$ of his day at school. What fraction of his day is spent doing things besides sleeping and going to school?

4-7 Adding, Subtracting, and Multiplying Decimals

Add or subtract. Estimate to check whether each answer is reasonable.

25. $-3.817 + 4.2$

26. $7.624 - 18.34$

27. $-4.77 - 12.053$

28. $30.62 - (-9.18)$

Multiply. Estimate to check whether each answer is reasonable.

29. $-8.7 \cdot 3.12$

30. $1.89 \cdot 0.07$

31. $-5.21 \cdot (-43.6)$

32. $0.58 \cdot (-3.1)$

33. Fresh ground beef is on sale for $4.90 per pound. How much will it cost to buy 8.30 pounds of ground beef?

4-8 Dividing Decimals

Divide. Estimate to check whether each answer is reasonable.

34. $48 \div 3.2$

35. $-13.6 \div 1.6$

36. $72 \div (-3.2)$

37. $-154 \div (-0.35)$

38. Jordan used 32.46 gallons of gas to drive his van 584.28 miles. How many miles per gallon did Jordan get?

4-9 Metric Measurements

Choose the most appropriate metric unit for the measurement. Justify your answer.

39. The width of your driveway

Convert each measure.

40. 1,270 g to kg

41. 890 cm to mm

42. 750 mL to L

43. 122 km to m

44. Rosa walks 1.5 km to the library. Meghan walks 2,200 m to the library. Who walks farther? Use estimation to explain why your answer makes sense.

4-10 Solving Equations Containing Decimals

Solve.

45. $t - 0.94 = 18.5$

46. $w + 28.52 = -16.03$

47. $0.27x = -8.1$

48. $\dfrac{k}{-0.36} = 8.5$

49. Shea bought CDs for $11.65 each. She spent a total of $163.10. How many CDs did Shea buy?

Holt Mathematics

Big Ideas

Answer these questions to summarize the important concepts from Chapter 4 in your own words.

1. Explain the guidelines for rounding fractions.

2. Explain the difference between adding or subtracting fractions with unlike denominators, and multiplying fractions with unlike denominators.

3. Explain how to multiply decimals.

4. Explain how to divide an integer by a decimal.

For more review of Chapter 4:

- Complete the Chapter 4 Study Guide and Review on pages 222–224 of your textbook.
- Complete the Ready to Go On quizzes on pages 184, 200, and 218 of your textbook.

Holt Mathematics

LESSON 5-1 Ratios

Lesson Objectives

Identify, write, and compare ratios

Vocabulary

ratio (p. 232) ____

____

Additional Examples

Example 1

Twenty students are asked to choose their favorite music category. Eight chose pop, seven chose hip hop, and five chose rock. Write each ratio in all three forms.

A. rock to hip hop

There were ☐ students that chose rock and ☐ students that chose hip hop.

The ratio of rock to hip hop is ☐ to ☐, which can be written as follows:

☐

B. hip hop to pop

There were ☐ students that chose hip hop and ☐ students that chose pop.

The ratio of hip hop to pop is ☐ to ☐, which can be written as follows:

☐

C. rock to pop and hip hop

There were ☐ students that chose rock and ☐ + ☐ = ☐ students that chose hip hop and pop.

The ratio of rock to hip hop and pop is ☐ to ☐, which can be written as follows:

☐

Holt Mathematics

Example 2

On average, most people can read about 600 words in 3 minutes. Write the ratio of words to minutes in simplest form.

$$\frac{\text{words}}{\text{minutes}} = \frac{\boxed{} \text{ words}}{\boxed{} \text{ minutes}}$$

Write the ratio as a fraction.

$$\frac{\text{words}}{\text{minutes}} = \frac{600 \div \boxed{}}{3 \div \boxed{}}$$

Simplify.

$$\frac{\text{words}}{\text{minutes}} = \frac{\boxed{} \text{ words}}{1 \text{ minute}}$$

For every minute, $\boxed{}$ words are read.

The ratios in simplest form are: $\boxed{}$.

Example 3

Honey lemon cough drops come in packages of 30 drops per 10-ounce bag. Cherry cough drops come in packages of 24 drops per 6-ounce bag. Tell which package has the greater ratio of drops to ounces.

Honey: $\dfrac{\text{drops}}{\text{ounces}} = \dfrac{\boxed{} \text{ drops}}{\boxed{} \text{ ounces}} = \dfrac{\boxed{}}{\boxed{}}$

Write the ratios as fractions with common denominators.

Cherry: $\dfrac{\text{drops}}{\text{ounces}} = \dfrac{\boxed{} \text{ drops}}{\boxed{} \text{ ounces}} = \dfrac{\boxed{}}{\boxed{}}$

Because $\boxed{} > \boxed{}$ and the denominators are the $\boxed{}$, the bag of $\boxed{}$ has the greater ratio of drops to ounces.

Holt Mathematics

Check It Out!

1. Nineteen students are asked to choose their favorite sport. Nine choose rock climbing, four choose kite surfing, and six choose snow boarding. Write the ratio in all three forms.

   snow boarding to rock climbing

2. At Casitas Middle School there are 456 microscopes for 152 students. Write the ratio of microscopes to students in simplest form.

3. Jelly beans come in small packages of 25 per 5-ounce package and large packages of 56 per 8-ounce package. Tell which bag has the greater ratio of jelly beans per ounce.

Holt Mathematics

LESSON 5-2 Rates

Lesson Objectives

Find and compare unit rates, such as average speed and unit price

Vocabulary

rate (p. 236) ______________________________

____

unit rate (p. 236) ______________________________

Additional Examples

Example 1

Find each rate.

A. A Ferris wheel revolves 35 times in 105 minutes. How many minutes does 1 revolution take?

$\dfrac{\boxed{}\text{ minutes}}{\boxed{}\text{ revolutions}}$ Write a rate that compares minutes and revolutions.

$\dfrac{\boxed{}\text{ minutes} \div \boxed{}}{\boxed{}\text{ revolutions} \div \boxed{}}$ Divide the numerator and denominator by $\boxed{}$ to get an equivalent rate.

$\dfrac{\boxed{}\text{ minutes}}{1\text{ revolution}}$ Simplify.

The Ferris wheel takes $\boxed{}$ minutes for 1 revolution.

Holt Mathematics

B. Sue walks 6 yards and passes 24 security lights set along the sidewalk. How many security lights does she pass in 1 yard?

$$\frac{\boxed{}\ \text{lights}}{\boxed{}\ \text{yards}}$$

Write a rate that compares lights and yards.

$$\frac{\boxed{}\ \text{lights} \div \boxed{}}{\boxed{}\ \text{yards} \div \boxed{}}$$

Divide the numerator and denominator by $\boxed{}$ to get an equivalent rate.

$$\frac{\boxed{}\ \text{lights}}{1\ \text{yard}}$$

Simplify.

Sue walks past $\boxed{}$ security lights in 1 yard.

Example 2

Danielle is cycling 68 miles as a fundraising commitment. She wants to complete her ride in 4 hours. What should be her average speed in miles per hour?

$$\frac{\boxed{}\ \text{miles}}{\boxed{}\ \text{hours}}$$

Write the rate as a fraction.

$$\frac{\boxed{}\ \text{miles} \div \boxed{}}{\boxed{}\ \text{hours} \div \boxed{}} = \frac{\boxed{}\ \text{miles}}{1\ \text{hour}}$$

Divide the numerator and denominator by $\boxed{}$

to get an equivalent rate.

Her average speed should be  miles per hour.

Holt Mathematics

Example 3

A 12-ounce sports drink costs $0.99, and a 16-ounce drink costs $1.19. Which size is the best buy?

Divide the ☐ by the number of ☐ to find the unit price of each size.

$$\frac{\$\ \boxed{}}{\boxed{}\ \text{oz}} \approx \frac{\$\ \boxed{}}{\boxed{}\ \text{oz}} \qquad \frac{\$\ \boxed{}}{\boxed{}\ \text{oz}} \approx \frac{\$\ \boxed{}}{\boxed{}\ \text{oz}}$$

Since $\$\ ☐ < \$\ ☐$, the ☐-oz sports drink is the best buy.

Check It Out!

1. **A dog walks 696 steps in 12 minutes. How many steps does the dog take in 1 minute?**

2. **Rhett is a pilot and needs to fly 1191 miles to the next city. He wants to complete his flight in 3 hours. What should be his average speed in miles per hour?**

3. **A 1.5-gallon container costs $4.02, and a 3.5-gallon container costs $8.75. Which size is the best buy?**

Holt Mathematics

California Standards NS1.2

LESSON 5-3

Identifying and Writing Proportions

Know it! Note

Lesson Objectives

Find equivalent ratios and identify proportions

Vocabulary

equivalent ratios (p. 240) ______

proportion (p. 240) ______

Additional Examples

Example 1

Determine whether the ratios are proportional.

A. $\frac{24}{51}, \frac{72}{128}$

$\frac{24 \div 3}{51 \div 3} =$ ☐ Simplify $\frac{24}{51}$.

$\frac{72 \div 8}{128 \div 8} =$ ☐ Simplify $\frac{72}{128}$.

Since ☐ $\neq$ ☐, the ratios ☐ proportional.

B. $\frac{150}{105}, \frac{90}{63}$

$\frac{150 \div ☐}{105 \div ☐} = \frac{10}{7}$ Simplify $\frac{150}{105}$.

$\frac{90 \div 9}{63 \div 9} =$ ☐ Simplify $\frac{90}{63}$.

Since $\frac{10}{7}$ ☐ ☐, the ratios ☐ proportional.

Example 2

Directions for making 12 servings of rice call for 3 cups of rice and 6 cups of water. For 40 servings, the directions call for 10 cups of rice and 19 cups of water. Determine whether the ratios of rice to water are proportional for both servings of rice.

Write the ⬚ of rice to water for 12 servings and for 40 servings.

Ratio of rice to water, 12 servings: ⬚   Write the ratio as a fraction.

Ratio of rice to water, 40 servings: ⬚   Write the ratio as a fraction.

$$\frac{3}{6} = \frac{3 \cdot 19}{6 \cdot 19} = \boxed{}$$ Write the ratios with a ⬚

denominator, such as 114.

$$\frac{10}{19} = \frac{10 \cdot 6}{19 \cdot 6} = \boxed{}$$

Since ⬚ ≠ ⬚ , the two ratios ⬚ proportional.

Example 3

Find a ratio equivalent to each ratio. Then use the ratios to write a proportion.

A. $\frac{3}{5}$

$$\frac{3}{5} = \frac{3 \cdot 2}{5 \cdot 2} = \boxed{}$$ Multiply both the ⬚ and

⬚ by any number, such as 2.

⬚ = ⬚   Write a ⬚ .

B. $\frac{28}{16}$

$$\frac{28}{16} = \frac{28 \div 4}{16 \div 4} = \boxed{}$$ Divide both the ⬚ and

⬚ by any number, such as 4.

⬚ = ⬚   Write a ⬚ .

Holt Mathematics

Check It Out!

1. Determine whether the ratios are proportional.

   $\dfrac{135}{75}, \dfrac{9}{4}$

2. Use the data in the table to determine whether the ratios of beans to water are proportional for both servings of beans.

Servings of Beans	Cups of Beans	Cups of Water
8	4	3
35	13	9

3. Find a ratio equivalent to the ratio. Then use the ratios to write a proportion.

   $\dfrac{16}{12}$

Holt Mathematics

LESSON 5-4
Solving Proportions

Lesson Objectives

Solve proportions by using cross products

Vocabulary

cross product (p. 244) ________________________________

Additional Examples

Example 1

Use cross products to solve the proportion.

$$\frac{9}{15} = \frac{m}{5}$$

☐ $\cdot\, m =$ ☐ $\cdot\, 5$ The cross products are ☐.

☐ $m =$ ☐   Multiply.

☐ $=$ ☐   Divide each side by ☐.

$m =$ ☐

Example 2

The graph shows the time and distance Greg walked on his way to school. At this rate, how long would it take Greg to walk 7.5 miles?

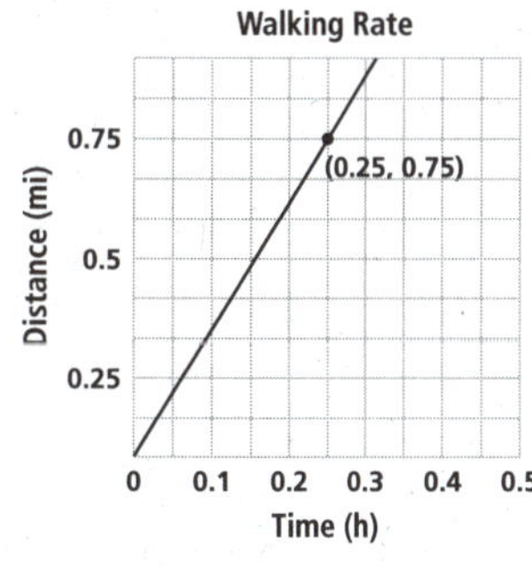

Set up a proportion in which each ratio compares distance to the time needed to walk that distance. Let t be the time needed to walk 7.5 miles.

$$\frac{0.75 \text{ mi}}{0.25 \text{ hr}} = \frac{7.5 \text{ mi}}{t \text{ hr}} \quad \begin{array}{l} \leftarrow \text{ Distance} \\ \leftarrow \text{ Time} \end{array}$$

Holt Mathematics

$$\boxed{} \cdot t = 0.25 \cdot \boxed{}$$ The cross products are $\boxed{}$.

$$\boxed{}\, t = \boxed{}$$ Multiply.

$$\frac{\boxed{}}{\boxed{}} = \frac{\boxed{}}{\boxed{}}$$ Divide each side by $\boxed{}$.

$$t = \boxed{}$$

It will take Greg $\boxed{}$ hours to walk 7.5 miles.

Example 3

PROBLEM SOLVING APPLICATION

If 3 volumes of Jennifer's encyclopedia take up 4 inches of space on her shelf, how much space will she need for all 26 volumes?

1. **Understand the Problem**
   Rewrite the question as a statement.

   • Find the space needed for $\boxed{}$ volumes of the encyclopedia.

   List the important information:

   • $\boxed{}$ volumes of the encyclopedia take up $\boxed{}$ inches of space.

2. **Make a Plan**
   Set up a proportion using the given information.

   $$\frac{3 \text{ volumes}}{4 \text{ inches}} = \frac{26 \text{ volumes}}{x}$$ Let x be the unknown space.

3. **Solve**

   $$\frac{3}{4} = \frac{26}{x}$$ Write the $\boxed{}$.

   $$\boxed{} \cdot x = 4 \cdot \boxed{}$$ The cross products are $\boxed{}$.

   $$\boxed{}\, x = 104$$ Multiply.

   $$\frac{\boxed{}}{} = \boxed{}$$ Divide each side by $\boxed{}$.

   $$x = \boxed{}$$

Holt Mathematics

She needs [____] inches for all 26 volumes.

4. Look Back

$$\frac{3}{4} = \frac{26}{34\frac{2}{3}}$$

$4 \cdot 26 = 104$

$3 \cdot 34\frac{2}{3} = 104$

The cross products are equal, so $34\frac{2}{3}$ is the answer.

Check It Out!

1. Use cross products to solve the proportion.

$$\frac{6}{7} = \frac{m}{14}$$

2. The graph shows the time and distance Paige ran in one marathon. At this rate, how long would it take Paige to run 8.5 miles?

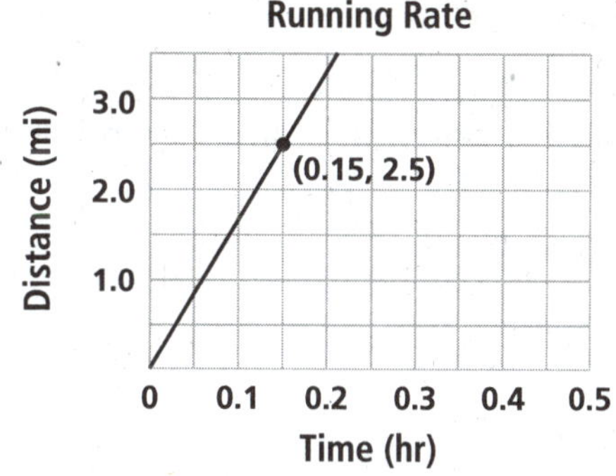

3. John filled his new radiator with 6 pints of coolant, which is at the 10-inch mark. How many pints of coolant would be needed to fill the radiator to the 25-inch level?

Holt Mathematics

LESSON 5-5

Customary Measurements

Lesson Objectives

Identify and convert customary units of measure

Additional Examples

Example 1

Choose the most appropriate customary unit for each measurement. Justify your answer.

A. the weight of a car

[____]—the weight of a car is similar to the weight of a

[____].

B. the diameter of a soup can

[____]—the diameter of a soup can is similar to the length of a

few [____].

C. the weight of a newborn baby

[____]—the weight of a newborn baby is similar to the weight of

more than a dozen [____].

Example 2

Convert 5,000 pounds to tons.

Write a proportion using a ratio of equivalent [____].

$$\frac{[\quad]}{[\quad]} \;\longrightarrow\; \frac{[\quad]}{[\quad]} = \frac{[\quad]}{[\quad]}$$

$$1 \cdot [\quad] = [\quad] \cdot x$$

$$[\quad] = x$$

5,000 pounds is equal to [____] tons.

Holt Mathematics

Example 3

**One mile is about 1.6 kilometers. What is the length in miles of a
10 kilometer race? Round to the nearest tenth of a mile.**

Write a proportion using 1 mi. $\approx$ 1.6 km. Let x be the length of a
10 kilometer race in miles.

$$\frac{\text{miles}}{\text{kilometers}} \longrightarrow \frac{1}{1.6} = \frac{x}{10}$$

$\boxed{} \cdot x = 1 \cdot \boxed{}$ The cross products are $\boxed{}$.

$\boxed{} x = 10$ Multiply.

$\boxed{} = \boxed{}$ Divide each side by $\boxed{}$.

$x = \boxed{}$ Round to the nearest tenth of a mile.

The length of a 10 kilometer race is about $\boxed{}$ mi.

Check It Out!

1. **Choose the most appropriate customary unit for the measure. Justify
   your answer.**

   the capacity of a jar of peanut butter

2. **Convert 24 pints to cups.**

3. **One cup is 8 fluid ounces. What is the amount of cups of a
   35 fluid ounce container? Round to the nearest tenth of a cup.**

Holt Mathematics

Similar Figures and Proportions

LESSON 5-6

Lesson Objectives

Use ratios to determine if two figures are similar

Vocabulary

similar (p. 258) _______________________________________

____

corresponding sides (p. 258) __________________________

____

corresponding angles (p. 258) _________________________

____

Additional Examples

Example 1

Tell whether the triangles are similar.

Write each set of corresponding sides as a ratio.

$\overline{AB}$ corresponds to ⬚.

$\overline{BC}$ corresponds to ⬚.

$\overline{AC}$ corresponds to ⬚.

$$\frac{AB}{DE} \overset{?}{=} \frac{BC}{EF} \overset{?}{=} \frac{AC}{DF}$$

Write ⬚ using the corresponding sides.

$$\boxed{} \overset{?}{=} \boxed{} \overset{?}{=} \boxed{}$$

Substitute the lengths of the sides.

$$\boxed{} = \boxed{} = \boxed{}$$

Simplify each ratio.

Since the ratios of the corresponding sides are ⬚,

the triangles ⬚ similar.

Holt Mathematics

Example 2

Tell whether the figures are similar.

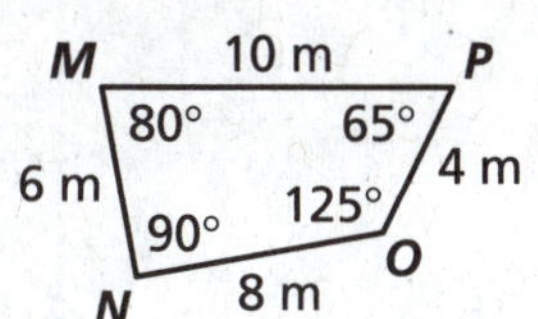

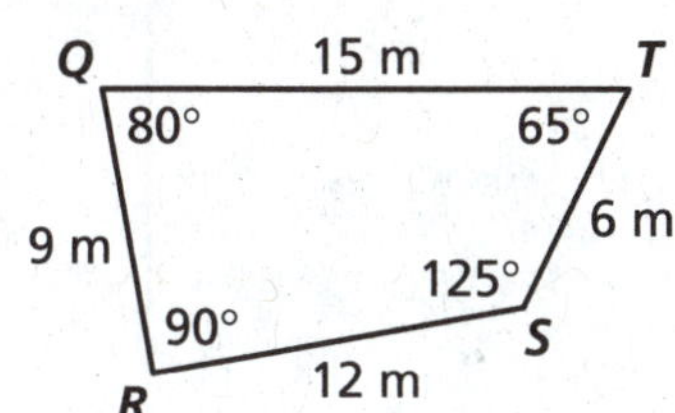

The [____] angles of the figures have [____] measures.

Write each set of sides as a ratio.

 $\overline{MN}$ corresponds to $\overline{QR}$.

 $\overline{NO}$ corresponds to $\overline{RS}$.

 $\overline{OP}$ corresponds to $\overline{ST}$.

[____] $\overline{MP}$ corresponds to $\overline{QT}$.

Determine whether the ratios of the lengths of the corresponding sides are [____].

$$\frac{MN}{QR} \stackrel{?}{=} \frac{NO}{RS} \stackrel{?}{=} \frac{OP}{ST} \stackrel{?}{=} \frac{MP}{QT}$$

Write ratios using [____] sides.

$$\frac{6}{9} \stackrel{?}{=} \frac{8}{12} \stackrel{?}{=} \frac{4}{6} \stackrel{?}{=} \frac{10}{15}$$

Substitute the lengths of the sides.

$$[\ \ ] = [\ \ ] = [\ \ ] = [\ \ ]$$

Write the ratios with [____].

Since the ratios of the corresponding sides are [____], the figures [____] similar.

Holt Mathematics

Check It Out!

1. Identify the corresponding sides in the pair of triangles. Then use ratios to determine whether the triangles are similar.

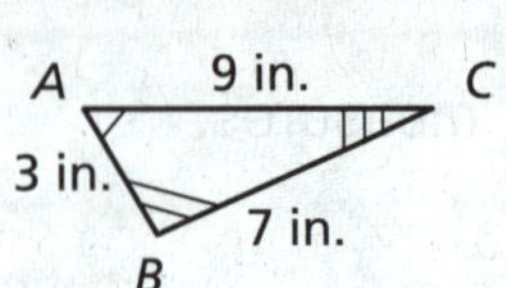

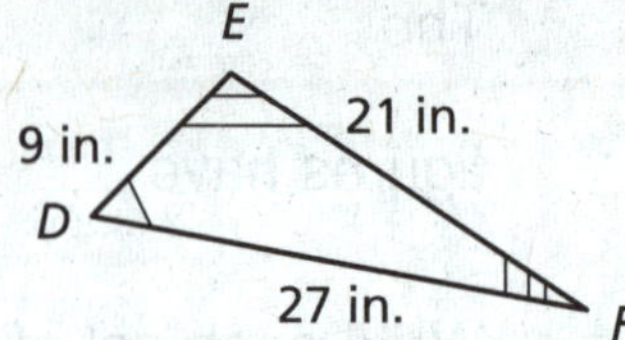

2. Tell whether the figures are similar.

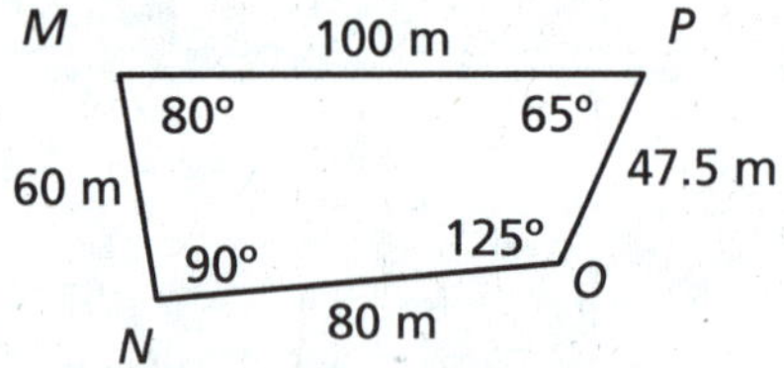

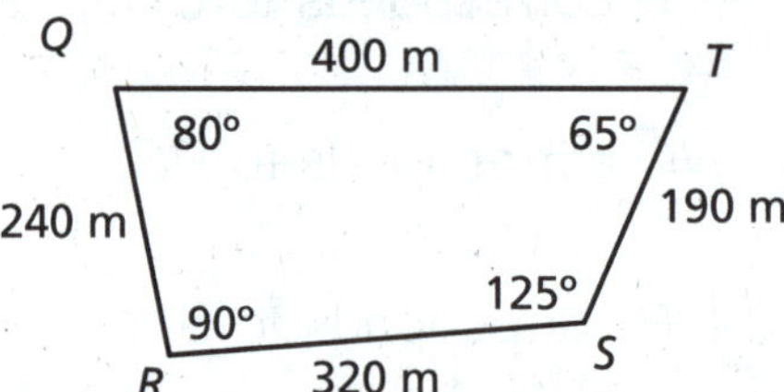

Holt Mathematics

LESSON 5-7
Using Similar Figures

Lesson Objectives

Use similar figures to find unknown lengths

Vocabulary

indirect measurement (p. 262) ________________________

____

Additional Examples

Example 1

Find the unknown length in the similar figures.

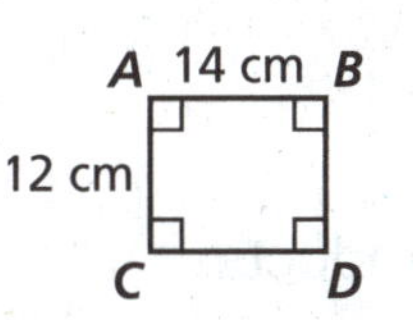

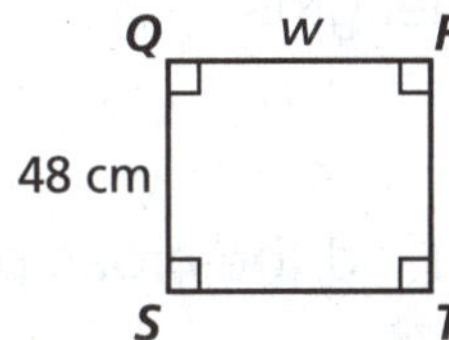

$$\frac{AC}{QS} = \frac{AB}{QR}$$

Write a proportion using corresponding

[   ].

$$\boxed{} = \frac{14}{w}$$

Substitute the lengths of the [   ].

$12 \cdot w = \boxed{} \cdot 14$ Find the [   ] products.

$\boxed{}\, w = \boxed{}$ Multiply.

$\boxed{} = \boxed{}$ Divide each side by [   ].

$w = \boxed{}$

QR is [   ] centimeters.

Holt Mathematics

Example 2

The inside triangle is similar in shape to the outside triangle. Find the length of the base of the inside triangle.

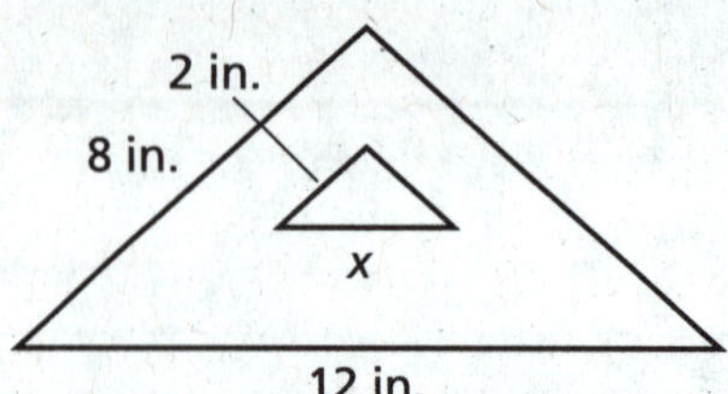

Let x = the ⬚ of the base of the inside triangle.

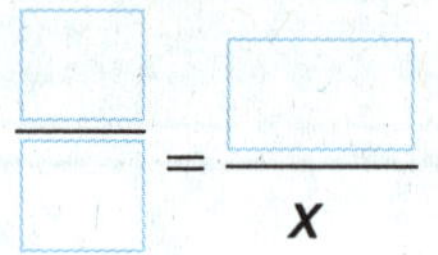

Write a proportion using corresponding side lengths.

$8 \cdot x = $ ⬚ $\cdot$ ⬚

Find the cross products.

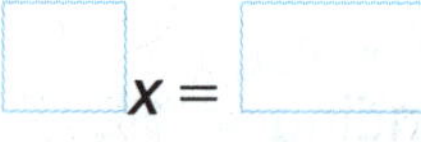

Multiply.

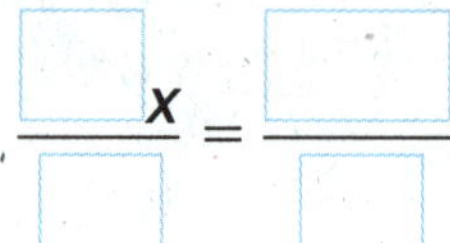

Divide each side by ⬚.

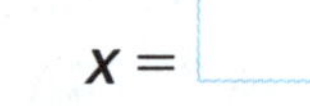

$x = $ ⬚

The length of the base of the inside triangle is  inches.

Holt Mathematics

Example 3

City officials want to know the height of a traffic light. Estimate the height of the traffic light.

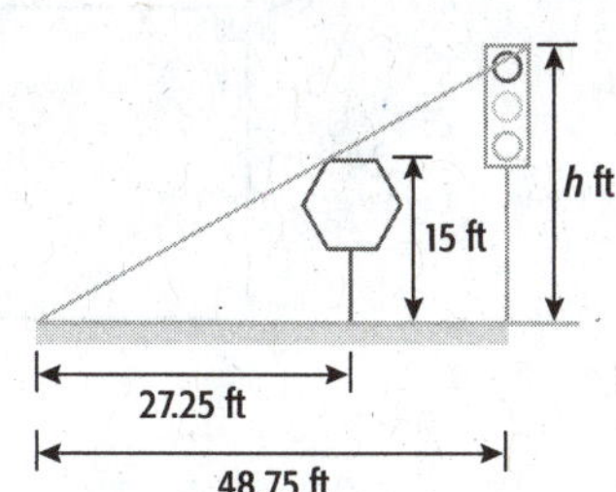

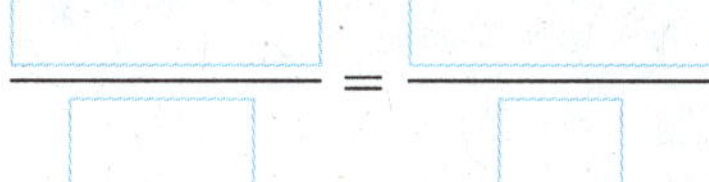 Write a ____________.

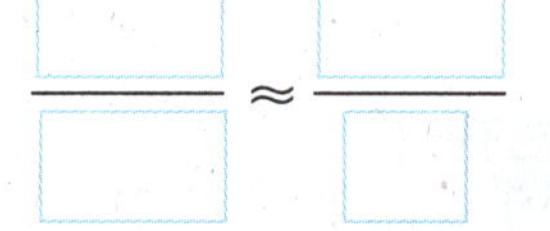 Use __________ numbers to estimate.

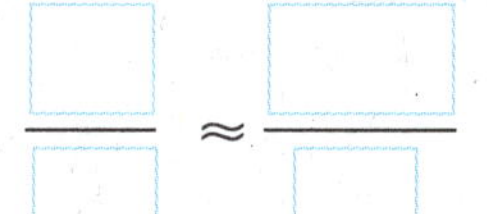 Simplify.

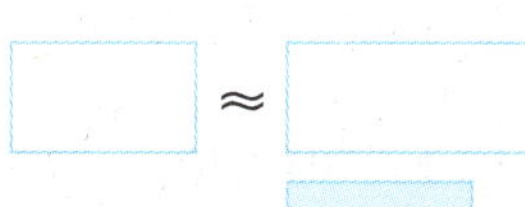 Cross multiply.

 $h \approx$  Divide each side by 5.

The height of the traffic light is about ________ feet.

Holt Mathematics

Check It Out!

1. Find the unknown length in the similar figures.

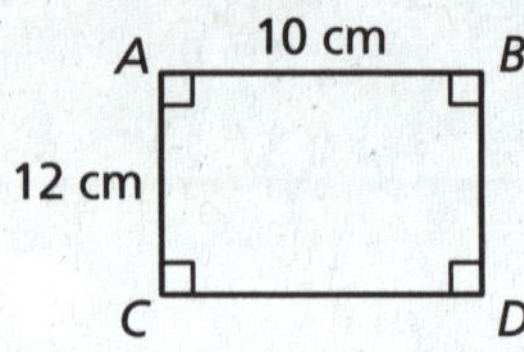

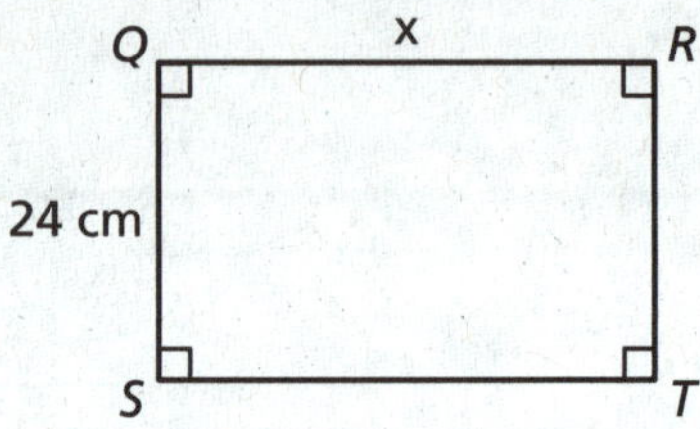

2. The rectangle on the left is similar in shape to the rectangle on the right. Find the width of the right rectangle.

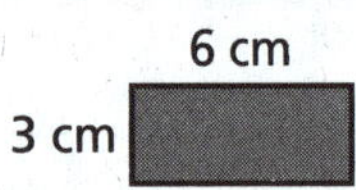

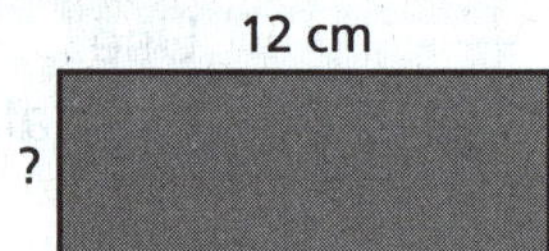

3. The inside triangle is similar in shape to the outside triangle. Find the height of the outside triangle.

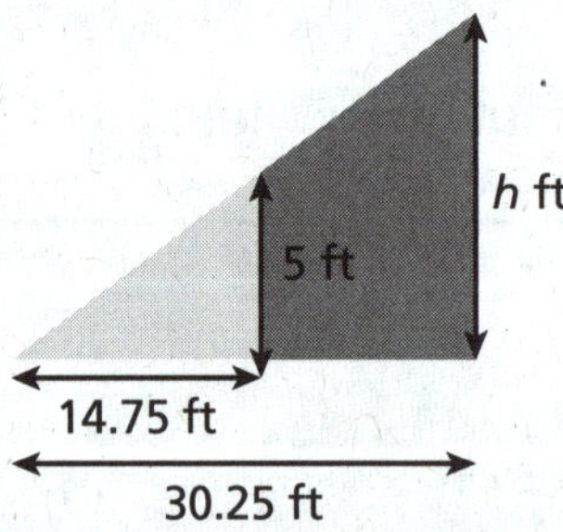

Holt Mathematics

LESSON 5-8

Scale Drawings and Scale Models

Lesson Objectives

Understand ratios and proportions in scale drawings; use ratios and proportions with scale

Vocabulary

scale model (p. 266) _______________________________

____

scale factor (p. 266) _______________________________

____

scale (p. 266) ____________________________________

____

scale drawing (p. 266) ______________________________

____

Additional Examples

Example 1

Identify the scale factor.

	Room	Blueprint
Length (in.)	144	18
Width (in.)	108	13.5

$\dfrac{\text{blueprint length}}{\text{room length}} = \boxed{}$ Write a $\boxed{}$ using one of the dimensions.

$= \boxed{}$ Simplify.

The scale factor is $\boxed{}$.

Holt Mathematics

Example 2

A photograph was enlarged and made into a poster. The poster is 20.5 inches by 36 inches. The scale factor is $\frac{5}{1}$. Find the size of the photograph to the nearest tenth of an inch.

Think: $\dfrac{\text{poster}}{\text{photo}} = \dfrac{5}{1}$

$\dfrac{36}{l} = \dfrac{5}{1}$ Write a proportion to find the length l.

$5l = \boxed{}$ Find the $\boxed{}$ products.

$l = \boxed{}$ Divide.

$\dfrac{20.5}{w} = \dfrac{5}{1}$ Write a proportion to find the width w.

$\boxed{}\, w = \boxed{}$ Find the cross $\boxed{}$.

$w = \boxed{}$ Divide.

The photo is  in. long and $\boxed{}$ in. wide.

Example 3

On a road map with a scale of 1.5 inches = 60 miles, the distance between Pittsburgh and Philadelphia measures 7.5 inches. What is the actual distance between the two cities?

Let d be the actual distance between the cities.

$\boxed{} = \boxed{}$ Write a proportion.

$\boxed{} \cdot d = \boxed{} \cdot \boxed{}$ Find the cross products.

$\boxed{}\, d = \boxed{}$ Multiply.

$\boxed{} = \boxed{}$ Divide both sides by 1.5.

$d = \boxed{}$

The distance between the cities is  miles.

Holt Mathematics

Check It Out!

1. Identify the scale factor.

	Model Aircraft	Blueprint
Length (in.)	12	2
Wing span (in.)	18	3

2. Mary's father made her a dollhouse which was modeled after the blueprint of their home. The blueprint is 24 inches by 45 inches. The scale factor is $\frac{1.5}{1}$. Find the size of the dollhouse.

3. On a road map with a scale of 1 inch = 50 kilometers, the distance between Dallas and Houston is 7 inches. What is the actual distance between the two cities?

135

Holt Mathematics

5-1 Ratios

Larry has a bag of colored dominoes. In the bag there are 20 orange dominoes, 16 red dominoes, 17 green dominoes, and 11 yellow dominoes.

Write each ratio in all three forms.

1. red dominoes to orange dominoes

2. yellow dominoes to green dominoes

3. Twelve boys showed up to football practice on Wednesday night. There are a total of 29 boys on the team. Write the ratio in all three forms of the number of boys at practice to the total number of boys on the team.

5-2 Rates

Find each rate.

4. A lawn service company charges Mrs. Smith $75 for $2\frac{1}{2}$ hours of work. What is their fee per hour?

5. A chartered bus drove 650 miles in 13 hours. What was the average rate of speed of the bus?

5-3 Identifying and Writing Proportions

Determine whether the ratios are proportional.

6. $\frac{4}{8}$, $\frac{8}{10}$

7. $\frac{2}{9}$, $\frac{10}{45}$

8. $\frac{3}{5}$, $\frac{27}{45}$

9. $\frac{11}{12}$, $\frac{22}{27}$

Complete each table of equivalent ratios.

10.

bird	8	14	22	
lion		7		16

11.

pyramid	5		15	
prism	3	6		12

Holt Mathematics

5-4 Solving Proportions

Use cross products to solve each proportion.

12. $\dfrac{4}{17} = \dfrac{y}{68}$ **13.** $\dfrac{9}{x} = \dfrac{3}{7}$ **14.** $\dfrac{p}{13} = \dfrac{33}{39}$ **15.** $\dfrac{2}{9} = \dfrac{q}{54}$

16. Kathy walked 2.5 miles in 35 minutes. Use a proportion to find how long it would take her to walk 6 miles at the same speed.

5-5 Customary Measurements

Choose the most appropriate customary unit for each measurement.

17. the weight of a tractor trailer truck   **18.** the length of a pencil

Convert each measure.

19. $8\dfrac{1}{2}$ feet to inches   **20.** 64 quarts to gallons

21. $9\dfrac{1}{4}$ pounds to ounces   **22.** 5 miles to feet

23. A chef has 4 gallons of soup. If she serves twelve 8-ounce bowls, then how many gallons of soup are remaining?

5-6 Similar Figures and Proportions

Use the properties of similarity to determine whether the figures are similar.

24. 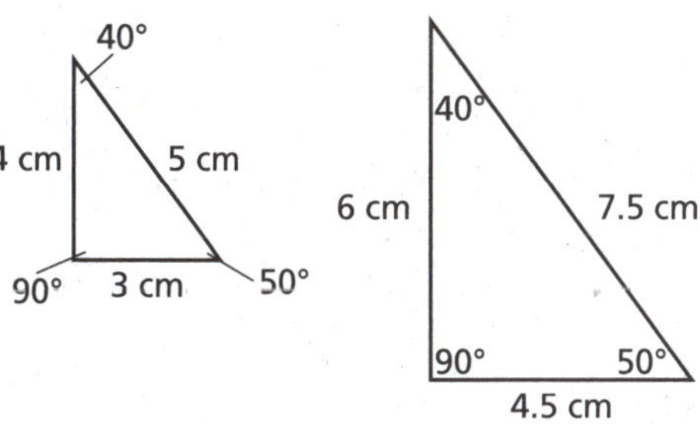

25. 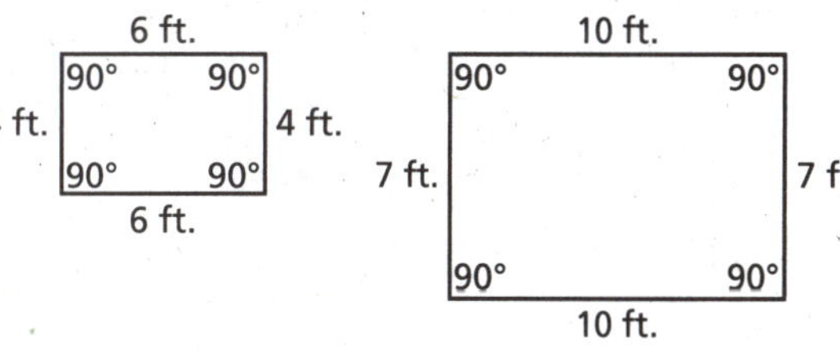

Holt Mathematics

5-7 Using Similar Figures

26. Mrs. Nuss planted two similar rectangular gardens. Her soybean garden measures 100 yards long and 60 yards wide. Her corn garden is 150 yards long. How many yards wide is her corn garden?

27. Ned is 5 ft 4 in. tall, and casts a shadow that is 3 ft 6 in. long. At the same time his dad's tool shed casts a shadow that is 7 ft long. Estimate the height of the tool shed.

5-8 Scale Drawings and Scale Models

Identify the scale factor.

28.

	Library	Model
Height (ft)	56	4

29.

	Car	Model
Length (in.)	96	8

30. In Joe's World Atlas the distance between Cleveland and Cincinnati is $5\frac{1}{2}$ cm. What is the actual distance between the two cities if the map scale is $\frac{1}{2}$ cm = 20 miles?

Holt Mathematics

Big Ideas

Answer these questions to summarize the important concepts from Chapter 5 in your own words.

1. Darin drove 245 miles in 5 hours. Explain how to find the unit rate.

2. Explain how to solve the proportion $\frac{14}{9} = \frac{x}{54}$ using cross products.

3. What is true about corresponding angles and corresponding sides of similar figures?

4. Two cities are 3.5 cm apart on a map. The scale factor is 2 cm = 25 miles. Explain how to find the actual distance d between the cities.

For more review of Chapter 5:

- Complete the Chapter 5 Study Guide and Review on pages 274–276 of your textbook.

- Complete the Ready to Go On quizzes on pages 254 and 270 of your textbook.

Holt Mathematics

 **LESSON 6-1**

Introduction to Percents

Lesson Objectives

Model and write percents as equivalent fractions and decimals

Vocabulary

percent (p. 286) ____

____

Additional Examples

Example 1

Write the percent modeled by each grid.

A.

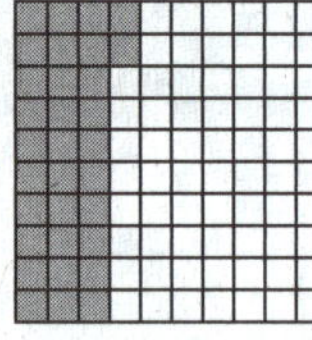

$\dfrac{\text{shaded}}{\text{total}} \rightarrow \dfrac{\boxed{}}{100} = \boxed{}\%$

B.

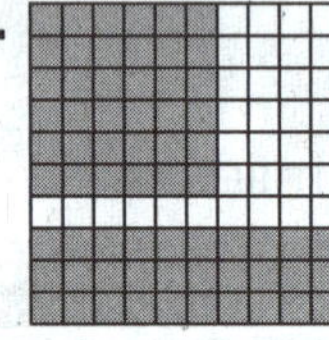

$\dfrac{\text{shaded}}{\text{total}} \rightarrow \dfrac{\boxed{}}{100} = \boxed{}\%$

Example 2

Write 28% as a fraction in simplest form.

$28\% = \dfrac{\boxed{}}{100}$ Write the percent as a fraction with a

$\boxed{}$ of 100.

$= \boxed{}$ Simplify.

So 28% can be written as $\boxed{}$.

Holt Mathematics

Example 3

Write 17% as a decimal.

17% = ⬚   Write the percent as a fraction with

a denominator of ⬚.

= ⬚   Divide ⬚ by 100.

Check It Out!

1. Write the percent modeled by the grid.

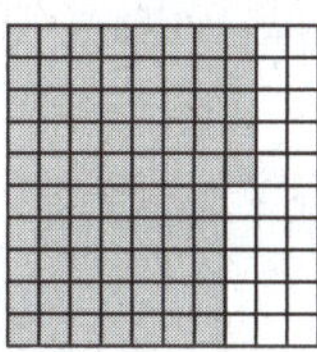

2. Write 90% as a fraction in simplest form.

3. Write 24% as a decimal.

Holt Mathematics

Fractions, Decimals, and Percents

LESSON 6-2

Lesson Objectives

Write decimals and fractions as percents

Additional Examples

Example 1

Write 0.7 as a percent.

$0.7 = \boxed{} = \boxed{}$ 　　Write the decimal as a fraction with a denominator of $\boxed{}$.

$= \boxed{}\%$ 　　Write the $\boxed{}$ with a percent sign.

Example 2

Write $\frac{5}{8}$ as a percent.

$\frac{5}{8} = 5 \div 8$ 　　Use $\boxed{}$ to write the fraction as a decimal.

$= \boxed{}$

$= \boxed{}\%$ 　　Write the decimal as a percent.

Holt Mathematics

Example 3

If 27 out of 50 people have the newspaper delivered to their homes, what percent of these people have the newspaper delivered to their homes?

27 out of 50 $= \dfrac{\boxed{}}{\boxed{}}$ Set up a ratio.

$= \boxed{} \div \boxed{}$ Use division to write the fraction as a

$\boxed{}$.

$= \boxed{}$

$= \boxed{}\%$ Write the decimal as a percent.

$\boxed{}$ of the people have the newspaper delivered to their home.

Check It Out!

1. Write 0.3 as a percent.

2. Write $\dfrac{3}{5}$ as a percent.

3. If 11 out of 50 students surveyed have blue backpacks, what percent of the students have blue backpacks?

Holt Mathematics

Estimating with Percents

LESSON 6-3

Lesson Objectives

Estimate percents

Additional Examples

Example 1

Use a fraction to estimate 27% of 63.

27% of 63 ≈ ☐ · 63   Think: 27% is about 25% and 25% is

equivalent to ☐.

≈ ☐ · 60   Change 63 to a compatible number.

≈ ☐   Multiply.

27% of 63 is approximately ☐.

Example 2

Tara's T's is offering 2 T-shirts for $16, while Good-T's is running their buy one for $9.99, get one for 50% off sale. Which store offers the better deal?

First find the discount price for 2 T-shirts at Good T's.

50% of $9.99 = ☐ · $9.99   Think: 50% is equivalent to ☐.

≈ ☐ · $10   Change $9.99 to a compatible number.

≈ $☐   Multiply.

The second shirt costs approximately $☐. Since $10 + $5 = $15, the two T-shirts for $15 at Good T's is the better deal.

Holt Mathematics

Example 3

Use 1% or 10% to estimate the percent of each number.

A. 4% of 18

18 is about 20, so find 4% of 20.

1% of 20 = ☐

4% of 20 = 4 · ☐ = ☐   4% equals ☐ · 1%.

4% of 18 is about ☐.

B. 29% of 80

29% is about 30, so find 30% of 80.

10% of 80 = ☐

30% of 80 = 3 · ☐ = ☐   30% equals ☐ · 10%.

29% of 80 is about ☐.

Example 4

Tim spent $58 on dinner for his family. About how much money should he leave for a 15% tip?

Since $58 is about $60, find 15% of $60.

15% = 10% + 5%   Think: 15% is 10% + 5%.

10% of $60 = $☐

5% of $60 = $6 ÷ 2 = $☐   5% is $\frac{1}{2}$ of ☐% so divide $6 by 2.

$6 + $3 = $☐   ☐ the 10% and 5% estimates.

Tim should leave about $☐ for a 15% tip.

Holt Mathematics

Check It Out!

1. Use a fraction to estimate 48% of 91.

2. Billy's Office Supply Store is offering 25% off a leather notebook, originally priced at $9.75. K's Office Supply Store offers the same notebook, not on sale, at $7.00. Which store offers the better deal?

3. Use 1% or 10% to estimate 5% of 14.

4. Amanda spent $12 on a hair cut. About how much money should she leave for a 15% tip?

146

Holt Mathematics

Percent of a Number

LESSON 6-4

Lesson Objectives

Find the percent of a number

Additional Examples

Example 1

Find the percent of each number.

A. 30% of 50

$$\boxed{} = \frac{n}{50}$$ Write a $\boxed{}$.

$\boxed{} \cdot 50 = \boxed{} \cdot n$ Set the cross $\boxed{}$ equal.

$\boxed{} = \boxed{} n$ Multiply.

$\boxed{} = \boxed{}$ Divide each side by $\boxed{}$.

$\boxed{} = n$ 30% of 50 is $\boxed{}$.

B. 200% of 24

$$\boxed{} = \frac{n}{24}$$ Write a $\boxed{}$.

$\boxed{} \cdot 24 = \boxed{} \cdot n$ Set the $\boxed{}$ products equal.

$\boxed{} = \boxed{} n$ Multiply.

$\boxed{} = \boxed{}$ Divide each side by $\boxed{}$.

$\boxed{} = n$ 200% of 24 is $\boxed{}$.

Holt Mathematics

Example 2

Find the percent of each number. Check whether your answer is reasonable.

A. 9% of 80

$$9\% \text{ of } 80 = \boxed{} \cdot 80 \qquad \text{Write the percent as a decimal.}$$

$$= \boxed{} \qquad \text{Multiply.}$$

Check

Since 10% of 80 is 8, a reasonable answer for 9% of 80 is 7.2.

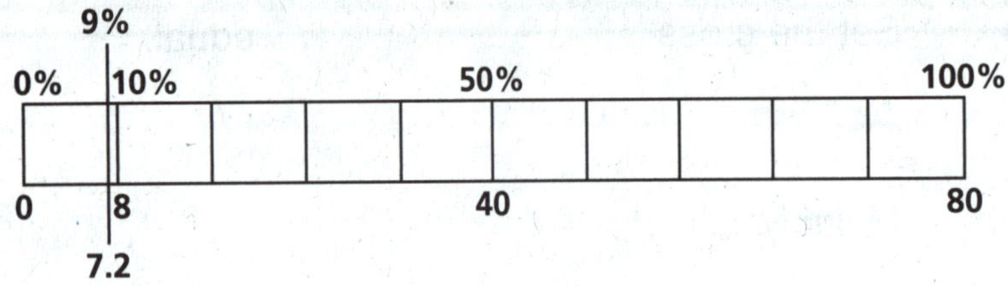

B. 3% of 12

$$3\% \text{ of } 12 = \boxed{} \cdot 12 \qquad \text{Write the percent as a decimal.}$$

$$= \boxed{} \qquad \text{Multiply.}$$

Check

5% · 12 = 0.6, so 3% of 12 is a little less than 0.6. Thus, 0.36 is a reasonable answer.

Holt Mathematics

Example 3

The estimated world population in 2001 was 6,157 million. About 40% of the people were 19 or younger. What was the approximate number of people 19 or younger, to the nearest million?

Find 40% of 6,157 million

[____] · 6,157   Write the percent as a decimal.

[____]   Multiply.

[____]   Round to the nearest million.

The number of people 19 or under was about [____] million.

Check It Out!

1. Find the percent of the number.

150% of 64

2. Find the percent of the number. Check whether your answer is reasonable.

21% of 40

3. The estimated world population in 2001 was 6,157 million. About 60% of the people were above 19 years of age. What was the approximate number of people 19 or older, to the nearest million?

Holt Mathematics

Solving Percent Problems

LESSON 6-5

Lesson Objectives

Solve problems involving percents

Additional Examples

Example 1

Solve.

A. What percent of 40 is 25?

$$\boxed{} = \frac{25}{40}$$ Write a $\boxed{}$.

$$\boxed{} \cdot 40 = \boxed{} \cdot 25$$ Set the $\boxed{}$ products equal.

$$40\boxed{} = \boxed{}$$ Multiply.

$$\boxed{} = \boxed{}$$ Divide each side by $\boxed{}$.

$$n = \boxed{}$$ 25 is $\boxed{}$% of 40.

B. 15 is 25% of what number?

$$\boxed{} = \frac{15}{n}$$ Write a $\boxed{}$.

$$n \cdot \boxed{} = \boxed{} \cdot 15$$ Set the cross $\boxed{}$ equal.

$$\boxed{} n = \boxed{}$$ Multiply.

$$\boxed{} = \boxed{}$$ Divide each side by $\boxed{}$.

$$n = \boxed{}$$ 15 is 25% of $\boxed{}$.

Holt Mathematics

Example 2

Solve.

A. 35 is 28% of what number?

$35 = 28\% \cdot n$ — Write an ________.

$35 = \boxed{} \cdot n$ — Write 28% as a decimal.

$\boxed{} = \boxed{}$ — Divide each side by ________.

$\boxed{} = n$

35 is 28% of ________.

B. What percent of 9 is 18?

$18 = n \cdot 9$ — Write an ________.

$\dfrac{\boxed{}}{\boxed{}} = \dfrac{n \cdot 9}{\boxed{}}$ — ________ each side by ________.

$\boxed{} = n$

$200\% = n$ — Write the decimal as a percent.

18 is ________% of 9.

Holt Mathematics

Example 3

A portable DVD player costs $225 before tax at an appliance warehouse. What is the sales tax rate if the tax is $18?

Restate the question: What percent of 225 is 18?

   Write a __________.

$n \cdot$  $= 100 \cdot$    Set the cross products equal.

$225n =$ __________   Multiply.

__________ $=$ __________

$n =$ __________   Divide each side by __________.

__________ % of $225 is $18. The sales tax rate is __________ %.

Check It Out!

1. Solve.

8 is 40% of what number?

2. 36 is 24% of what number?

3. A new flat screen TV costs $800 before tax at an appliance warehouse. What is the sales tax rate if the tax is $56?

Holt Mathematics

LESSON 6-6 Percent of Change

Lesson Objectives

Solve problems involving percent of change

Vocabulary

percent of change (p. 308) __________________________________

____

percent of increase (p. 308) __________________________________

____

percent of decrease (p. 308) __________________________________

____

Additional Examples

Example 1

Find each percent of change. Round answers to the nearest tenth of a percent, if necessary.

A. 65 is decreased to 38.

$$65 - 38 = \boxed{}$$ Find the amount of $\boxed{}$.

$$\text{percent of change} = \frac{27}{65}$$ Substitute values into formula.

$$\approx 0.4153846$$ Divide.

$$\approx \boxed{}\%$$ Write as a percent. Round.

The percent of decrease is about $\boxed{}$%.

B. 41 is increased to 92.

$$92 - 41 = \boxed{}$$ Find the amount of change.

$$\text{Percent of change} = \frac{51}{41}$$ Substitute values into formula.

$$\approx 1.2439$$ Divide.

$$\approx \boxed{}\%$$ Write as a percent. Round.

The percent of increase is about $\boxed{}$%.

Holt Mathematics

Example 2

The regular price of a bicycle helmet is \$42.99. It is on sale for 20% off. What is the sale price?

Step 1: Find the amount of the discount.

$20\% \cdot 42.99 = d$ Think: 20% of \$42.99 is what number?

$\boxed{} \cdot 42.99 = d$ Write the percent as a decimal.

$\boxed{} = d$

$\$\boxed{} \approx d$ Round to the nearest cent.

The amount of the discount is $\$\boxed{}$.

Step 2: Find the sale price.

regular price − amount of discount = sale price

$\$42.99 - \$\boxed{} = \$\boxed{}$

The sale price is $\$\boxed{}$.

Example 3

A boutique buys hand-painted T-shirts for \$12.60 each and sells them after a price increase of 110%. What is the retail price of the T-shirts?

Step 1: Find the amount n of increase.
Think: 110% of \$12.60 is what number?

$110\% \cdot 12.60 = n$

$\boxed{} \cdot 12.60 = n$ Write the percent as a decimal.

$\boxed{} = n$ Multiply.

The amount of increase is $\$\boxed{}$.

Holt Mathematics

Step 2: Find the retail price.
Think: retail price = wholesale price + amount of increase.

$p = \$12.60 + \$$ ⬚

$p = \$$ ⬚

The retail price of the hand-painted T-shirts is $ ⬚ each.

Check It Out!

1. **Find the percent of change. Round answers to the nearest tenth of a percent, if necessary.**

   70 is decreased to 45.

2. **The regular price of a computer game is $49.88. It is on sale for 15% off.**

   Find the sale price.

3. **William makes T-shirts for $7.00 each and sells them after a price increase of 125%. What is the retail price of the T-shirts?**

Holt Mathematics

LESSON 6-7 · Simple Interest

Lesson Objectives

Solve problems involving simple interest

Vocabulary

interest (p. 312) ____

____

simple interest (p. 312) _______________________________________

____

principal (p. 312) ____

____

Additional Examples

Example 1

Find each missing value.

A. $I = \rule{1cm}{0.1pt}$, $P = \$575$, $r = 8\%$, $t = 3$ years

$I = P \cdot r \cdot t$

$I = \boxed{} \cdot \boxed{} \cdot \boxed{}$ Substitute. Use 0.08 for 8%.

$I = \$\boxed{}$ Multiply.

The simple interest is $\$\boxed{}$.

B. $I = \$204$, $P = \$1{,}700$, $r = \rule{1cm}{0.1pt}$, $t = 6$ years

$I = P \cdot r \cdot t$

$\boxed{} = \boxed{} \cdot r \cdot 6$ Substitute.

$\boxed{} = \boxed{}\, r$ Multiply.

$\boxed{} = \boxed{}$ Divide each side by $\rule{2cm}{0.1pt}$.

$\boxed{} = r$ The interest rate is $\boxed{}$%.

Holt Mathematics

Example 2

Avery deposits $6,000 in an account that earns 4% simple interest. How long will it take for the total amount in his account to reach $6,800?

1. **Understand the Problem**
   Rewrite the question as a statement:

   • Find the number of years it will take for Avery's account to reach $⬚.

   List the important information:

   • The principal is $⬚.

   • The interest rate is ⬚%.

   • His account balance will be $⬚.

2. **Make a Plan**
   Avery's account balance A includes the principal plus the interest:
   $A = P + I$. Once you solve for I, you can use $I = P \cdot r \cdot t$ to find the time.

3. **Solve**

   $$A = P + I$$

   ⬚ = ⬚ + I Substitute.

   $-6{,}000 \qquad -6{,}000$

   ⬚ = I

   $I = P \cdot r \cdot t$ Subtract ⬚ from each side.

   ⬚ = ⬚ · ⬚ · t Substitute. Use 0.04 for 4%.

   ⬚ = ⬚ t Multiply.

   ⬚ = ⬚   Divide each side by ⬚.

   ⬚ $\approx t$ Round to the nearest hundredth.

   It will take 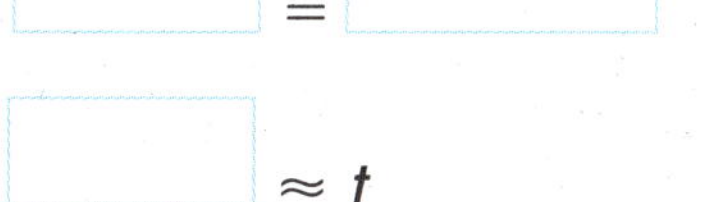 ⬚ years.

Holt Mathematics

4. Look Back

After exactly $3\frac{1}{3}$ years, Avery's money will have earned $800 in simple interest and his account balance will be $6,800.

$$I = 6{,}000 \cdot 0.04 \cdot 3\frac{1}{3} = 800$$

So it will take $3\frac{1}{3}$ years to reach $6,800.

Check It Out!

1. Find the missing value.

$I = \$600,\ P = \$2{,}000,\ r = \rule{1cm}{0.4cm},\ t = 3$ years

2. Linda deposits $10,000 in an account that earns 8% simple interest. How long will it take for the total amount in her account to reach $12,000?

Holt Mathematics

CHAPTER 6

Chapter Review

6-1 Introduction to Percents

Write the percent modeled by each grid.

1. 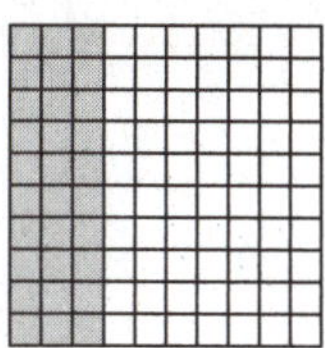

2. 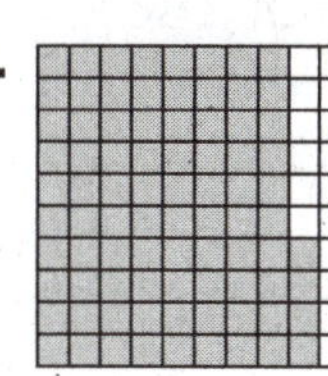

Write each percent as a fraction in simplest form.

3. 27%   **4.** 64%   **5.** 35%   **6.** 6%

6-2 Fractions, Decimals, and Percents

Write each decimal as a percent.

7. 0.37   **8.** 0.045   **9.** 0.05   **10.** 0.627

11. Sam asked 20 friends if they liked peanut butter and jelly sandwiches or grilled cheese sandwiches. Thirteen of his friends said peanut butter and jelly. What percent liked peanut butter and jelly?

6-3 Estimating with Percents

Use a fraction to estimate the percent of each number.

12. 19% of 61   **13.** 76% of 62   **14.** 49% of 98   **15.** 19% of 86

Estimate.

16. 15% of $41.07   **17.** 32% of 211   **18.** 1% of 95

19. Alex has $15.00. He finds an item on sale for 20% off the regular price of $19.99. Does he have enough money to buy the toy? Explain.

Holt Mathematics

6-4 Percent of a Number

Find the percent of each number. If necessary, round to the nearest tenth.

20. 64% of 313　　　　**21.** 7% of 186　　　　**22.** 138% of 52

23. Hillview School has 440 students. If 55% of the students are girls, how many of the students are girls?

6-5 Solving Percent Problems

Solve. Round to the nearest tenth, if necessary.

24. 12 is what percent of 60?　　　　**25.** 5 is what percent of 14?

26. 9 is 75% of what number?　　　　**27.** 26 is 34% of what number?

6-6 Percent of Change

Find each percent of change. Round answers to the nearest tenth of a percent, if necessary.

28. 150 to 220　　　　　　　　**29.** 37 to 31

30. A store buys milk from a dairy for $1.90 a gallon. They sell it to their customers for $2.29 a gallon. What percent increase is this?

6-7 Simple Interest

Find each missing value.

31. $I = $ ▨ , $P = \$2{,}000$, $r = 3\%$, $t = 4$ years

32. $I = \$87.50$, $P = $ ▨ , $r = 5\%$, $t = 5$ years

33. $I = \$105$, $P = \$750$, $r = $ ▨ , $t = 42$ months

34. Oliver deposits $500 in an account that earns 4.75% simple interest. How long will it be before the total amount is $750 dollars?

Holt Mathematics

Big Ideas

Answer these questions to summarize the important concepts from Chapter 6 in your own words.

1. Explain how to write 45% as a fraction.

2. Explain how to find 150% of 350.

3. Explain how to find the percent change when 32 is decreased to 21.

4. Explain how to find the interest rate when the simple interest is $360, the principal is $1,600, and the time is 2 years.

For more review of Chapter 6:

- Complete the Chapter 6 Study Guide and Review on pages 320–322 of your textbook.

- Complete the Ready to Go On quizzes on pages 306 and 316 of your textbook.

Holt Mathematics

Mean, Median, Mode, and Range

LESSON 7-1

Lesson Objectives

Find the mean, median, mode, and range of a data set

Vocabulary

mean (p. 331) ______________________________

____

median (p. 332) ______________________________

____

mode (p. 332) ______________________________

____

range (p. 332) ______________________________

____

Additional Examples

Example 1

Find the mean of each data set.

A.

Depth of Puddles (in.)						
5	8	3	5	4	2	1

$5 + 8 + 3 + 5 + 4 + 2 + 1 =$ ☐   ☐ all values.

$28 \div$ ☐ $=$ ☐   ☐ the sum by

the ☐ of items.

The mean is ☐ inches.

Holt Mathematics

Example 2

Find the mean, median, mode, and range of the data set.

Car Wash Totals			
6th grade	12	7th grade	11
8th grade	14	9th grade	15

mean: $\dfrac{12 + 11 + 14 + 15}{4} = \boxed{}$ Add all values. Divide the sum by the number of values.

median: Write the data in numerical order: $\boxed{}$

11, (12, 14,) 15   There are an even number of items,

$\dfrac{12 + 14}{2} = \boxed{}$ so find the $\boxed{}$ of the two middle values.

mode: $\boxed{}$ No value occurs most often.

range: $15 - 11 = \boxed{}$ Subtract the least value from the greatest value.

The mean is $\boxed{}$ cars washed; the median is $\boxed{}$ cars washed; there is $\boxed{}$ mode; and the range is $\boxed{}$ cars washed.

Check It Out!

1. Find the mean of the data set.

Rainfall per Month (in.)						
1	2	10	2	5	6	9

2. Find the mean, median, mode, and range of the data set.

Bake Sale Profits ($)			
6th Grade	17	7th Grade	11
8th Grade	22	9th Grade	14

Holt Mathematics

LESSON 7-2

Additional Data and Outliers

Lesson Objectives

Learn the effects of additional data and outliers

Vocabulary

outlier (p. 335) ____

Additional Examples

Example 1

A. Find the mean, median, mode, and range of the data in the table.

EMS Football Games Won				
Year	1998	1999	2000	2001	2002
Games	11	5	7	5	7

mean: $\dfrac{11 + 5 + 7 + 5 + 7}{} = \boxed{}$

median: Write the data in numerical order: 5, 5, 7, 7, 11.

mode: [ ]   The values [ ] and [ ] occurs most often.

range: $11 - 5 = $ [ ]   Subtract the least value from the greatest value.

B. EMS also won 13 games in 1997 and 8 games in 1996. Add this data to the data in the table and find the mean, median, mode, and range.

mean: [ ]   The mean increased by 1.

median: [ ]   The median stayed the same.

modes: [ ]   The modes stayed the same.

range: [ ]   The range increased by 2.

Holt Mathematics

Example 2

The table shows the prices of television sets at a discount store. Which price represents an outlier?

Television Prices			
$141	$225	$849	$246
$269	$165	$258	$159

Step 1: Draw a number line.

Step 2: For each television price, use an x on the number line to represent its price in dollars.

Prices of Televisions ($)

The line plot shows that the value [____] is much [________] than the other values in the set. The price [________] represents an outlier.

Example 3

Ms. Gray is 25 years old. She took a class with students who were 55, 52, 59, 61, 63, and 58 years old. Find the mean, median, mode, and range with and without Ms. Gray's age.

Data with Ms. Gray's age:

mean: ≈ [____]   mode: [____]   median: [____]   range: [____]

Data without Ms. Gray's age:

mean: [____]   mode: [____]   median: [____]   range: [____]

When you add Ms. Gray's age, the mean decreases by about 4.7, the [____] stays the same, the [________] decreases by 0.5, and the [____] increases by 27. The [____] and the [____] are most affected by the [________].

Holt Mathematics

Check It Out!

1. Find the mean, median, mode, and range of the data in the table.

MA Basketball Games Won					
Year	1998	1999	2000	2001	2002
Games	13	6	4	6	11

2. The table shows the number of inches of hair cut from a salon's last eight customers. Which length represents an outlier?

Length of Hair Cut (in.)			
12	3	4	2
2	1	4	1

3. Ms. Pink is 56 years old. She volunteered to work with people who were 25, 22, 27, 24, 26, and 23 years old. Find the mean, median, mode, and range with and without Ms. Pink's age.

Holt Mathematics

LESSON 7-3 Choosing the Most Useful Measure

Lesson Objectives

Identify the most useful measure for describing a data set.

Additional Examples

Example 1

The heights of players on a basketball team are 72, 86, 74, 73, and 75 inches. What are the mean and median? Is one measure more useful than the other for describing the typical height of a player on the team? Explain.

Step 1: Find the mean and median.

mean:

median:

Step 2: Choose the most useful measure.

The ____________ is a more useful description of the typical player. There is only one player taller than the mean.

Example 2

The number of hours Jordan spent studying for his last five exams are 4, 0.5, 3.5, 3, and 0.5. Should Jordan use the mean, median, or mode to convince his teacher that he spends enough time studying? Explain.

mean: **median:**   **mode:**

Jordan should use the ____________ because it makes the number of hours spent studying seem greatest.

Holt Mathematics

Check It Out!

1. The shoe size of players on a soccer team are 11, 10, 12, 11, and 16. What are the mean and median? Is one measure more useful than the other for describing the typical shoe size of a player on the team? Explain.

2. Elisa is shopping for skates and found the following prices: $35, $42, $75, $40, $47, $34, $45, and $40. Elisa wants to convince her parents to buy her skates. Should Elisa use the mean, median, or mode to describe the data set?

Holt Mathematics

LESSON 7-4: Analyzing Data Displays

Lesson Objectives

Analyze data displays and evaluate claims based on data displays

Vocabulary

bar graph (p. 342) ______________________________

____

circle graph (p. 342) ______________________________

____

sector (p. 342) ______________________________

____

line graph (p. 343) ______________________________

____

Additional Examples

Example 1

Use the bar graph to answer the questions.

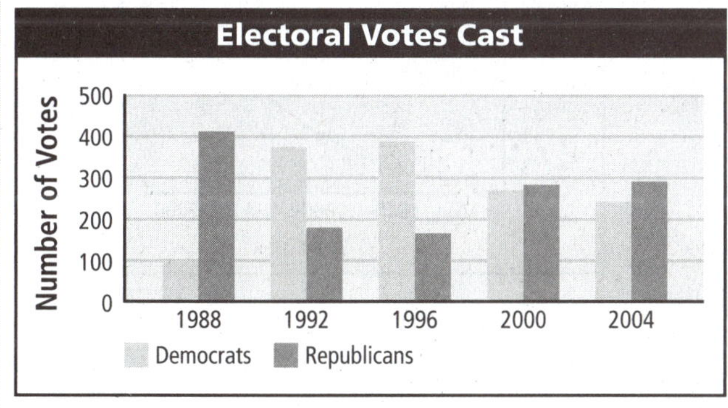

A. In which year did Democrats cast the fewest number of electoral votes?

The bar for ________ is the shortest, so Democrats cast the fewest

number of electoral votes in ________ .

B. Marco claims that Republicans cast about twice as many electoral votes in 2004 as they did in 1996. Is his claim valid? Explain.

________ They cast about ________ electoral votes in 1996 and almost

________ in 2004.

Holt Mathematics

Example 2

Leon surveyed 30 people about pet ownership. The circle graph shows his results. Use the graph to answer each question.

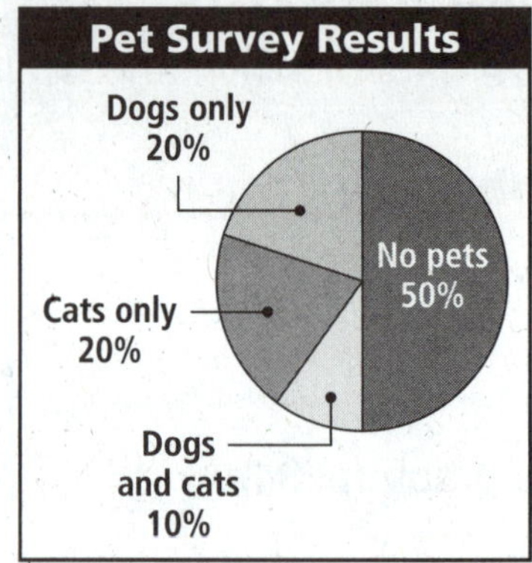

A. How many people own both cats and dogs?

Since 20% is 6 people, 10% is ____ people.

________ people own both cats and dogs.

B. Maya claims that about $\frac{1}{2}$ of the people surveyed do not own a cat. Is her claim valid? Explain.

________ The graph shows that ____ % do not own pets and ____ %

own dogs only. In all, ____ % do not own cats, and ____ % ____ $\frac{1}{2}$.

Example 3

Use the line graph to answer the question.

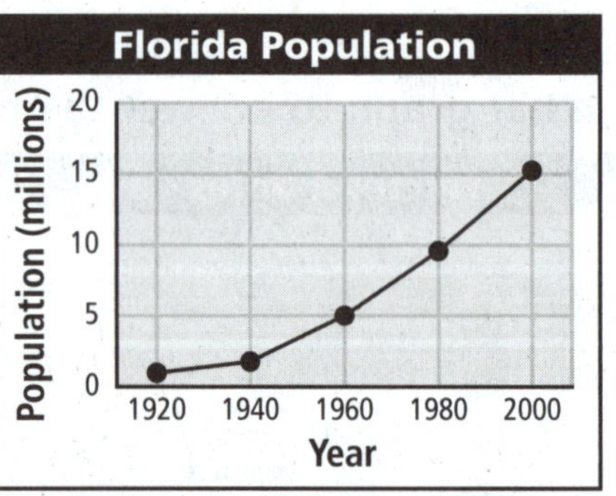

A. In approximately what year did Florida's population first reach 5 million?

The graph shows that Florida's population

reached 5 million people in ________ .

B. Roy claims that Florida's population more than tripled between 1960 and 2000. Is his claim valid? Explain.

________ , the population in 1960 was about ____ million, and the

population in 2000 was more than ____ million.

Holt Mathematics

Check It Out!

Use the bar graph to answer the question.

1. **About how many more pounds of apples than pounds of grapes were eaten per person?**

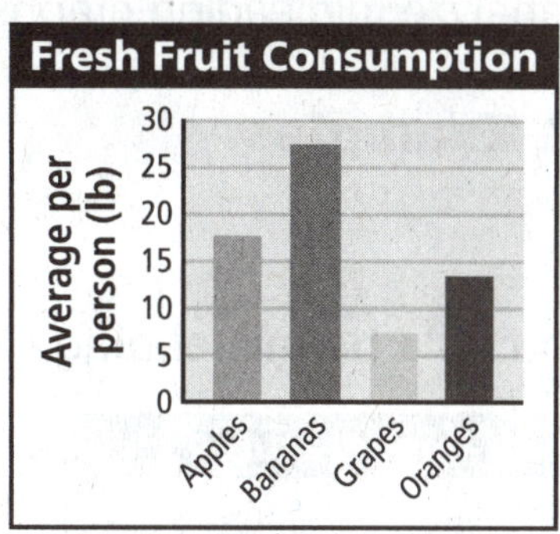

2. **Fifty students were asked which instrument they could play. The circle graph shows the responses. Use the graph to answer the question. How many students do not play an instrument?**

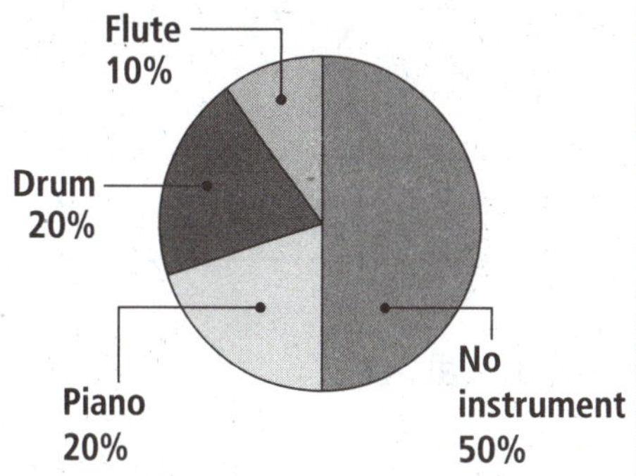

3. **What was the approximate population of Florida in 1970?**

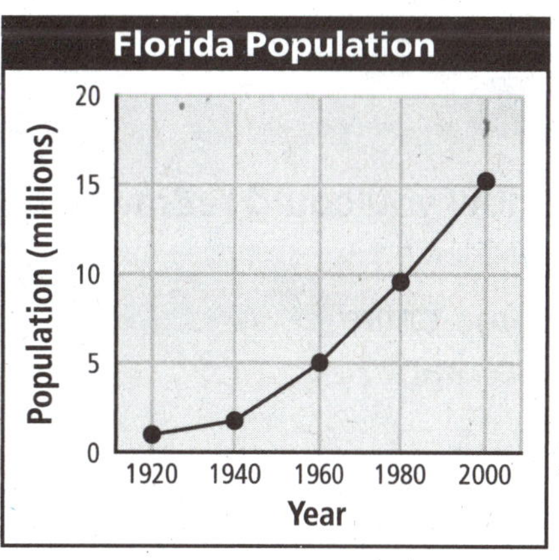

Holt Mathematics

LESSON 7-5
Misleading Graphs

Lesson Objectives

Identify and analyze midleading graphs

Additional Examples

Example 1

Which graph could be misleading? Why?

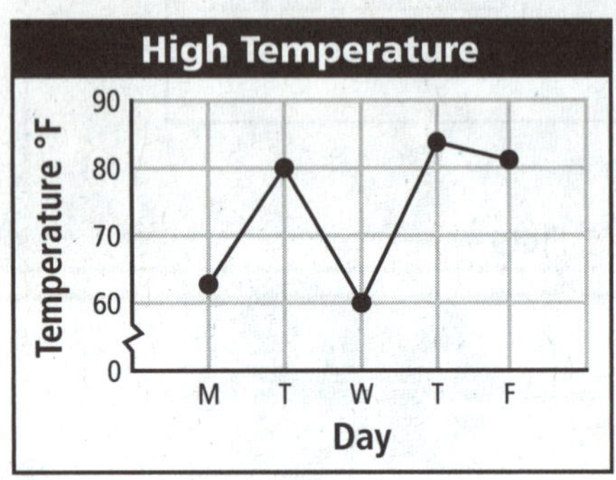

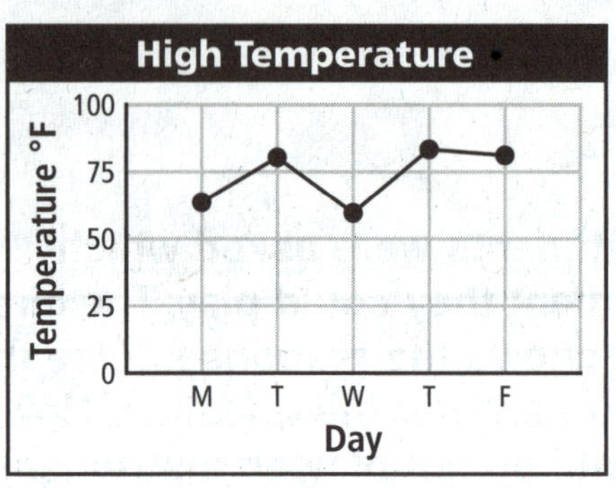

The graph at [ ] could be misleading. It gives the impression of

[ ] temperature change because the [ ]

axis does not begin at zero.

Example 2

Explain how you could redraw each graph so it would *not* be misleading.

A. Draw the entire [ ] scale
on the graph.

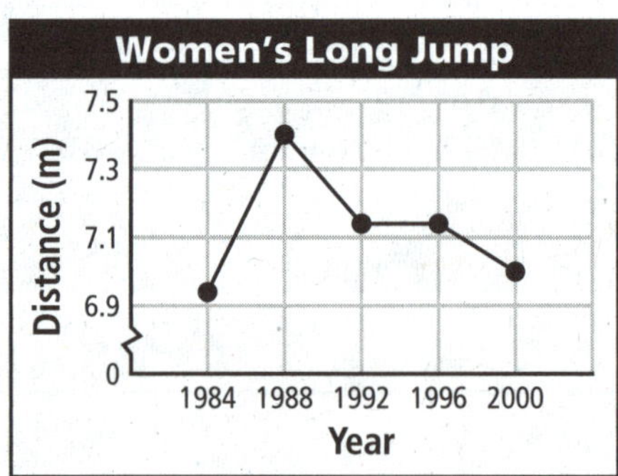

Holt Mathematics

B. Make the icons for cars, light trucks, and heavy trucks _______ size.

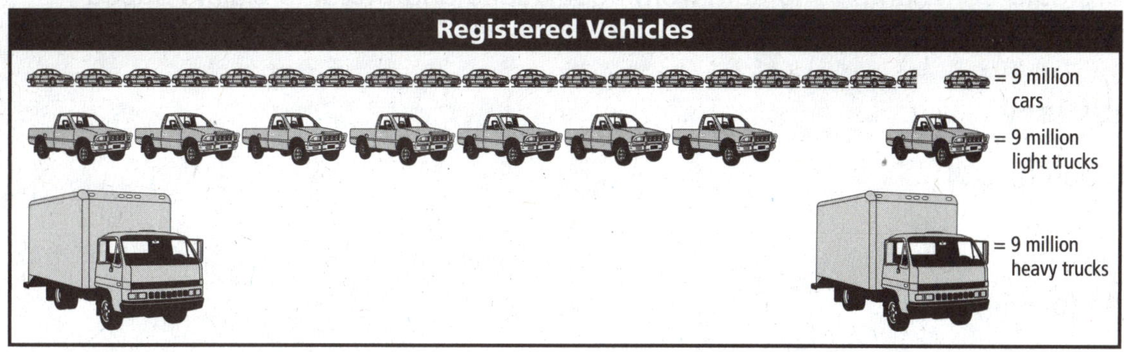

Check It Out!

1. Which graph could be misleading? Why?

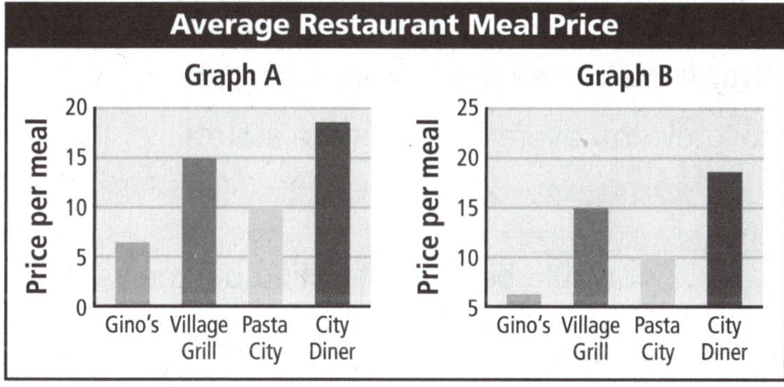

2. Explain how you could redraw the graph so it would _not_ be misleading.

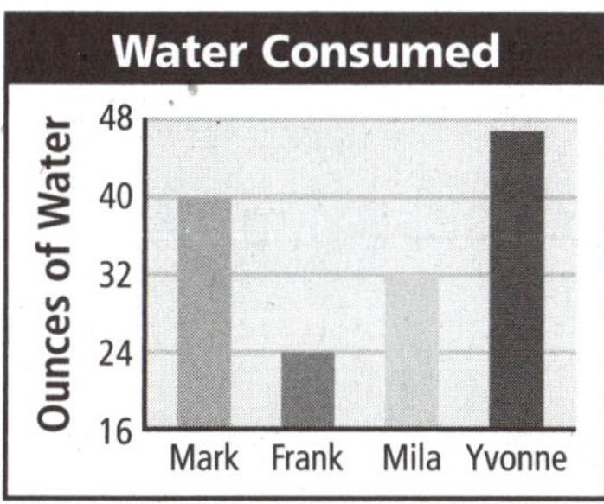

Holt Mathematics

Populations and Samples

LESSON 7-6

Lesson Objectives

Compare data from samples to data from populations and evaluate claims based on samples

Vocabulary

population (p. 354) ____

____

sample (p. 354) ____

random sample (p. 354) ____

____

Additional Examples

Example 1

For each situation, explain whether it makes sense to use a sample.

A. The manager of a store wants to know the average age of the store's customers.

The entire population is __________ . It would be difficult to find out the

age for every customer. It __________ make sense to use a sample.

B. The manager of a store wants to know the average salary of the store's 8 employees.

The entire population is __________ . It __________ make sense to use a sample because every employee can be evaluated.

Holt Mathematics

Example 2

About 39% of all U.S. households have houseplants. Lee surveys a random sample of households from two towns in his state. Compare the samples with the national percent.

Houseplant Ownership		
Sample	With Plants	Without Plants
Town A	40	60
Town B	60	40

For each sample, find the percent of the households that have houseplants.

Town A: $\dfrac{\text{\# of households with plants}}{\text{total number of households}} = \dfrac{40}{40 + 60} = \dfrac{40}{100}$

$$= \boxed{} = \boxed{}\ \%$$

Town B: $\dfrac{\text{\# of households with plants}}{\text{total number of households}} = \dfrac{60}{60 + 40} = \dfrac{60}{100}$

$$= \boxed{} = \boxed{}\ \%$$

The percent of households with houseplants in Town A ($\boxed{}$ %) is $\boxed{}$ to the national percent. The percent of households in Town B ($\boxed{}$ %) is $\boxed{}$ than the national percent.

Example 3

A Web site consists of 400 pages. A Web designer estimates that 60 of the Web pages have broken links. In a random sample of 20 pages, 7 of the pages have broken links. Determine whether the manager's estimate is likely to be accurate. Explain.

Set up a proportion to predict the total number of broken links.

$$\dfrac{\text{broken links in sample}}{\text{pages sampled}} = \dfrac{\text{total \# of broken links}}{\text{\# of web site pages}}$$

$\dfrac{7}{20} = \dfrac{x}{400}$ \qquad Let x represent the number of actual links broken.

$7 \cdot 400 = 20 \cdot x$ \qquad The cross products are equal.

$\boxed{} = 20x$ \qquad Multiply.

Holt Mathematics

$$\frac{\boxed{}}{\boxed{}} = \frac{20x}{\boxed{}} \qquad \text{Divide each side by } \boxed{}.$$

$$\boxed{} = x$$

The estimate is ____________________ because based on the sample, the

number of pages with broken links is likely to be about ________.

Check It Out!

1. **For each situation, explain whether it makes sense to use a sample.**

    A veterinarian wants to know the average number of pets in her town.

2. **About 22% of all U.S. households have pet fish. Rylan surveys a random sample of households from two towns in his state. Compare the samples with the national percent.**

Pet Fish Ownership		
Sample	With Pet Fish	Without Pet Fish
Town A	25	75
Town B	55	45

    For each sample, find the percent of the households that have pet fish.

3. **The owner of a large chain restaurant with 1,200 employees estimates that about 250 employees will ask for winter vacation. A random sample of 40 employees showed that 8 of them will ask for the time off. Determine whether the owner's estimate is likely to be accurate. Explain.**

Holt Mathematics

LESSON 7-7 Selecting Samples

Lesson Objectives

Identify sampling methods and choose representative samples

Vocabulary

systematic sample (p. 358) ____

____

convenience sample (p. 358) ____

____

self-selected sample (p. 358) ____

____

Additional Examples

Example 1

The manager of a company wants to know how many employees have a laptop computer at home. Identify each type of sampling method.

A. The manager randomly chooses 40 names from a list of all employees.

This is a ____________ sample because the employees are ____________.

B. The manager surveys the first 50 employees as they arrive at the office.

This is a ____________ sample because the group of employees is ____________.

C. The manager places a stack of survey forms in the company cafeteria.

This is a ____________ sample because the employees ____________ whether to complete the surveys.

177

Holt Mathematics

Example 2

Determine which sampling method will better represent the entire population. Justify your answer.

Band Uniform Style	
Sampling Method	**Results**
Maria surveys only the band students she knows personally.	84% want blue uniforms
Jon writes each band student's name on a card. He questions those students whose name he draws.	61% want blue uniforms

Jon's method is ____________ ; it uses a ____________ sample, and

Maria's method uses a ____________ sample.

Check It Out!

1. **You want to know how often students in high school take tests. Identify the type of sampling method.**

   You survey the first 50 students as they arrive at school.

2. **Determine which sampling method will better represent the entire population. Justify your answer.**

Swimming Scheduling	
Sampling Method	**Results**
Ferdinand surveys every other swimmer on the team.	72% want practice early
Anna-Maria asks swimmers in her Biology class.	50% want practice early

178

Holt Mathematics

LESSON 7-8 Identifying Sampling Errors and Bias

Lesson Objectives

Identify biased samples and biased survey questions

Vocabulary

biased sample (p. 362) ___________________________

____

biased question (p. 362) __________________________

____

Additional Examples

Example 1

Determine whether each sample may be biased. Explain.

A. An employee of a phone company randomly chooses 80 customers to ask whether they are happy with their service.

The sample is ____________. It is a _______ sample.

B. The first 25 students to arrive at school are surveyed to find out how they get to school.

The sample is __________. It is likely that the first 25 students arrived

by the ________ method, such as the bus.

Example 2

Determine whether each survey question may be biased. Explain.

A. Do you prefer broccoli or corn?

The question is ____________. It _________ lead people to
choose one item over the other.

B. Would you rather drive this luxurious and roomy sedan or a tiny compact car?

The question is __________. People may be _______ likely to
choose a car that is described as luxurious and roomy than one that is
described as tiny and compact.

Holt Mathematics

Example 3

Mari conducts a survey to find out which animals at the zoo are the most popular among visitors. Determine whether Mari's claim is valid. Explain.

Sample: 30 visitors outside the monkey house
Question: Which animals at the zoo are your favorite?
Claim: Monkeys are the most popular animal.
Results:

Favorite Animal	Responses
Monkeys	10
Bears	8
Lions	6

The claim ______ be valid. The sample is ______ because visitors standing outside the monkey house may be ______ interested in monkeys.

Check It Out!

1. Determine whether each sample may be biased. Explain.

A sales manager of a large department store randomly chooses 40 previous customers to ask whether they were satisfied with the service they received.

2. Determine whether each survey may be biased. Explain.

Would you rather have a new wide screen or an old small screen television?

3. Jed conducts a survey to find out which animals at the zoo are the most popular. Determine whether Jed's claim is valid. Explain.

Sample: 50 visitors selected at random throughout the day
Question: Which animals at the zoo are your favorite?
Claim: Lions are the most popular animal.
Results:

Favorite Animal	Responses
Monkeys	12
Bears	18
Lions	20

Holt Mathematics

CHAPTER 7

Chapter Review

7-1 Mean, Median, Mode, and Range

Find the mean, median, mode, and range of each data set.

1.

Bowling Scores		
89	133	123

2.

Number of Seconds in Each Commercial				
29	18	45	60	18

3.

Distance (km)							
8	11	8	4	12	6	9	6

4.

Homework Scores							
21	18	24	16	12	23	20	18

5. Margie's first six test scores were 88, 98, 82, 86, 88, and 98. Create a table using this data. Then find the mean, median, mode, and range.

7-2 Additional Data and Outliers

The table shows the number of miles of Interstate 70 in the states of the Great Plains and Midwest.

CO	IL	IN	KA	MD	MO	OH	PA	UT	WV
451	126	157	424	94	252	226	168	232	14

6. What is the median number of miles of Interstate 70 in the states through which the interstate passes?

7. What is the mean number of miles, to the nearest mile, of Interstate 70 in the states through which the Interstate passes?

8. What is the mean number of miles, to the nearest mile, of Interstate 70 in the states excluding West Virginia?

Holt Mathematics

7-3 Choosing the Most Useful Measure

9. Marquis called several pizza places and was told the following prices for a large pizza: $10, $11, $8, $17, and $9. What are the mean and the median prices? Is one more useful than the other for describing the typical price? Explain.

10. The number of miles that Amarisse drove her parents' car for the last 5 days are 25, 5, 31, 31, and 28. Should Amarisse use the mean, median or mode to convince her parents that she isn't driving their car too much?

7-4 Analyzing Data Displays

Use the bar graph for questions 11 and 12.

11. Which months have the most days above 80°?

12. How many more days does it reach 80° in September compared to May?

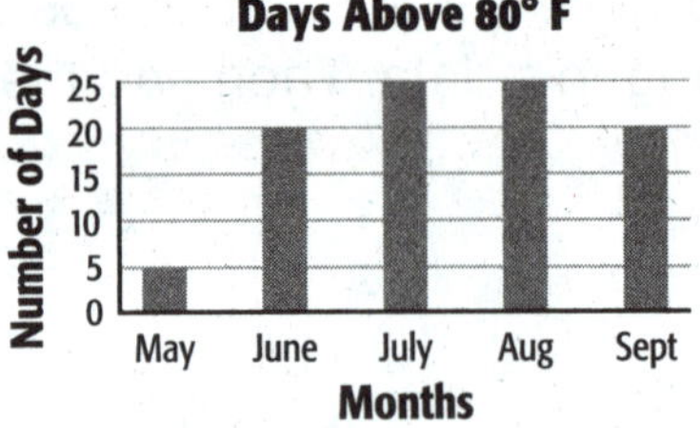

7-5 Misleading Graphs

13. Which graph could be misleading? Why?

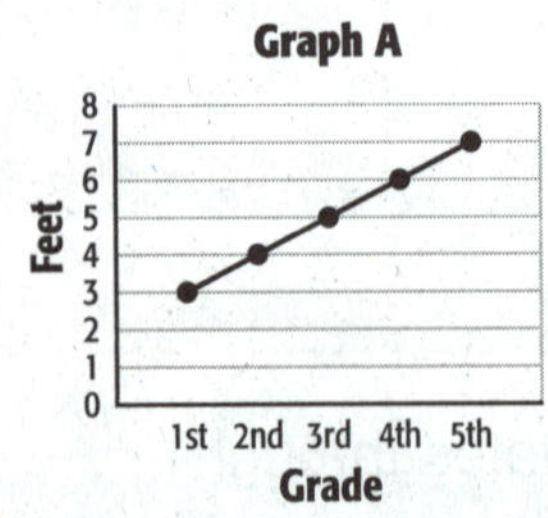

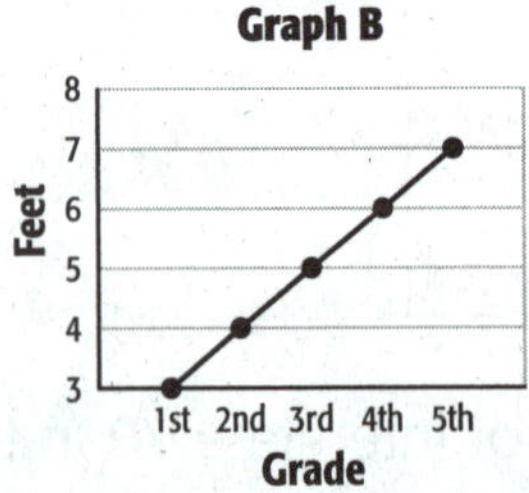

Holt Mathematics

7-6 Population and Samples

Determine whether each sample may be biased. Explain.

14. A school principal randomly chooses 75 students for a survey on the cafeteria food.

A reporter surveys 120 people leaving a baseball game to find out their favorite baseball team.

7-7 Selecting Samples

15. Determine which sampling method will better represent the entire population. Justify your answer.

Field Trip Location	
Sampling Method	**Results**
Tony asks his friends where they would like to have the field trip.	86% chose the amusement park
Ed picks names randomly from a list of all students going on the trip.	48% chose the amusement park

7-8 Indentifying Sampling Errors and Bias

Determine whether each sample or question is biased. Explain.

16. People buying gasoline are surveyed to find out how many times a week they ride the bus.

17. Would you rather paint the room blue or gray?

Holt Mathematics

Answer these questions to summarize the important concepts from Chapter 7 in your own words.

1. Explain how to find the mean, median, mode, and range of the data set.

   5, 8, 10, 12, 6, 5, 3

2. How does an outlier affect the mean, median and mode?

3. Give an example of a biased sample and explain why it is biased.

4. What things can be done to a graph to make it misleading?

For more review of Chapter 7:

- Complete the Chapter 7 Study Guide and Review on pages 370–372 of your textbook.
- Complete the Ready to Go On quizzes on pages 352 and 366 of your textbook.

Holt Mathematics

California Standards ←SDAP3.3
LESSON 8-1
Probability

Lesson Objectives

Use informal measures of probability

Vocabulary

experiment (p. 832) _______________________________________

____

trial (p. 832) _______________________________________

____

outcome (p. 832) _______________________________________

____

event (p. 832) _______________________________________

____

probability (p. 832) _______________________________________

____

complement (p. 833) _______________________________________

____

Additional Examples

Example 1

Determine whether each event is impossible, unlikely, as likely as not, likely, or certain.

A. rolling an odd number on a number cube

There are 6 possible outcomes:

Odd	*Not* Odd
1, 3, 5	2, 4, 6

___________ of the outcomes are odd.

Rolling an odd number is ___________.

Holt Mathematics

B. rolling a number less than 2 on a number cube
There are 6 possible outcomes:

Less than 2	*Not* Less than 2
1	2, 3, 4, 5, 6

Only [ ] outcome is less than 2.

Rolling a number less than 2 is [ ].

Example 2

A bag contains 22 circular chips that are the same size and weight. There are 8 purple, 4 pink, 8 white, and 2 blue chips in the bag. The probability of drawing a pink chip is $\frac{2}{11}$. What is the probability of not drawing a pink chip?

$P(\text{event}) + P(\text{complement}) = \Box$

$P(\text{pink}) + P(\text{not pink}) = \Box$

$\Box + P(\text{not pink}) = \Box$ Substitute [ ] for $P(\text{pink})$.

$- \Box \qquad\qquad\qquad - \Box$ Subtract [ ] from both sides.

$P(\text{not pink}) = \Box$ Simplify.

The probability of not drawing a pink chip is [ ].

Check Find the sum of the probabilities of drawing a pink chip and not drawing a pink chip.

$P(\text{pink}) + P(\text{not pink}) = \frac{2}{11} + \frac{9}{11} = \frac{11}{11} = 1$

The sum of the probabilities is 1, so the answer is reasonable.

Holt Mathematics

Example 3

Mandy's science teacher almost always introduces a new chapter by conducting an experiment. Mandy's class finished a chapter on Friday. Should Mandy expect the teacher to conduct an experiment next week? Explain.

Since the class will be starting a new chapter, it is __________ the teacher will conduct an experiment.

Check It Out!

1. **Determine whether each event is impossible, unlikely, as likely as not, likely, or certain.**

   A. rolling a 3 or more on a number cube

   B. rolling a 2 or 4 on a number cube

2. **A bag contains circular buttons that are the same size and weight. There are 7 maroon buttons, 3 sky buttons, 5 white buttons, and 5 lavender buttons in the bag. The probability of drawing a sky button is $\frac{3}{20}$. What is the probability of not drawing a sky button?**

3. **After completing a unit chapter, Alice's keyboarding class usually begins the next class day with a time trial exercise, practicing the previously learned skills. It is Wednesday and a unit chapter was completed the previous day. Will the class start with a time trial exercise?**

Holt Mathematics

Experimental Probability

Lesson Objectives

Find experimental probability

Vocabulary

experimental probability (p. 386) ______________________________

____

Additional Examples

Example 1

During skating practice, Sasha landed 7 out of 12 jumps. What is the experimental probability that she will land her next jump? Write your answer as a ratio, as a decimal, and as a percent. Then explain why your answer is reasonable.

$$P(\text{event}) \approx \frac{\text{number of times an event occurs}}{\text{total number of trails}}$$

$$P(\text{jumps landed}) \approx \frac{\text{number of jumps} \quad \boxed{}}{\text{total number of jumps} \quad \boxed{}}$$

$= \boxed{}$ Substitute data from the experiment.

$\approx \boxed{} \approx \boxed{}$ %   Write as a decimal and as a percent.

The experimental probability that Sasha will land her next jump is ________ or

__________, or ________ %.

Sasha landed about half, or 50% of the 12 jumps, so an answer of 58.3% is reasonable.

Holt Mathematics

Example 2

Students have checked out 55 books from the library. Of these, 32 books are fiction.

What is the experimental probability that the next book checked out will be fiction?

$$P(\text{fiction}) \approx \frac{\text{number of \rule{2cm}{0.4pt} books checked out}}{\text{total number of books checked out}}$$

$$\approx \rule{1.5cm}{0.4pt} \qquad \text{Substitute data.}$$

The experimental probability that the next book checked out will be fiction is \rule{1.5cm}{0.4pt}.

Check It Out!

1. **During basketball practice, Martha made 9 out of 10 free throws. What is the experimental probability that she will make her next attempt? Write your answer as a ratio, as a decimal, and as a percent. Then explain why your answer is reasonable.**

2. **Students have a fruit choice of either an apple or a pear. So far 18 of 47 students have selected pears.**

   A. What is the experimental probability that the next fruit selected will be a pear?

   B. What is the experimental probability that the next fruit selected will be an apple?

Holt Mathematics

Theoretical Probability

LESSON 8-3

Lesson Objectives

Find the theoretical probability of an event

Vocabulary

theoretical probability (p. 390) _______________________________________

____

Additional Examples

Example 1

Andy has 20 marbles in a bag. Of these, 9 are clear and 11 are blue. Find the probability of each event. Write your answer as a fraction, a decimal, and a percent.

drawing a clear marble

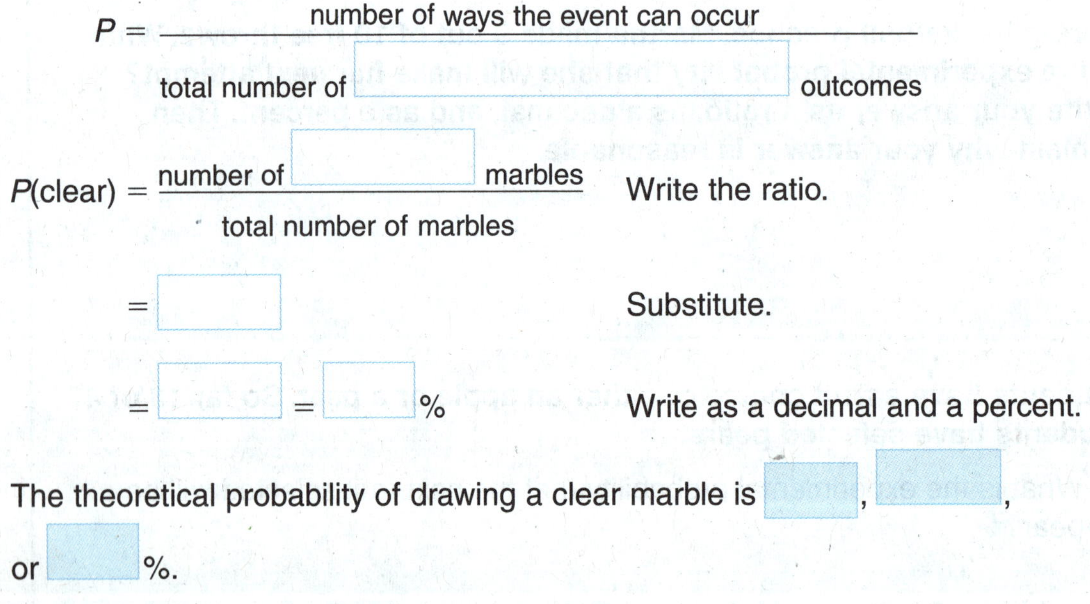

$$P = \frac{\text{number of ways the event can occur}}{\text{total number of } \boxed{} \text{ outcomes}}$$

$$P(\text{clear}) = \frac{\text{number of } \boxed{} \text{ marbles}}{\text{total number of marbles}} \qquad \text{Write the ratio.}$$

$$= \boxed{} \qquad\qquad \text{Substitute.}$$

$$= \boxed{} = \boxed{}\% \qquad \text{Write as a decimal and a percent.}$$

The theoretical probability of drawing a clear marble is $\boxed{}$, $\boxed{}$, or $\boxed{}$ %.

Holt Mathematics

Example 2

There are 13 boys and 10 girls on the track team. The name of each team member is written on an index card. A card is drawn at random to choose a student to run a sprint and the card is replaced in the stack.

A. Find the theoretical probability of drawing a boy's name.

$$P(\text{boy}) = \frac{\text{number of } \boxed{} \text{ on the team}}{\text{number of } \boxed{} \text{ on the team}} \qquad \text{Find the theoretical probability.}$$

$$= \boxed{} \qquad \text{Substitute.}$$

B. Find the theoretical probability of drawing a girl's name.

$$P(\text{boy}) + P(\text{girl}) = 1$$

$$\boxed{} + P(\text{girl}) = 1 \qquad \text{Substitute } \boxed{} \text{ for } P(\text{boy}).$$

$$-\boxed{} \qquad\qquad -\boxed{} \qquad \text{Subtract } \boxed{} \text{ from both sides.}$$

$$P(\text{girl}) = \boxed{} \qquad \text{Simplify.}$$

Check It Out!

1. Find the probability of each event. Jane has 20 marbles in a bag. Of these 8 are green. Find the probability of drawing a green marble from the bag. Write your answer as a ratio, a decimal, and a percent.

2. There are 15 boys and 12 girls in a class. A teacher has written the name of each student on a piece of paper and randomly draws a paper to determine which student will present the answer to the problem of the day. Find the theoretical probability that a girl's name will be drawn.

Holt Mathematics

Sample Spaces

LESSON 8-4

Lesson Objectives

Use counting methods to determine possible outcomes

Vocabulary

sample space (p. 394) _______________________________

____

compound event (p. 394) _______________________________

____

Fundamental Counting Principle (p. 395) _______________________________

____

____

Additional Examples

Example 1

One bag has a red tile, a blue tile, and a green tile. A second bag has a red tile and a blue tile. Vincent draws one tile from each bag. Use a table to find all the possible outcomes. What is the theoretical probability of each outcome?

Let R = red tile, B = blue tile, and G = green tile.
Record each possible outcome.

Bag 1	Bag 2

: 2 red tiles   P(2 red tiles) = ☐

: 1 red, 1 blue tile   P(1 red, 1 blue tile) = ☐

: 1 blue, 1 red tile

: 2 blue tiles   P(2 blue tiles) = ☐

: 1 green, 1 red tile   P(1 green, 1 red tile) = ☐

: 1 green, 1 blue tile   P(1 green, 1 blue tile) = ☐

Holt Mathematics

Example 2

There are 4 cards and 2 tiles in a board game. The cards are labeled N, S, E, and W. The tiles are numbered 1 and 2. A player randomly selects one card and one tile. Use a tree diagram to find all the possible outcomes. What is the probability that the player will select the E card and the 2 card?

Make a [____] diagram to show the sample space.

List each letter on the cards. Then list each number on the tiles.

N		S		E		W

There are [____] possible outcomes in the sample space.

Find the probability of each outcome.

P(E and 2 card) = $\dfrac{\text{number of ways the event can occur}}{\text{total number of [\_\_\_\_] outcomes}}$

= [____]

The probability that the player will select the E and 2 card is [____].

Example 3

Carrie rolls two 1–6 number cubes. How many outcomes are possible?

The first number cube has [____] outcomes.

The second number cube has [____] outcomes.

[____] · [____] = [____]   Use the Fundamental Counting Principle.

There are [____] possible outcomes when Carrie rolls two number cubes.

Holt Mathematics

Check It Out!

1. Darren has two bags of marbles. One has a green marble and a red marble. The second bag has a blue and a red marble. Darren draws one marble from each bag. Use a table to find all the possible outcomes. What is the theoretical probability of each outcome?

2. There are 3 cubes and 2 marbles in a board game. The cubes are numbered 1, 2, and 3. The marbles are pink and green. A player randomly selects one cube and one marble. Use a tree diagram to find all the possible outcomes. What is the probability that the player will select the cube numbered 1 and the green marble?

3. A sandwich shop offers wheat, white, and sourdough bread. The choices of sandwich meat are ham, turkey, and roast beef. How many different one-meat sandwiches could you order?

Holt Mathematics

LESSON 8-5
Disjoint Events

Lesson Objectives

Find the probability of disjoint events

Vocabulary

disjoint events (p. 402) ______________________________

____

Additional Examples

Example 1

Determine whether each set of events is disjoint. Explain.

A. choosing a dog or a poodle from the animals at an animal shelter

The event ____________________. A poodle is a type of dog, so it is possible to choose an animal that is both a dog and a poodle.

B. choosing a fish or a snake from the animals at a pet store

The event ____________________. Fish and snakes are different types of animals, so you cannot choose an animal that is both a fish and a snake.

Example 2

Find the probability of each set of disjoint events.

choosing an *A* or an *E* from the letters in the word *mathematics*

$P(\text{A}) = \boxed{}$ $P(\text{E}) = \boxed{}$

$P(\text{A or E}) = P(\text{A}) + P(\text{E})$ Add the probabilities of the individual events.

$= \boxed{} + \boxed{} = \boxed{}$

The probability of choosing a 3 or 4 is $\boxed{}$.

Holt Mathematics

Example 3

Sharon rolls two number cubes. What is the probability that the sum of the numbers shown on the cubes is 2 or 8?

Step 1: Use a grid to find the sample space.

First Roll

	1	2	3	4	5	6
1	②	3	4	5	6	7
2	3	4	5	6	7	⑧
3	4	5	6	7	⑧	9
4	5	6	7	⑧	9	10
5	6	7	⑧	9	10	11
6	7	⑧	9	10	11	12

(Second Roll)

The grid shows all possible sums.

There are 36 equally likely outcomes in the sample space.

Step 2: Find the probability of the set of disjoint events.

$P(\text{sum of 2}) =$ $\qquad$ $P(\text{sum of 8}) =$

$P(\text{sum of 2 or sum of 8}) = P(\text{sum of 2}) + P(\text{sum of 8})$

$$= \boxed{} + \boxed{} = \boxed{} = \boxed{}$$

The probability that the sum of the cubes is a 2 or 8 is $\boxed{}$.

Holt Mathematics

Check It Out!

1. Determine whether each set of events is disjoint. Explain.

A. choosing a bowl of soup or a bowl of chicken noodle soup from the cafeteria

B. choosing a bowl of chicken noodle soup or broccoli cheese soup

2. Find the probability of each set of disjoint events.

A. choosing an *I* or an *E* from the letters in the word *centimeter*

B. spinning a 2 or a 4 on a spinner with six equal sectors numbered 1–6

3. Sun Li rolls two number cubes. What is the probability that the sum of the numbers shown on the cubes is 3 or 4?

197

Holt Mathematics

LESSON 8-6 Independent and Dependent Events

Lesson Objectives

Identify independent and dependent events and find the probability of independent events

Vocabulary

independent events (p. 406) _______________________________________

____

dependent events (p. 406) _______________________________________

____

Additional Examples

Example 1

Decide whether each set of events are dependent or independent. Explain your answer.

A. Kathi draws a 4 from a set of cards numbered 1–10 and rolls a 2 on a number cube.

Since the outcome of drawing the card does not ______________ the

outcome of rolling the cube, the events are ______________.

B. Yuki chooses a book from the shelf to read, and then Janette chooses a book from the books that remain.

Since Janette cannot pick the same book that Yuki picked, and since there are fewer books for Janette to choose from after Yuki chooses, the events

are ______________.

C. Imad chooses a pencil from a drawer, puts it back, and then chooses a second pencil. Both pencils are red. The drawer holds the same pencils each time.

Since Imad replaces the first pencil, the outcome of picking the first pencil

does not ______________ the outcome of picking the second pencil. The

events are ______________.

Holt Mathematics

Example 2

Find the probability of choosing a green marble at random from a bag of 5 green and 10 white marbles and then flipping a coin and getting tails.

The outcome of choosing the marble does not [____] the

outcome of flipping the coin, so the events are [____].

P(green and tails) = P(green) · P(tails)

= [__] · [__]

The probability of choosing a green marble and a coin landing on tails

is [__].

Example 3

A basketball player has a 60% chance of making a free throw on each attempt. If the chance of making one free throw is independent of the chance of making the next free throw, what is the probability that the player will make 2 free throws in a row?

P(making 1st free throw = and 2nd free throw) P(1st free throw) · P(2nd free throw)

= [__] % · [__] %   Substitute [__]% for P(1st free throw) and [__]% for P(2nd free throw).

= 0.[__] · 0.[__]   Write the percents as decimals.

= 0.[__]   Multiply.

= [__] %   Write the decimal as a percent.

The probability of the basketball player making 2 free throws in a row is [__]%.

Holt Mathematics

Check It Out!

1. **Decide whether the set of events are dependent or independent. Explain your answer.**

   A. Joann flips a coin and gets a head. Then she rolls a 6 on a number cube.

   B. Annabelle chooses a blue marble from a set of three, each of different colors, and then Louise chooses a second marble from the remaining two marbles.

   C. Lisa chooses a pen from a bag, puts it back, and then chooses a second pen. Both pens are blue. The bag holds the same pens each time.

2. **Find the probability of choosing a red marble at random from a bag containing 5 red and 5 white marbles and then flipping a coin and getting heads.**

3. **A professional bowler has a 40% chance of bowling a strike on each attempt. If the chance of bowling a strike is independent of the chance of bowling a strike in the next frame, what is the probability that the player will bowl 2 strikes in a row?**

Holt Mathematics

Making Predictions

LESSON 8-7

Lesson Objectives

Use probability to predict future events

Vocabulary

prediction (p. 410) _______________________________

____

Additional Examples

Example 1

A. A store claims that 78% of shoppers end up buying something. Out of 1,000 shoppers, how many would you predict will buy something?

You can write a proportion. Remember that percent means "per hundred."

$$\frac{78}{100} = \frac{x}{1,000}$$

Think: ☐ out of 100 is how many out of ☐ ?

$$100 \cdot x = 78 \cdot 1,000$$

The cross products are ☐.

$$☐ \quad x = ☐$$

$$\frac{100x}{100} = \frac{78,000}{100}$$

☐ both sides by ☐.

$$x = ☐$$

You can predict that about ☐ out of 1,000 customers will buy something.

Holt Mathematics

Example 2

If you roll a number cube 30 times, how many times do you except to roll a number greater than 2?

$$P(\text{greater than 2}) = \frac{4}{6} = \frac{2}{3}$$

$\dfrac{2}{3} = \dfrac{x}{30}$ Think: 2 out of 3 is how many out of 30?

$3 \cdot x = 2 \cdot 30$ The cross products are [ ].

[ ]$x = 60$

$\dfrac{3x}{3} = \dfrac{60}{3}$ [ ] both sides by [ ].

$x =$ [ ]

You can expect to roll a number greater than 2 about [ ] times.

Example 3

A stadium sells yearly parking passes. If you have a parking pass, you can park at that stadium for any event during that year. The managers of the stadium estimate that the probability that a person with a pass attending any one event is 50%. The parking lot has 400 spaces. If the managers want the lot to be full at every event, how many passes should they sell?

1. Understand the Problem
The answer will be the number of parking passes they should sell.
List the important information:

- P(person with pass attends event): = [ ] %

- There are [ ] parking spaces.

2. Make a Plan
The managers want to fill all [ ] spaces. But on average, only [ ] % of parking pass holders will attend. So 50% of the pass holders must equal 400. You can write an equation to find this number.

Holt Mathematics

3. Solve

$$\frac{50}{100} = \frac{400}{x}$$ Think: 50 out of [ ] is 400 out of how many?

$$100 \cdot 400 = 50 \cdot x$$ The cross products are [ ].

$$40,000 = [\ ]x$$

$$\frac{40,000}{50} = \frac{50x}{50}$$ [ ] both sides by 50.

[ ] $= x$ The managers should sell [ ] parking passes.

4. Look Back

If the managers sold only 400 passes, the parking lot would not usually be full because only about 50% of the people with passes will attend any one event. The managers should sell more than 400 passes, so 800 is a reasonable answer.

Check It Out!

1. A store claims 62% of shoppers end up buying something. Out of 1,000 shoppers, how many would you predict will buy something?

2. If you roll a number cube 30 times, how many times do you expect to roll a number greater than 3?

3. The concert hall managers sell annual memberships. If you have an annual membership, you can attend any event during that year.

The manager estimates that the probability of a person with a membership attending any one event is 60%. The concert hall has 600 seats. If the manager want the seats to be full at every event, how many memberships should she sell?

Holt Mathematics

Chapter Review

8-1 Probability

Determine whether each event is impossible, unlikely, as likely as not, likely, or certain.

1. rolling a 7 on a number cube

2. flipping a coin and getting heads

3. drawing a red marble from a bag with 7 blue marbles and 10 red marbles

4. Charlie rolls two number cubes. The probability the sum is less than 4 is $\frac{2}{21}$. What is the probability of having a sum of 4 or greater?

5. Anna exercises for at least 45 minutes on days she has to work. If it is Monday and Anna has to work, would you expect her to exercise over 30 minutes? Explain.

8-2 Experimental Probability

6. David made 16 out of 28 free throws at basketball practice. What is the experimental probability of making his next free throw?

7. Christina scored an A on 7 out of 10 math quizzes this quarter. What is the experimental probability that she scores an A on her next math quiz?

8. For the past two weeks, Courtney has picked 9 long sleeve and 6 short sleeve shirts to wear to school.

   a) What is the probability that the next shirt she picks will be short sleeve?

   b) What is the probability that the next shirt she picks will be long sleeve?

Holt Mathematics

8-3 Theoretical Probability

Find the probability of each event. Write your answer as a fraction, a decimal, and a percent.

9. randomly drawing a heart from a shuffled deck of 52 cards with 13-card suits: diamonds, hearts, clubs and spades

10. randomly drawing one of the 4-D Scrabble tiles from a complete set of 100 Scrabble Tiles

A twelve-sided polyhedron with numbered faces that are each regular, congruent polygons is rolled. What is the probability of each event?

11. P(even #)

12. P(greater than 10)

13. P(less than 6)

14. P(9)

15. Lucy and her cousins are drawing names to buy gifts for each other. She has 6 boy cousins and 7 girl cousins. If Lucy is randomly drawing one of her cousin's names, what is the probability she draws a girl?

8-4 Sample Spaces

16. Josh and Jennifer are playing a game with a spinner and a coin. The spinner is divided into 6 equal sections labeled 1–6. A turn consists of one spin of the spinner and one flip of the coin. Find all the possible outcomes. What is the probability the spinner will land on 6 and the coin will land on tails?

17. McKenzie has a sundae bar for her birthday party. It has vanilla, chocolate and strawberry ice cream. For toppings it has hot fudge, caramel sauce, and marshmallow topping. How many different sundaes can she make with one scoop of ice cream and one topping?

Holt Mathematics

8-5 Disjoint Events

18. Determine whether the set of events is disjoint. Explain.

Choosing a coffee drink and choosing a cold drink

19. Find the probability of the set of disjoint events.

Choosing a vowel or an *L* from the letters in the word *parallel*.

8-6 Independent and Dependent Events

Decide whether each set of events is independent or dependent. Explain.

20. A man chooses a movie at the video store and then chooses a second movie from those remaining.

21. A child takes a coin out of his piggybank and then picks another one after replacing the first coin.

22. Julio has a bag of marbles that contains 6 red, 11 blue, 5 green, and 10 yellow. What is the probability Julio picks a green marble first and then picks a red marble without replacing the green marble?

8-7 Making Predictions

23. Based on a sample survey, a broadcasting company claims that 78% of the household televisions were tuned into the new reality series on Tuesday night. Out of 40,000 households, how many would you predict watched the new reality series?

24. A sack holds 4 orange marbles, 2 green marbles, 3 red marbles, and 1 clear marble. You pick a marble from the sack, record its color, and place the marble back in the sack. If you repeat this process 50 times, how many times do you expect to pick a red marble from the sack?

Holt Mathematics

Big Ideas

Answer these questions to summarize the important concepts from Chapter 8 in your own words.

1. Tony answered 27 out of 30 questions correctly. Explain how to find the experimental probability that Tony will answer the next question correctly.

2. Explain how to find the theoretical probability of rolling a number greater than 4 on a fair number cube.

3. Explain the difference between disjoint events, independent events, and dependent events.

For more review of Chapter 8:

- Complete the Chapter 8 Study Guide and Review on pages 418–420 of your textbook.
- Complete the Ready to Go On quizzes on pages 400 and 414 of your textbook.

Holt Mathematics

LESSON 9-1 Introduction to Geometry

Lesson Objectives

Identify and describe geometric figures

Vocabulary

point (p. 428) _______________________________________

line (p. 428) _______________________________________

____

plane (p. 428) _______________________________________

____

ray (p. 429) _______________________________________

____

line segment (p. 429) _______________________________________

____

congruent (p. 429) _______________________________________

____

Additional Examples

Example 1

Identify the figures in the diagram.

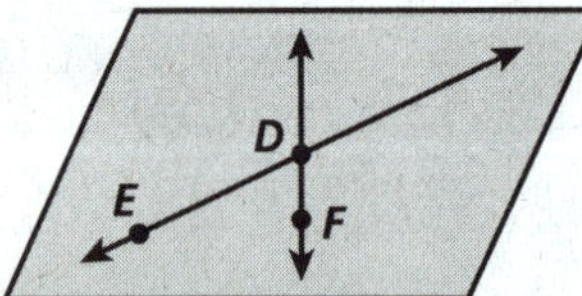

A. three points [____________]

B. two lines [________]   Choose any [____] points on a line to
                                    name a line.

C. a plane [__________]   Choose any [____] points not on
                                    the same line to name a plane.

Holt Mathematics

Example 2

Identify the figures in the diagram.

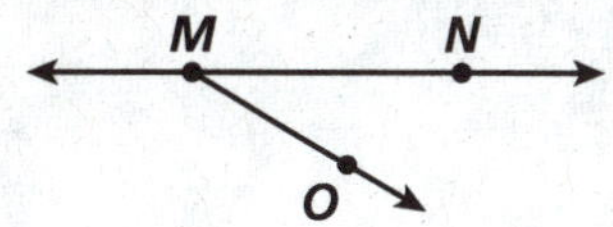

A. three rays

Name the [ ] of a ray first.

B. two line segments

Use the [ ] in any order to name a line segment.

Example 3

Identify the line segments that are congruent in the figure.

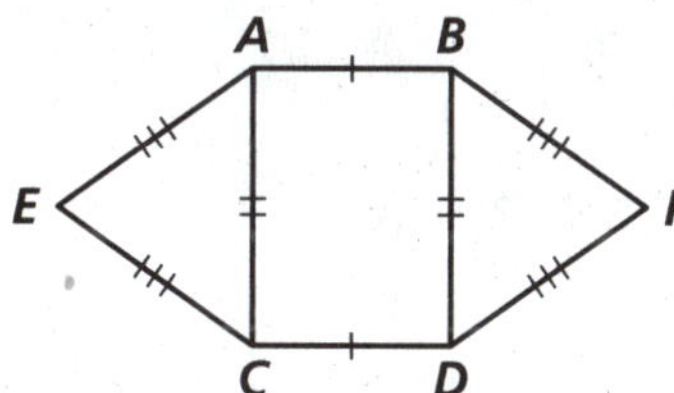

[ ] ≅ [ ]   One tick mark

[ ] ≅ [ ]   Two tick marks

[ ] ≅ [ ] ≅ [ ] ≅ [ ]   Three tick marks

Holt Mathematics

Check It Out!

1. Identify four points, two lines, and a plane in the diagram.

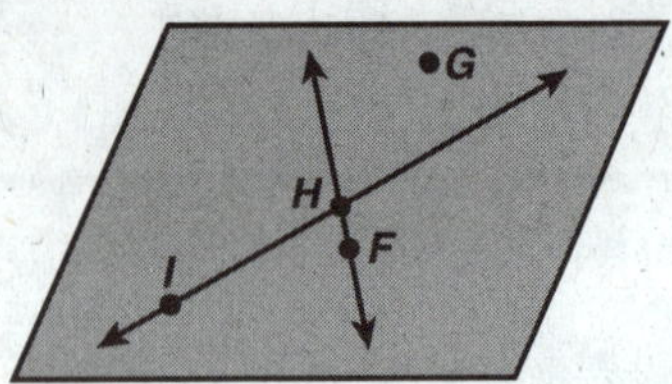

2. Identify three rays and three line segments in the diagram.

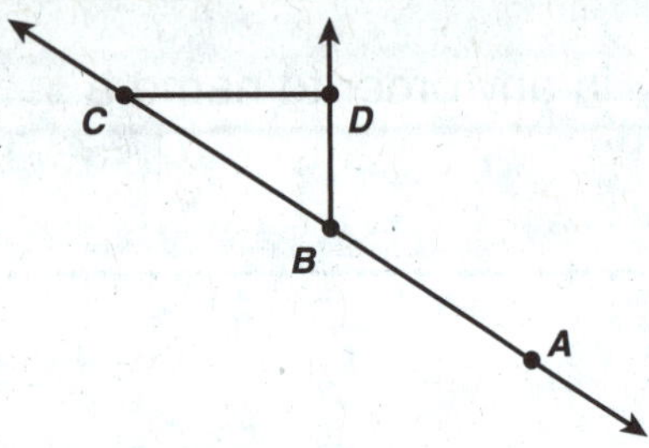

3. Identify the line segments that are congruent in the figure.

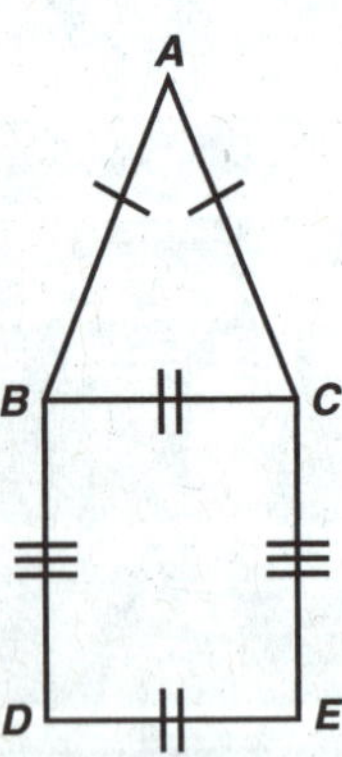

Holt Mathematics

LESSON 9-2
Measuring and Classifying Angles

Lesson Objectives

Name, measure, draw, and classify angles

Vocabulary

angle (p. 432) ____

____

vertex (p. 432) ____

____

acute angle (p. 433) ____

____

right angle (p. 433) ____

____

obtuse angle (p. 433) ____

____

straight angle (p. 433) ____

____

Additional Examples

Example 1

Use a protractor to measure the angle.

- Place the [ ] point of the

  protractor on the [ ]

  of the angle.

- Place the protractor so [ ] passes through the [ ]° mark.

Holt Mathematics

- Using the scale that starts with ☐° along $\overrightarrow{GH}$, read the measure where

  ☐ crosses.

- The measure of $\angle FGH$ is ☐°. Write this as m$\angle FGH$ = ☐°.

Example 2

Use a protractor to draw an angle that measures 80°.

- Draw a ☐ on a sheet of paper.

- Place the ☐ point of the protractor on the endpoint of the

  ☐. Make sure the ☐ passes through the ☐° mark.

- Make a mark at ☐° above the scale on the ☐.

- Draw a ☐ from the endpoint of the first ray through the mark at

  ☐°.

Holt Mathematics

Example 3

Classify each angle as acute, right, obtuse, or straight.

A.

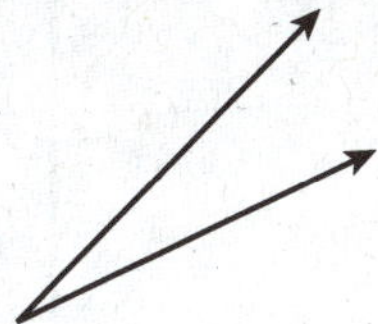

The angle measures __________ 90°, so it is an __________ angle.

B.

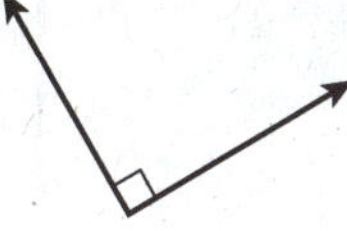

The angle measures __________ 90°, so it is a __________ angle.

Example 4

A welder used this piece of metal on his project. Classify ∠X, ∠Y, and ∠Z.

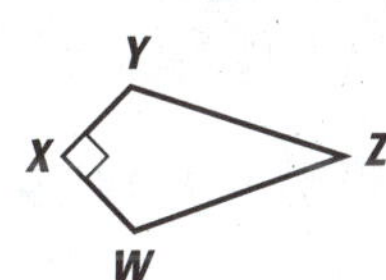

∠X __________ The angle is marked as a __________ angle.

∠Y __________ The angle measures more than __________° and less than __________°.

∠Z __________ The angle measures less than __________°.

Holt Mathematics

Check It Out!

1. Use a protractor to measure the angle.

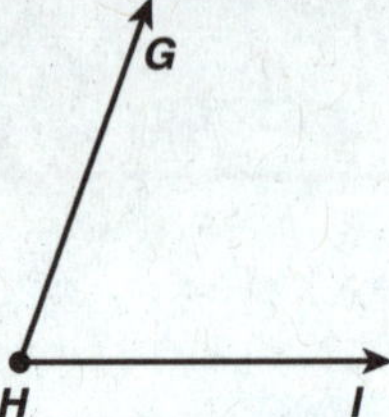

2. Use a protractor to draw an angle that measures 45°.

3. Classify the angle as acute, right, obtuse, or straight.

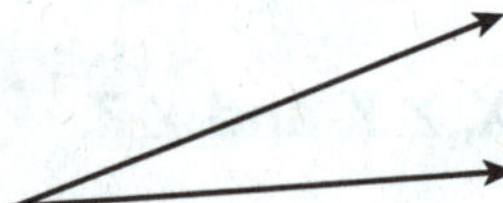

4. A metal jeweler used this piece of metal on her project. Classify ∠A, ∠B, and ∠D.

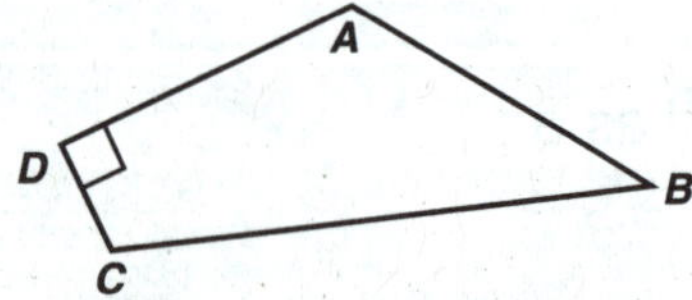

Holt Mathematics

Angle Relationships

Lesson Objectives

Identify and describe angle pairs

Vocabulary

vertical angles (p. 436) _______________________________

____

adjacent angles (p. 436) _______________________________

____

complementary angles (p. 437) __________________________

____

supplementary angles (p. 437) __________________________

____

Additional Examples

Example 1

Tell whether the numbered angles are vertical or adjacent.

A.

∠5 and ∠6 are ______________ each other and

are formed by two ______________ lines.

They are ______________ angles.

B.

∠7 and ∠8 are side by side and have a common

______________ and ______________.

They are ______________ angles.

Holt Mathematics

Example 2

Use the diagram to tell whether the angles are complementary, supplementary, or neither.

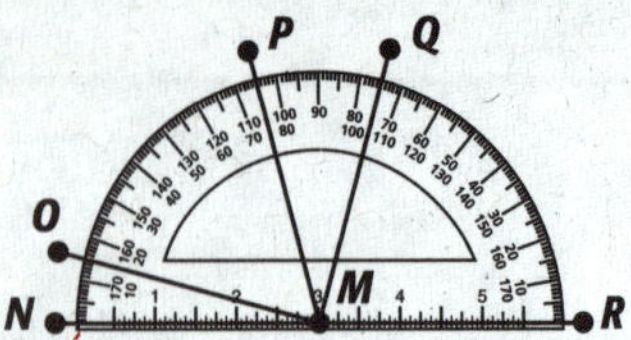

A. ∠*OMP* and ∠*PMQ*

To find m∠*PMQ*, start with the measure that *QM* crosses, ☐°, and

subtract the measure that *MP* crosses, ☐°.

m∠*PMQ* = ☐° − ☐° = ☐°.

m∠*OMP* = ☐° − ☐° = ☐°.

Since ☐° + ☐° = ☐°, ∠*OMP* and ∠*PMQ* are ________.

B. ∠*NMO* and ∠*OMR*

m∠*NMO* = ☐° and m∠*OMR* = ☐°

Since ☐° + ☐° = ☐°, ∠*NMO* and ∠*OMR* are ________.

C. ∠*PMQ* and ∠*QMR*

m∠*PMQ* = ☐° − ☐° = ☐°.

m∠*QMR* = ☐°.

Since ☐° + ☐° = ☐°, ∠*PMQ* and ∠*QMR* are ________.

Holt Mathematics

Check It Out!

1. Tell whether the numbered angles are adjacent or vertical.

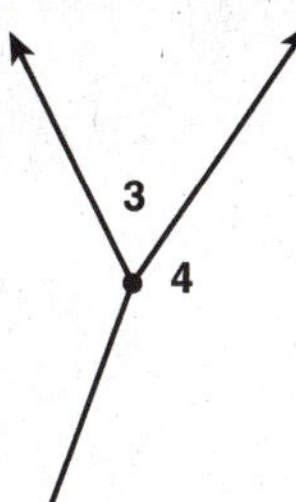

2. Use the diagram to tell whether the angles are complementary, supplementary, or neither.

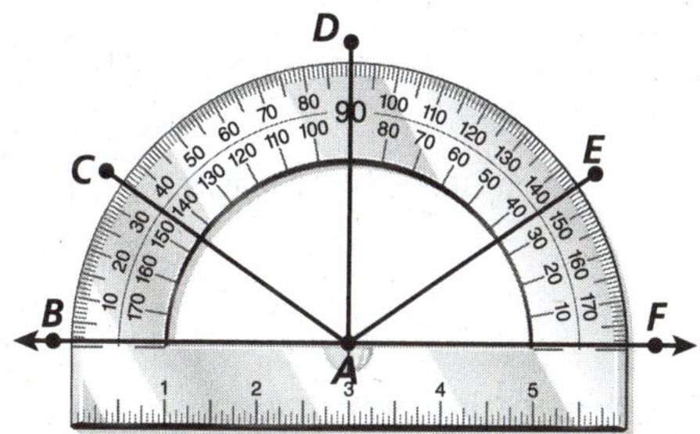

$\angle CAD$ and $\angle EAF$

Holt Mathematics

LESSON 9-4
Finding Angle Measures

Lesson Objectives

Use angle relationships to find angle measures

Additional Examples

Example 1

Find each unknown angle measure.

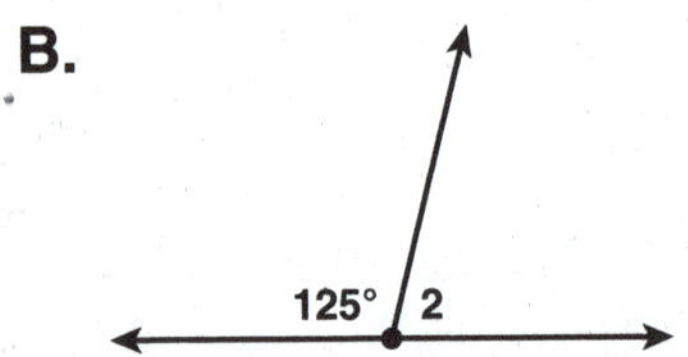

A.

The angles are complementary.

Since the angles are complementary, the sum of the angle measures is ☐°.

$$71° + m\angle 1 = \underline{\qquad}°$$

$$-\underline{\qquad}° \qquad -\underline{\qquad}°$$

Subtract ☐° from both sides.

$$m\angle 1 = \underline{\qquad}°$$

B.

The angles are supplementary.

Since the angles are supplementary, the sum of the angle measures is ☐°.

$$125° + m\angle 2 = \underline{\qquad}°$$

$$-\underline{\qquad}° \qquad -\underline{\qquad}°$$

Subtract ☐° from both sides.

$$m\angle 2 = \underline{\qquad}°$$

C.

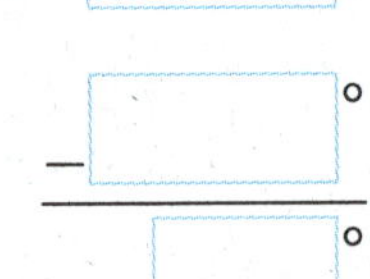

The angles are vertical angles.

$$m\angle 3 = \underline{\qquad}°$$

Congruent angles have the ☐ measure.

Holt Mathematics

Example 2

**Use the information in the diagram to find the unknown angle measures
a, *b*, and *c*. Show your work.**

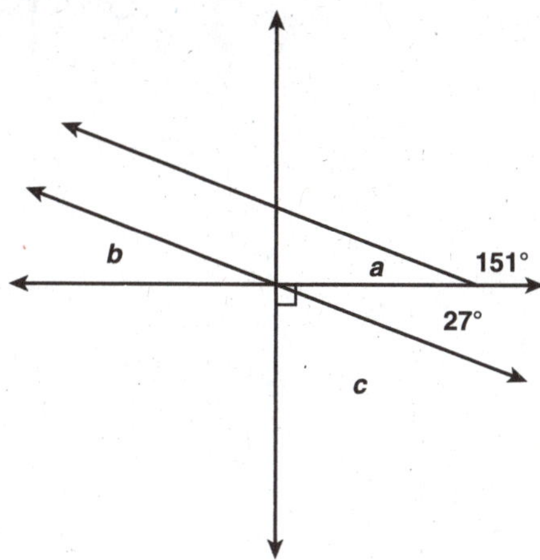

Step 1: The angles labeled *c* and 27° are ____________. To

find *c*, use properties of ____________ angles.

$27° + c =$ ____°   The sum of the measures is ____°.

$-$ ____° $-$ ____°   Subtract ____° from both sides.

$c =$ ____°

Step 2: The angles labeled *a* and 151° are ____________. To

find *a*, use properties of ____________ angles.

$151° + a =$ ____°   The sum of the measures is ____°.

$-$ ____° $-$ ____°   Subtract ____° from both sides.

$a =$ ____°

Step 3: The angles labeled *b* and 27° are ____________ angles. To find

b, use properties of ____________ angles.

$b =$ ____°   ____________ angles are congruent.

Holt Mathematics

Check It Out!

1. Find each unknown angle measure.

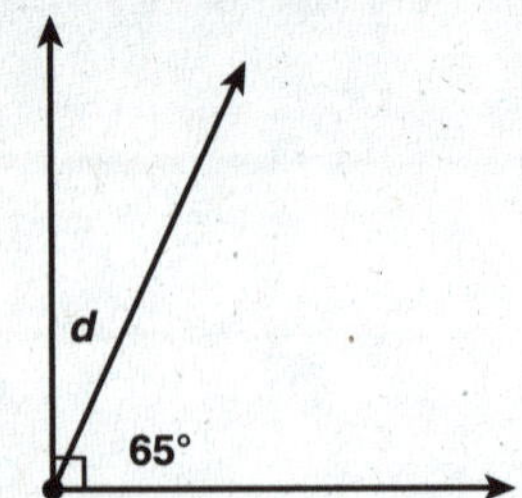

The angles are complementary.

2. Use the information in the diagram to find the unknown angle measures *x*, *y*, and *z*. Show your work.

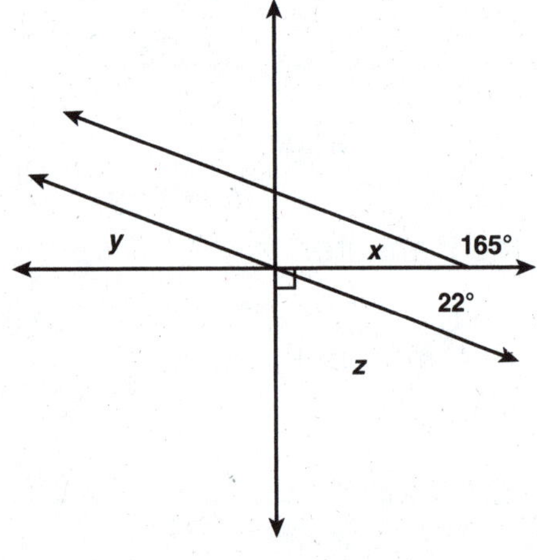

Holt Mathematics

LESSON 9-5 Classifying Polygons

Lesson Objectives

Identify and name polygons

Vocabulary

polygon (p. 448) ____

____

vertex (p. 448) ____

____

regular polygon (p. 449) ____

____

Additional Examples

Example 1

Determine whether each figure is a polygon. Explain your answer.

A.
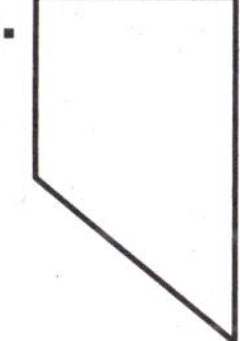

The figure ______ a polygon.

It is a ______________ figure with

4 line ______________ .

B.

The figure ______________ a

polygon. It is not a ______________

figure.

C.

The figure ______________ a

polygon. The figure is ______________

formed by line segments.

D.
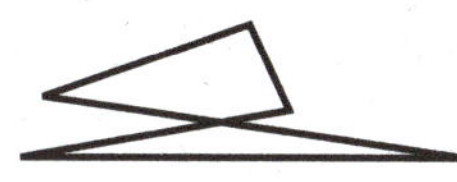

The figure ______________ a

polygon. There are sides that meet

______________ 2 other sides.

Holt Mathematics

Example 2

Name each polygon.

A. 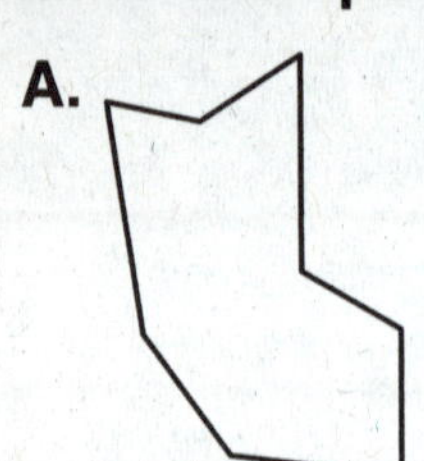

[   ]

[   ] sides, [   ] angles

B.

[   ]

[   ] sides, [   ] angles

Example 3

Name each polygon and tell whether it is a regular polygon. If it is not, explain why not.

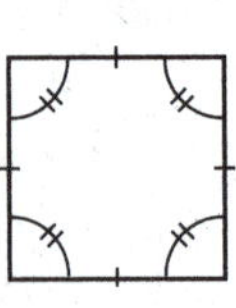

The figure is a [   ]. It [   ] a regular polygon

because all sides and angles are [   ].

Check It Out!

1. Determine whether the figure is a polygon. If it is not, explain why not.

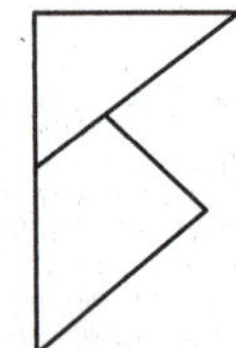

2. Name the polygon.

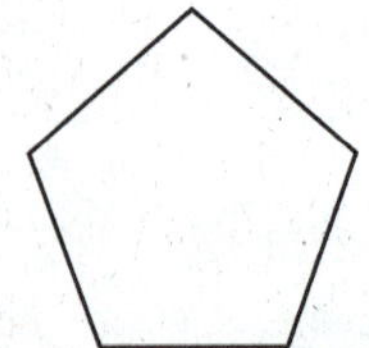

3. Name the polygon and tell whether it is a regular polygon. If it is not, explain why not.

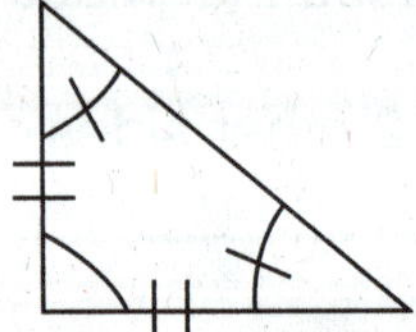

Holt Mathematics

Classifying Triangles

LESSON
9-6

Lesson Objectives

Classify triangles by their side lengths and angle measures

Vocabulary

scalene triangle (p. 452) _______________________________

____

isosceles triangle (p. 452) _____________________________

____

equilateral triangle (p. 452) ___________________________

____

acute triangle (p. 452) _________________________________

____

obtuse triangle (p. 452) ________________________________

____

right triangle (p. 452) _________________________________

Additional Examples

Example 1

Classify each triangle according to its sides and angles.

A.

Two congruent sides

Three acute angles

This is an ______________ ______________ triangle.

Classify each triangle according to its sides and angles.

B.

No congruent sides

One right angle

This is a ______________ ______________ triangle.

Holt Mathematics

Example 2

Identify the different types of triangles in the figure, and determine how many of each there are.

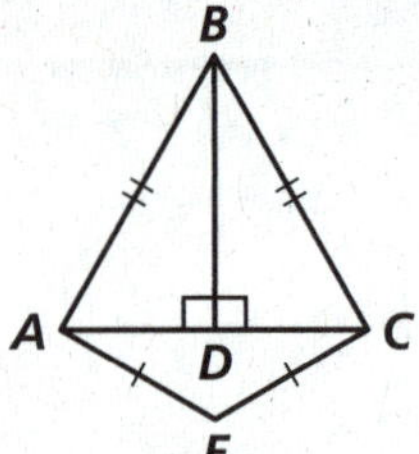

Type	How many	Name
Right		
Isosceles		
Acute		
Scalene		
Obtuse		

Check It Out!

1. Classify the triangle according to its sides and angles.

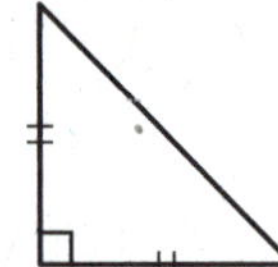

2. Identify the different types of triangles in the figure, and determine how many of each there are.

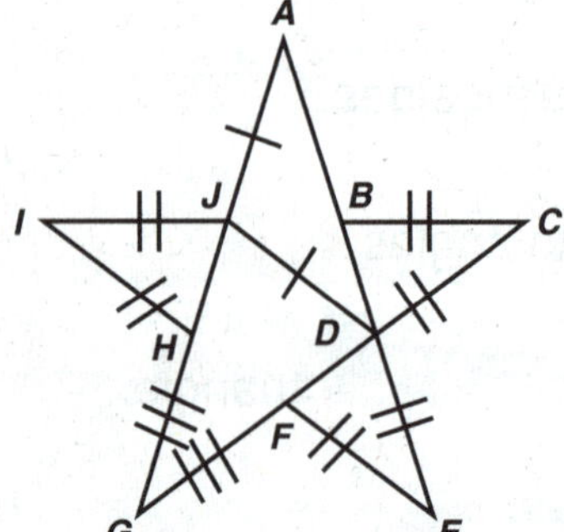

Holt Mathematics

LESSON 9-7 — Angle Measures in Triangles

Lesson Objectives

Find the measures of angles in triangles

Additional Examples

Example 1

Find the unknown measure in each triangle.

A.

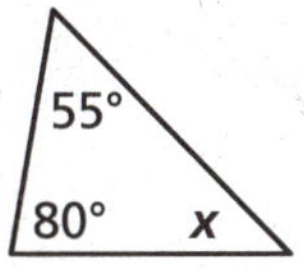

$80° + 55° + x = \boxed{}°$ The sum of the angle measures in a triangle is $\boxed{}°$.

$135° + x = \boxed{}°$ Add $80°$ and $55°$.

$-\boxed{}° \quad -\boxed{}°$ $\boxed{}$ $135°$ from both sides.

$x = \boxed{}°$

The measure of the unknown angle is $\boxed{}°$.

B.

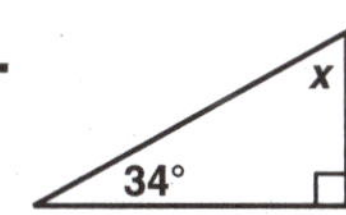

$34° + 90° + x = \boxed{}°$ The sum of the angle measures in a triangle is $\boxed{}°$.

$124° + x = \boxed{}°$ Add $34°$ and $90°$.

$-\boxed{}° \quad -\boxed{}°$ Subtract $\boxed{}$ from both sides.

$x = \boxed{}°$

The measure of the unknown angle is $\boxed{}°$.

Holt Mathematics

Example 2

The figure shows part of the support structure of a bridge. Find the unknown angle measure *x*. Show your work.

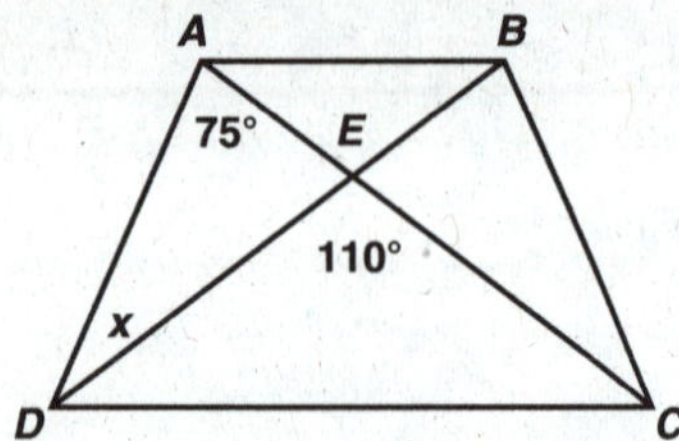

Step 1: Find the measure of $\angle DEA$.

$$\text{m}\angle DEA + \text{m}\angle DEC = \boxed{}^\circ$$

$$\text{m}\angle DEA + 110° = \boxed{}^\circ \qquad \text{Substitute } 110° \text{ for m}\angle DEC.$$

$$\text{m}\angle DEA = \boxed{}^\circ \qquad \boxed{} \; 110° \text{ from}$$

both sides.

Step 2: Find the angle measure *x*.

$$70° + 75° + x = \boxed{}^\circ \qquad \text{Sum of angle measures is } \boxed{}^\circ.$$

$$145° + x = \boxed{}^\circ \qquad \text{Add } 70° \text{ and } 75°.$$

$$x = \boxed{}^\circ \qquad \boxed{} \; 145° \text{ from}$$

both sides.

Holt Mathematics

Check It Out!

1. Find the unknown angle measure in each triangle.

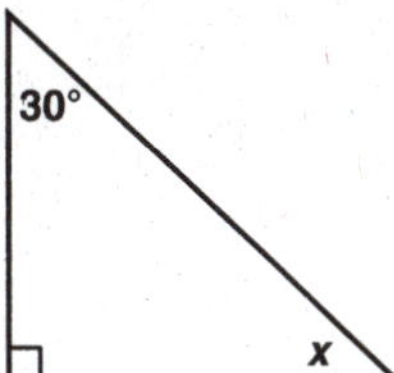

2. The figure shows a diagram of a design. Find the unknown angle measure *x*. Show your work.

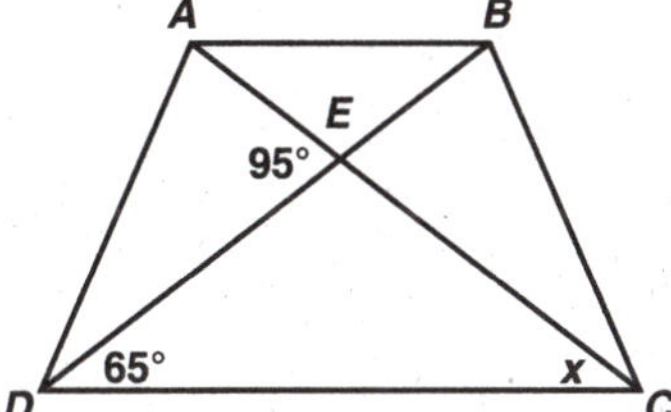

Holt Mathematics

LESSON 9-8 Classifying Quadrilaterals

Lesson Objectives

Name, identify, and draw types of quadrilaterals

Vocabulary

parallelogram (p. 462) _______________________________________

____

rectangle (p. 462) _______________________________________

____

rhombus (p. 462) _______________________________________

____

square (p. 462) _______________________________________

____

trapezoid (p. 462) _______________________________________

____

Additional Examples

Example 1

Give all the names that apply to the quadrilateral. Then give the name that best describes it.

A. 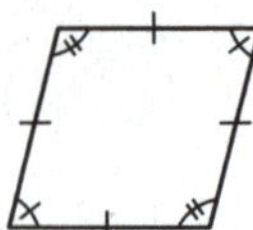

This figure has two pairs of parallel sides, so it is a

________________________________ .

It has four congruent sides, so it is also a ________________ .

________________ best describes this quadrilateral.

B. 

The figure has exactly one pair of opposite sides that are

parallel, so it is a ________________ .

________________ best describes the quadrilateral.

Holt Mathematics

Example 2

Draw each figure. If it is not possible to draw, explain why.

A. a rectangle that is not a rhombus.

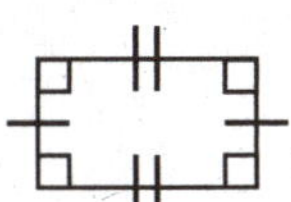

The figure has [   ] right angles and two pairs of

congruent sides. It [   ] have 4 congruent sides.

B. a square that is not a rhombus

Drawing the figure is [   ]. All squares are

[   ] because they have [   ] congruent sides.

Check It Out!

1. Give all the names that apply to the quadrilateral. Then give the name that best describes it.

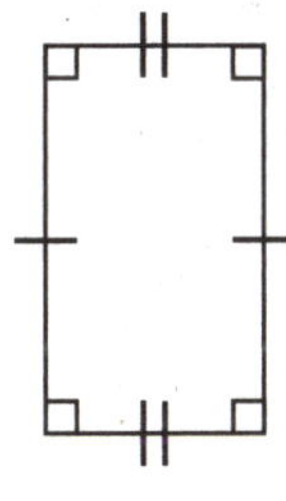

2. Draw each figure. If it is not possible to draw explain why.

a rhombus that is not a square

Holt Mathematics

LESSON 9-9
Congruent Figures

Lesson Objectives

Identify congruent figures and use congruence to solve problems

Vocabulary

Side-Side-Side Rule (p. 466) ____

____

Additional Examples

Example 1

Identify any congruent figures.

A. 

The sides of the octagons [   ] congruent. Each side of the outer figure is larger than each side of the inner figure.

B.

The sections in the figure [   ] congruent.

Example 2

Determine whether the triangles are congruent.

$AB =$ [   ] cm $PQ =$ [   ] cm

$BC =$ [   ] cm $PR =$ [   ] cm

$AC =$ [   ] cm $RQ =$ [   ] cm

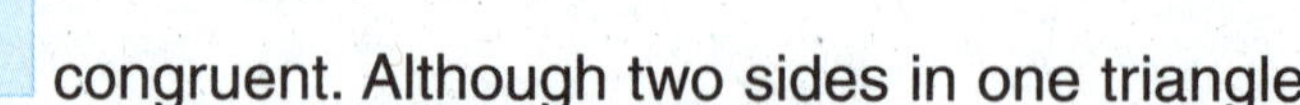
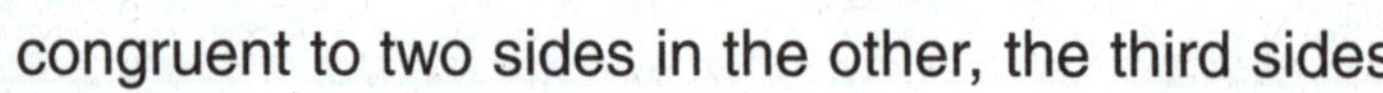

The triangles [   ] congruent. Although two sides in one triangle

[   ] congruent to two sides in the other, the third sides

[   ] congruent.

Holt Mathematics

Example 3

Determine the missing measures in the set of congruent polygons.

A.

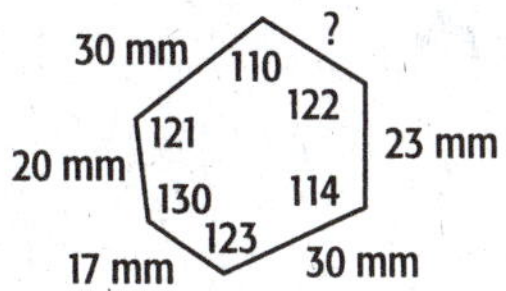

The corresponding angles of congruent polygons are

The missing angle measure is [ ]°.

B.

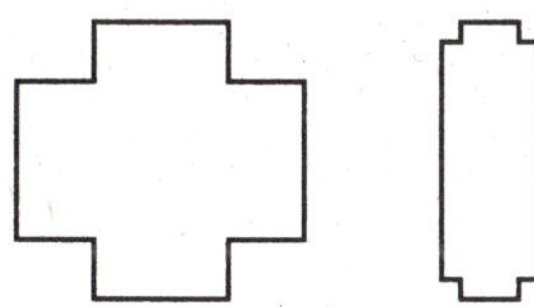

The corresponding sides of congruent polygons are

The missing side measure is [ ] mm.

Check It Out!

1. Identify any congruent figures.

2. Determine whether the triangles are congruent.

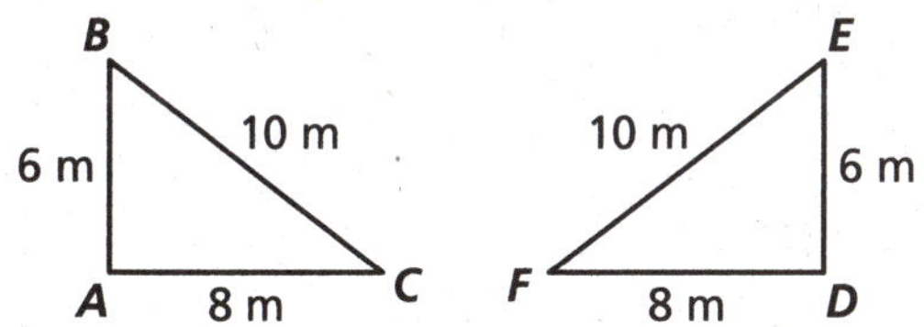

3. Determine the missing measures in the set of congruent polygons.

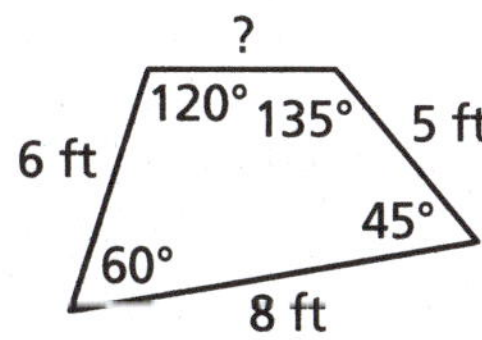
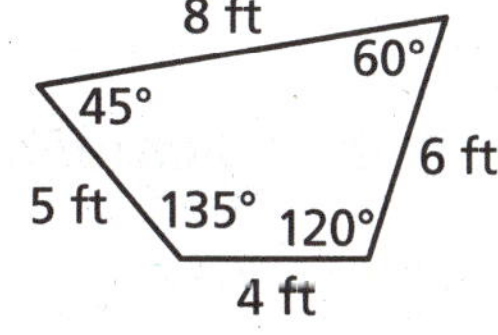

Holt Mathematics

Chapter Review

9-1 Introduction to Geometry

Identify the figures in the diagram.

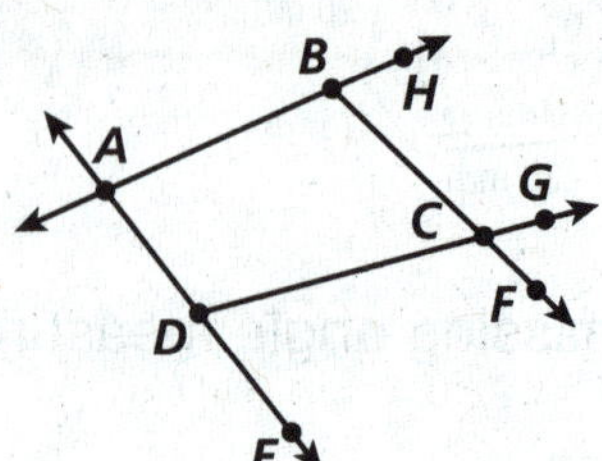

1. three points

2. two lines

3. a plane

4. three rays

9-2 Measuring and Classifying Angles

Classify each angle as acute, right, obtuse, or straight.

5. 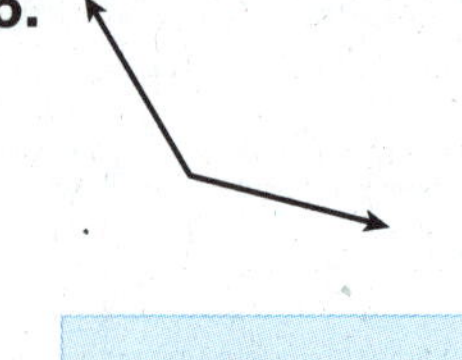

6. 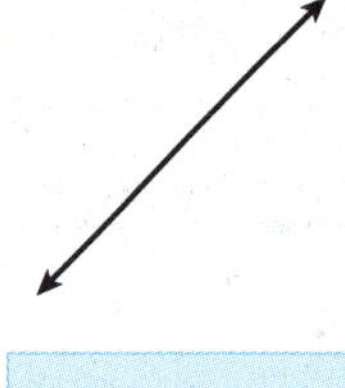

7. 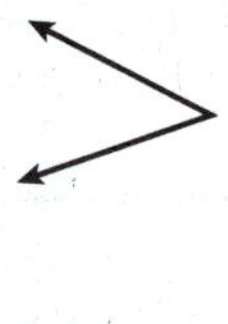

Use a protractor to draw an angle with each given measure.

8. 45°

9. 120°

10. 95°

9-3 Angle Relationships

11. If the m∠8 is 54°, what are the measures of ∠5, ∠6, and ∠7?

Find the measure of the angle that is complementary to each given angle.

12. 33°

13. 64°

14. 75°

15. 17°

Holt Mathematics

9-4 Finding Angle Measures

Find the unknown angle measures.

16. 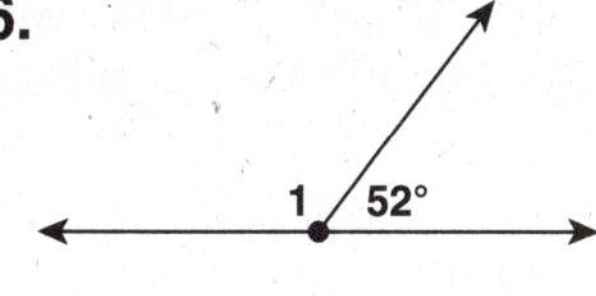

17. 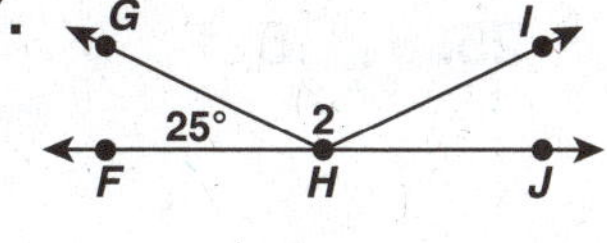

$\angle FHG \cong \angle JHI$;
$m\angle FHJ = 180°$

18. 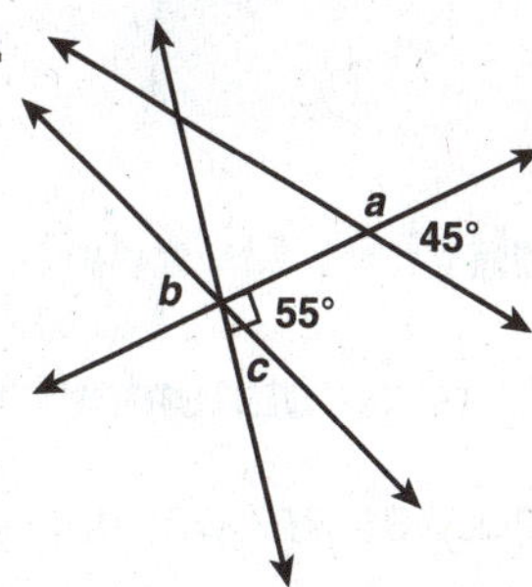

9-5 Classifying Polygons

Name each polygon, and tell whether it is a regular polygon. If it is not, explain why not.

19. 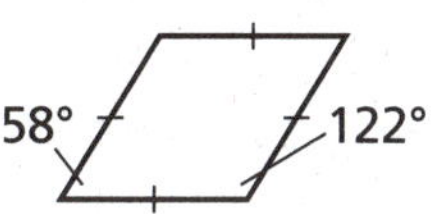

20. 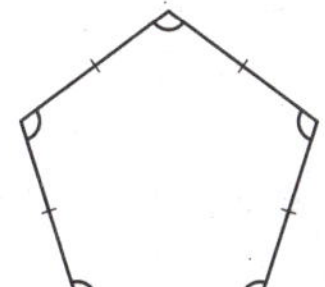

21. 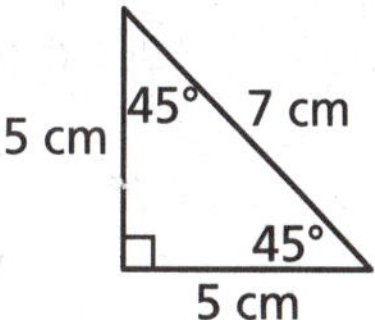

9-6 Classifying Triangles

22. Identify the different types of triangles in the figure, and determine how many of each there are.

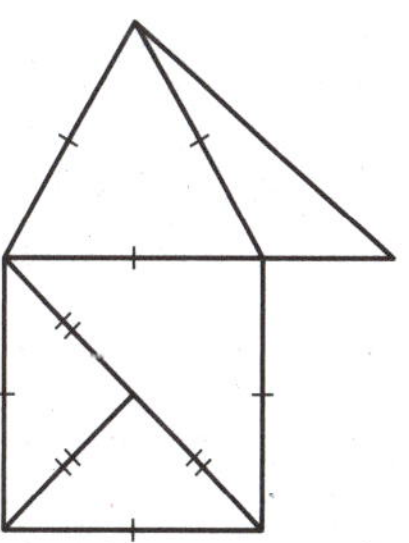

23. The sum of the lengths of the sides of triangle *ABC* is 38 in. The lengths of sides $\overline{AB}$ and $\overline{BC}$ are 14 inches and 11 inches. Find the length of side $\overline{AC}$ and classify the triangle.

Holt Mathematics

9-7 Angle Measures in Triangles

Find the unknown measure in each triangle, given two angle measures.

24. 36°, 19°

25. 61°, 52°

9-8 Classifying Quadrilaterals

Tell whether each statement is true or false. Explain your answer.

26. All rhombuses are parallelograms.

27. Some trapezoids are parallelograms.

28. Some squares are rectangles.

9-9 Congruent Figures

Determine the missing measures in each set of congruent polygons.

29. 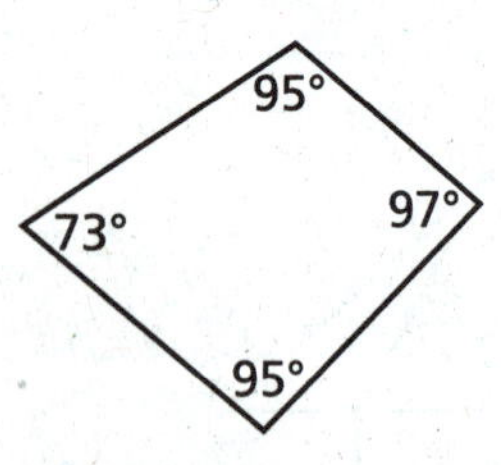

30. 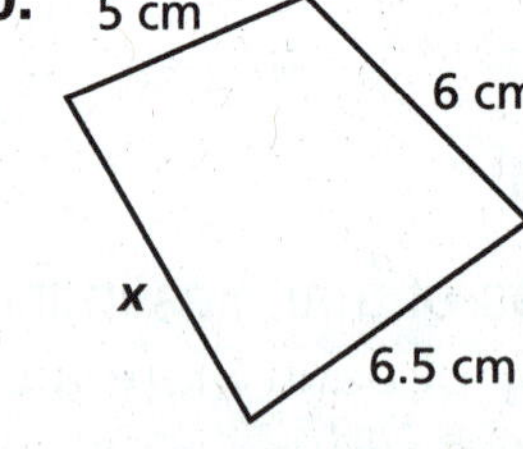 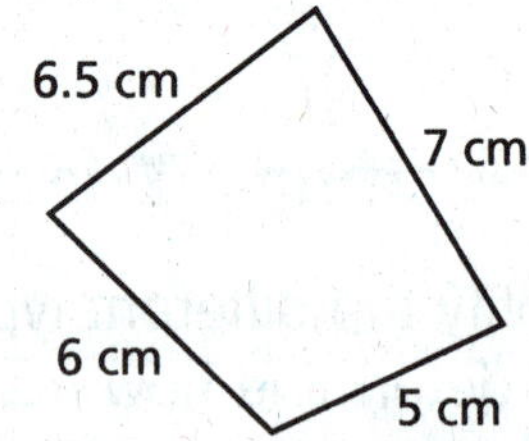

Holt Mathematics

Big Ideas

Answer these questions to summarize the important concepts from Chapter 9 in your own words.

1. Explain how to measure an angle with a protractor.

2. Explain the difference between complementary and supplementary angles.

3. Explain the difference between a polygon and a regular polygon.

4. Two angle measures in a triangle are 35° and 77°. Explain how to find the third angle measure in the triangle.

5. Explain how to determine if two polygons are congruent.

For more review of Chapter 9:

- Complete the Chapter 9 Study Guide and Review on pages 474–476.
- Complete the Ready to Go On quizzes on pages 446 and 470.

Holt Mathematics

Perimeter

LESSON 10-1

Lesson Objectives

Find the perimeter and missing side lengths of a polygon

Vocabulary

perimeter (p. 486) ____

____

Additional Examples

Example 1

Find the perimeter of the figure.

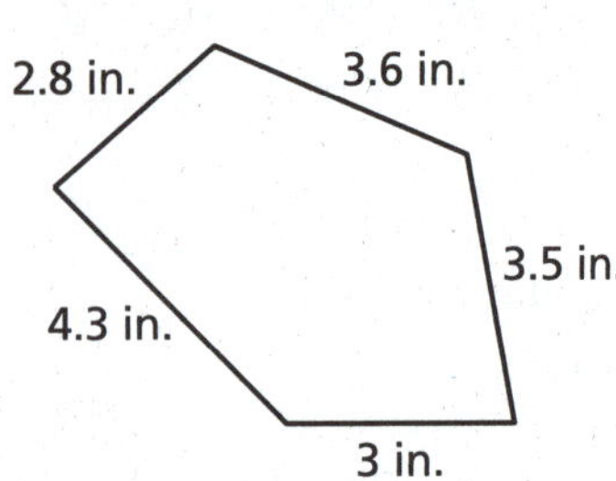

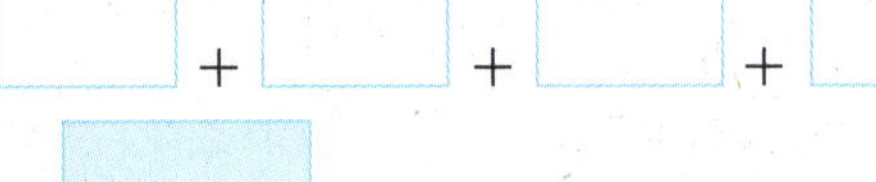 all the side lengths.

☐ + ☐ + ☐ + ☐ + ☐

= ☐

The perimeter is ☐ in.

Example 2

Find the perimeter P of the rectangle.

$P = 2w + 2l$

$P = (2 \cdot \boxed{}) + (2 \cdot \boxed{})$ Substitute ☐ for w and ☐ for l.

$P = \boxed{} + \boxed{}$ Multiply.

$P = \boxed{}$ Add.

The perimeter is  cm.

Holt Mathematics

Example 3

Find each unknown measure.

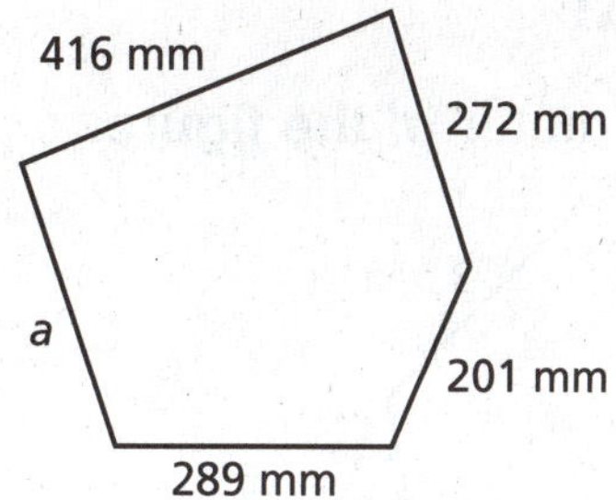

A. What is the length of side *a* if
the perimeter equals 1,471 mm?

P = sum of side lengths

Use the values you know.

1,471 = ☐ + ☐ + ☐ + ☐ + *a*

1,471 = ☐ + *a*   Add the known lengths.

1,471 − 1,178 = 1,178 + *a* − 1,178   Subtract ☐ from both sides.

☐ = *a*   Side *a* is ☐ mm long.

B. What is the perimeter of the polygon?

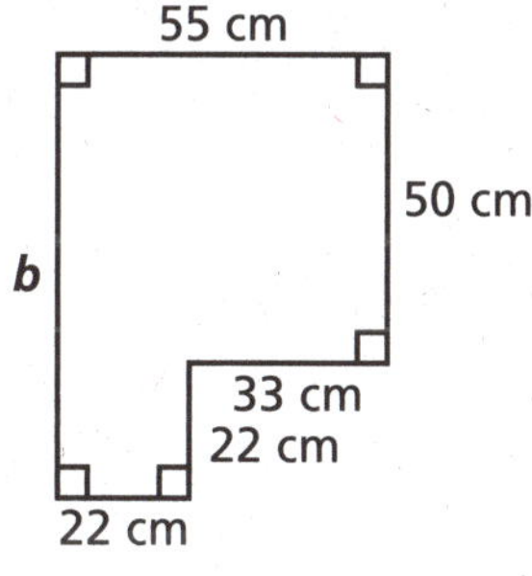

Step 1: Find *b*.

Find the sum of the lengths of the
sides ☐ *b*.

b = ☐ + ☐.

b = ☐

Side *b* is ☐ cm long.

Step 2: Find the perimeter.

P = ☐ + ☐ + ☐ + ☐ + ☐ + ☐

P = ☐

The perimeter of the polygon is ☐ cm.

Holt Mathematics

Check It Out!

1. Find the perimeter of the figure.

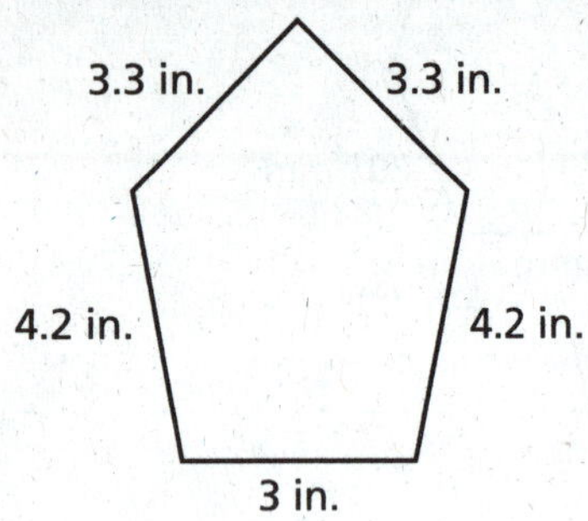

2. Find the perimeter P of the polygon.

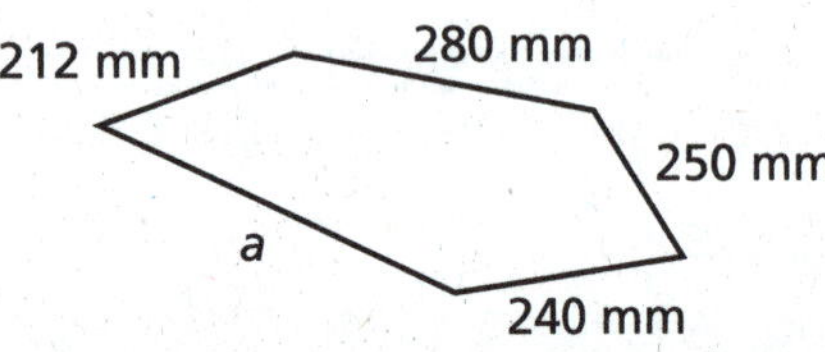

3. What is the length of side *a* if the perimeter equals 1,302 mm?

238

Holt Mathematics

LESSON 10-2 · Circles and Circumference

Lesson Objectives

Identify the parts of a circle and find the circumference of a circle

Vocabulary

circle (p. 492) ____

____

center (p. 492) ____

____

radius (radii) (p. 492) ____

____

diameter (p. 492) ____

____

circumference (p. 492) ____

____

pi (p. 492) ____

____

Additional Examples

Example 1

Name the circle, a diameter, and three radii.

The center is point ⬚, so this is circle ⬚.

⬚ is a diameter.

⬚, ⬚, and ⬚ are radii.

Holt Mathematics

Example 2

A skydiver is laying out a circular target for his next jump. Find the circumference of the target by using $\frac{22}{7}$ as an estimate for π.

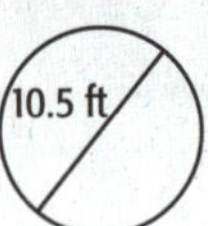

$C = \pi d$ — Use the formula.

$C \approx \boxed{} \cdot \boxed{}$ — Replace π with $\boxed{}$ and d with $\boxed{}$.

$C \approx \boxed{}$

The circumference of the target is $\boxed{}$ feet.

Example 3

Find the missing value to the nearest hundredth. Use 3.14 as an estimate for *pi*.

A.

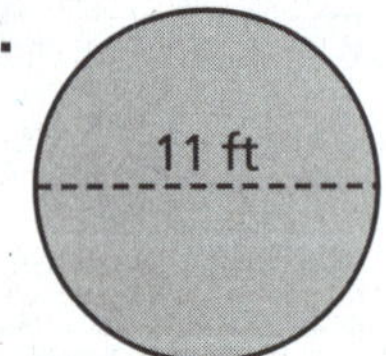

$d = 11$ ft; $C = ?$

$C = \pi d$ — Write the formula.

$C \approx \boxed{} \cdot \boxed{}$ — Replace π with $\boxed{}$ and

d with $\boxed{}$.

$C \approx \boxed{}$ ft

B.

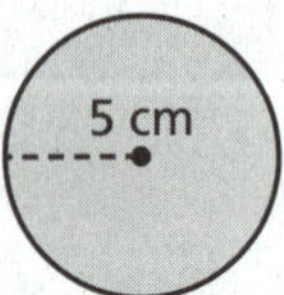

$r = 5$ cm; $C = ?$

$C = 2\pi r$ — Write the formula.

$C \approx 2 \cdot \boxed{} \cdot \boxed{}$ — Replace π with $\boxed{}$ and

r with $\boxed{}$.

$C \approx \boxed{}$ cm

Holt Mathematics

Check It Out!

1. Name the circle, a diameter, and three radii.

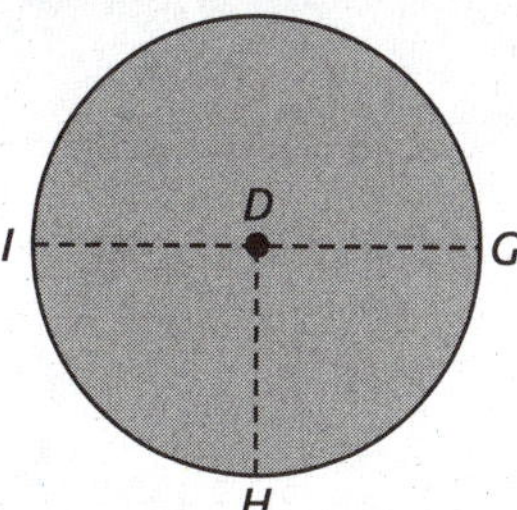

2. A concrete chalk artist is drawing a circular design. Estimate the circumference of the chalk design by using $\frac{22}{7}$ as an estimate for π.

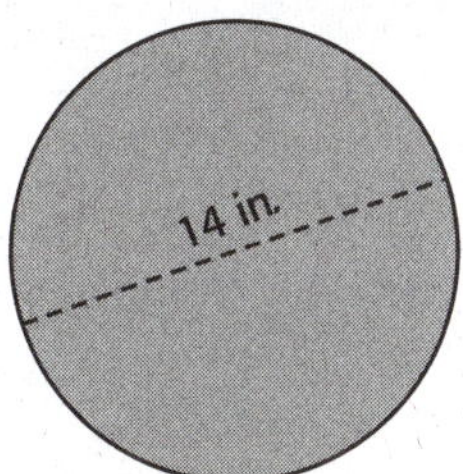

3. Find the missing value to the nearest hundredth. Use 3.14 as an estimate for π.

$d = 9$ ft; $C = ?$

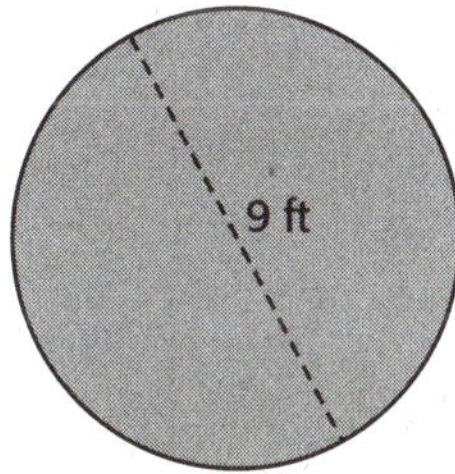

Holt Mathematics

Area of Parallelograms

LESSON 10-3

Lesson Objectives

Find the area of rectangles and other parallelograms

Vocabulary

area (p. 497) ______________________________

____

base (p. 497) ______________________________

____

height (p. 497) ______________________________

____

Additional Examples

Example 1

Find the area of the parallelogram.

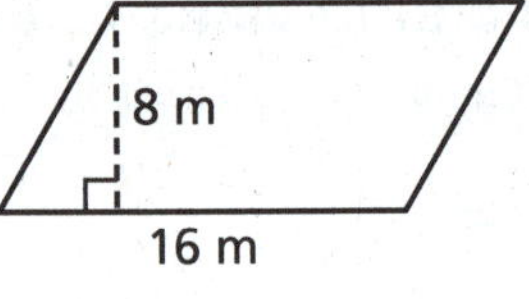

$A = bh$ Use the formula.

$A = $ ☐ · ☐ Substitute for b and h.

$A = $ ☐

The area of the parallelogram is ☐ m^2.

Example 2

Find the area of the rectangle.

$A = lw$ Use the formula.

$A = $ ☐ · ☐ Substitute for l and w.

$A = $ ☐ Multiply.

The area of the rectangle is ☐ in^2.

Holt Mathematics

Example 3

The area of a playing field is 1,470 ft and the length is 42 ft. What is the width of the field?

$A = lw$ Use the formula for the area of a rectangle.

$\boxed{} = \boxed{} \, w$ Substitute $\boxed{}$ for A and $\boxed{}$ for l.

$\boxed{} = \boxed{} \, w$ Divide both sides by $\boxed{}$ to isolate w.

$\boxed{} = w$

The width of the playing field is $\boxed{}$ feet.

Example 4

A carpenter is laying a wood floor measuring 4 yd by 5 yd. How many square feet of flooring material does she need?

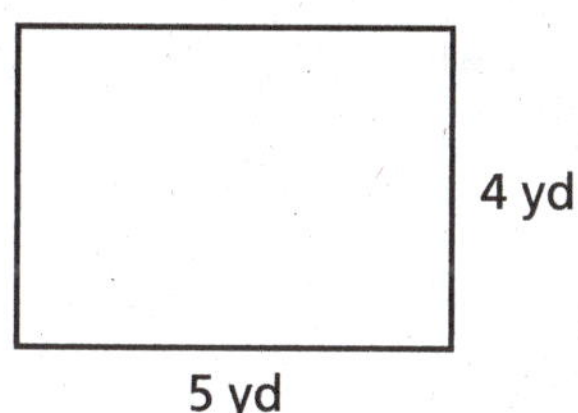

Step 1: Draw and label a diagram.

Step 2: Convert the units.

$4 \, \text{yd} \cdot \dfrac{3}{1 \, \text{yd}} = \boxed{} \, \text{ft}$ Convert yards to feet by multiplying by a ratio equal to 1.

$5 \, \text{yd} \cdot \dfrac{3}{1 \, \text{yd}} = \boxed{} \, \text{ft}$

Step 3: Find the area of the floor in square feet.

$A = lw$ Use the formula for the area of a rectangle.

$A = \boxed{} \cdot \boxed{}$ Substitute $\boxed{}$ for l and $\boxed{}$ for w.

$A = \boxed{}$ Multiply.

The carpenter needs $\boxed{}$ ft^2 of flooring material.

Holt Mathematics

Check It Out!

1. Find the area of the parallelogram.

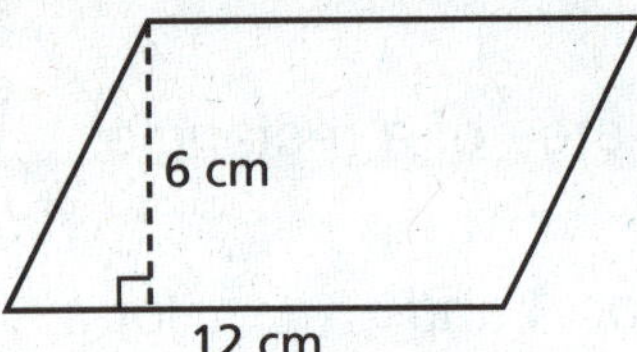

2. Find the area of the rectangle.

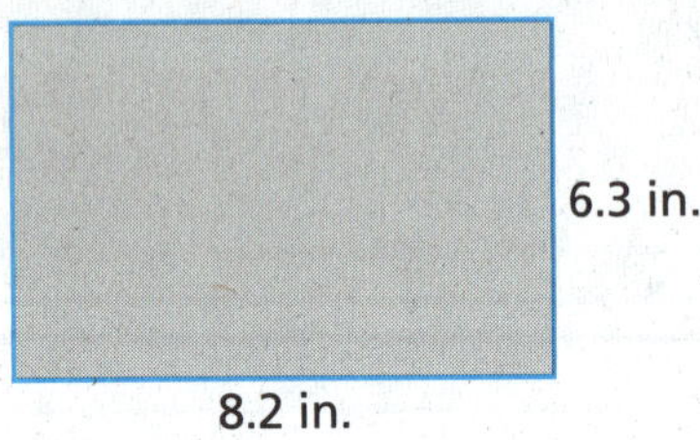

3. The area of a rectangular parking lot is 3,570 ft² and the width is 70 ft. What is the length of the parking lot?

4. A carpenter is laying a tile floor measuring 5 yd by 7 yd. How many square feet of tile material does she need?

Holt Mathematics

LESSON 10-4 # Area of Triangles and Trapezoids

Lesson Objectives

Find the area of triangles and trapezoids

Additional Examples

Example 1

Find the area of the triangle.

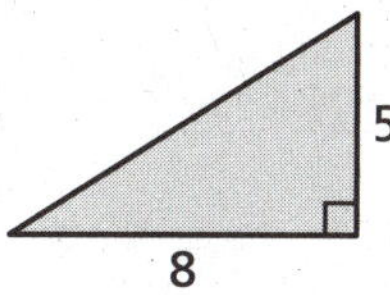

$A = \frac{1}{2}bh$ Use the formula.

$A = \frac{1}{2}(\boxed{} \cdot \boxed{})$ Substitute $\boxed{}$ for b and $\boxed{}$ for h.

$A = \boxed{}$

The area of the triangle is $\boxed{}$ square units.

Example 2

Find the area of the trapezoid.

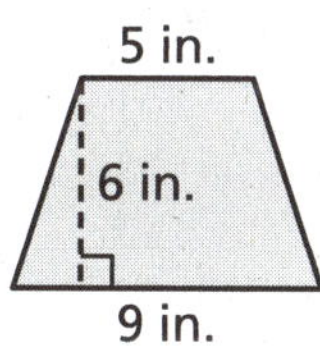

$A = \frac{1}{2}h(b_1 + b_2)$ Use the formula.

$A = \frac{1}{2} \cdot \boxed{}(\boxed{} + \boxed{})$ Substitute.

$A = \frac{1}{2} \cdot \boxed{}(\boxed{})$ Add.

$A = \boxed{}$ Multiply.

The area of the trapezoid is $\boxed{}$  in².

Holt Mathematics

Example 3

The state of Wisconsin is shaped somewhat like a trapezoid. What is the approximate area of the state?

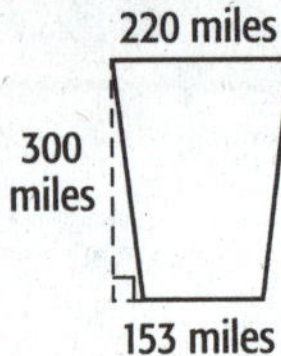

$A = \boxed{} \, h(b_1 + b_2)$ Use the formula.

$A = \boxed{} \cdot \boxed{} (\boxed{} + \boxed{})$ Substitute.

$A = \boxed{} \cdot \boxed{} (\boxed{})$ Add.

$A = \boxed{}$ Multiply.

The area of Wisconsin is about $\boxed{}$ square miles.

Check It Out!

1. Find the area of the triangle.

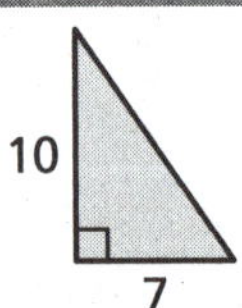

2. Find the area of the trapezoid.

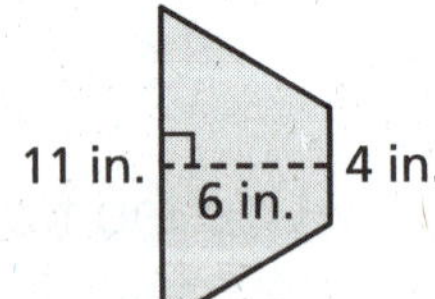

3. A large preserve has a similar trapezoid shape. What is the approximate area of the preserve?

Holt Mathematics

LESSON 10-5

Area of Circles

Lesson Objectives

Find the area of circles

Additional Examples

Example 1

Find the area of the circle by using a formula. Then use an estimate to check whether your answer is reasonable.

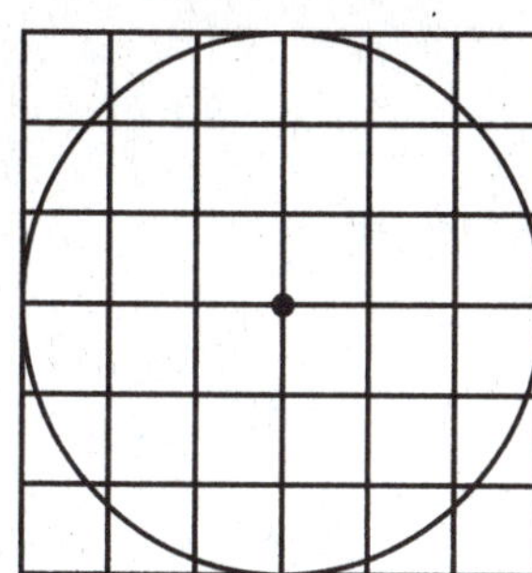

$A = \pi r^2$ — Use the formula.

$A \approx 3.14 \cdot \boxed{}^2$ — Use 3.14 as an estimate for π, and use $\boxed{}$ for r.

$A \approx 3.14 \cdot \boxed{}$ — Evaluate the power.

$A \approx \boxed{}$ square units — Multiply.

Check Use the grid to estimate the area.

$16 + 8 + \frac{1}{2}(8) = \boxed{}$ square units

16 squares are completely inside the circle.
8 squares are mostly inside the circle.
8 squares are halfway inside the circle.

Because $\boxed{}$ is close to $\boxed{}$, an answer of $\boxed{}$ square units is reasonable.

Holt Mathematics

Example 2

Find the area of each circle to the nearest tenth. Use 3.14 for π.

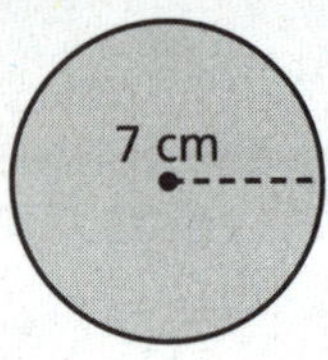

$A = \pi r^2$ Use the formula.

$A \approx 3.14 \cdot \boxed{}^{2}$ Substitute. Use $\boxed{}$ for r.

$A \approx 3.14 \cdot \boxed{}$ Evaluate the power.

$A \approx \boxed{}$ Multiply.

The area of the circle is about $\boxed{}$ cm^2.

Example 3

Park employees are fitting a top over a circular drain in the park. If the radius of the drain is 14 inches, what is the area of the top that will cover the drain? Use $\frac{22}{7}$ for π.

$A = \pi r^2$ Use the formula for the area of a circle.

$A \approx \frac{22}{7} \cdot \boxed{}^{2}$ Substitute. Use $\boxed{}$ for r.

$A \approx \frac{22}{7} \cdot \boxed{}$ Evaluate the power. Then simplify.

$A \approx 22 \cdot 28$

$A \approx \boxed{}$ Multiply.

The area of the top that will cover the drain is about  $\boxed{}$ in^2.

Holt Mathematics

Check It Out!

1. Find the area of the circle by using a formula. Then use an estimate to check whether your answer is reasonable.

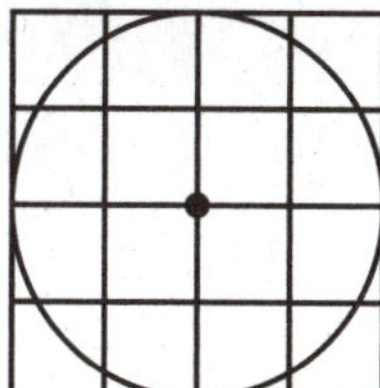

2. Find the area of the circle to the nearest tenth. Use 3.14 as an estimate for π.

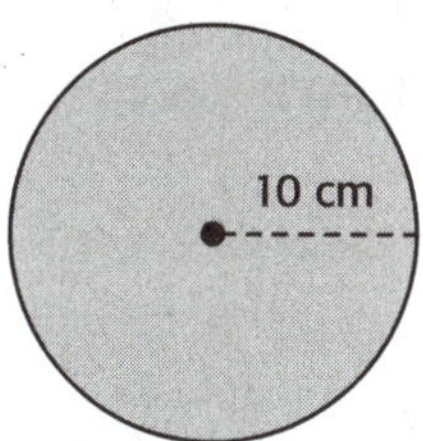

3. Albert was designing a cover for a spa. If the radius of the spa is 7 ft, what is the area of the cover that will be made? Use $\frac{22}{7}$ as an estimate for π.

Holt Mathematics

LESSON 10-6
Area of Irregular and Composite Figures

Lesson Objectives

Find the area of irregular and composite figures

Vocabulary

composite figure (p. 510) _______________________________

____

Additional Examples

Example 1

Estimate the area of the figure. Each square represents one square yard.

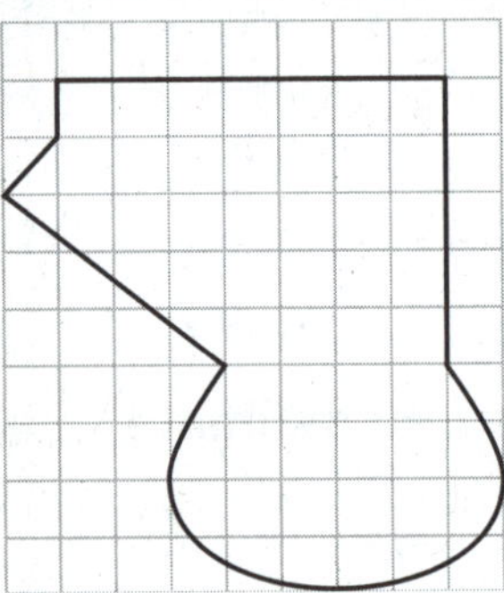

Count the number of filled or almost filled squares: ☐

Count the number of squares half-filled: ☐

Add the number of filled squares plus $\frac{1}{2}$ the number of half-filled squares:

☐ $+ (\frac{1}{2} \cdot$ ☐ $) =$ ☐ $+$ ☐ $=$ ☐ .

The area of the garden is about ☐ yds² .

Holt Mathematics

Example 2

Find the area of the composite figure. Use 3.14 as an estimate for π.

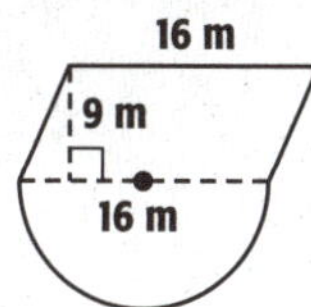

Step 1: Separate the figure into smaller, similar figures.

Step 2: Find the area of each smaller figure.
Area of the parallelogram:

$A = bh$ — Use the formula for the area of a parallelogram.

$A = \boxed{} \cdot \boxed{}$ — Substitute $\boxed{}$ for b and $\boxed{}$ for h.

$A = \boxed{}$ — Multiply.

Area of the semicircle:

$A = \frac{1}{2}(\pi r^2)$ — The area of a semicircle is $\frac{1}{2}$ the area of a circle.

$A \approx \frac{1}{2}(3.14 \cdot \boxed{}^2)$ — Substitute 3.14 for π and $\boxed{}$ for r.

$A \approx \frac{1}{2}(\boxed{}) \approx \boxed{}$ — Multiply.

Step 3: Add the areas to find the total area.

$A \approx \boxed{} + \boxed{} = \boxed{}$

The area of the irregular figure is about $\boxed{}$ m².

Holt Mathematics

Example 3

The Wrights want to tile their entry with square foot tiles. How much tile will they need?

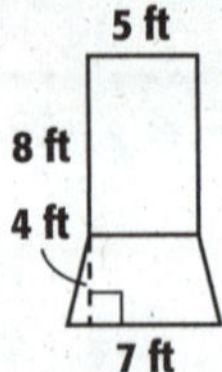

1. Understand the Problem

Rewrite the question as a statement.

- Find the amount of tile needed to cover the entry.

List the important information:

- The entry is a composite figure.

- The amount of tile needed is equal to the ⬚ of the entry.

2. Make a Plan

Find the area of the entry by separating the figure into familiar figures:

a ⬚ and a ⬚. Then add the areas of the rectangle and trapezoid to find the total area.

3. Solve

Find the area of each smaller figure.

Area of the rectangle:

$$A = lw$$

$$A = \boxed{} \cdot \boxed{}$$

$$A = \boxed{}$$

Area of the trapezoid:

$$A = \tfrac{1}{2}h(b_1 + b_2)$$

$$A = \tfrac{1}{2} \cdot \boxed{} (\boxed{} + \boxed{})$$

$$A = \tfrac{1}{2} \cdot 4(\boxed{}) = \boxed{}$$

Add the areas to find the total area.

$$A = \boxed{} + \boxed{} = \boxed{}$$

The Wrights need ⬚ ft^2 of tile.

4. Look Back

The area of the entry must be greater than the area of the rectangle (40 ft^2), so the answer is reasonable.

Holt Mathematics

Check It Out!

1. Estimate the area of the figure. Each square represents 1 yd².

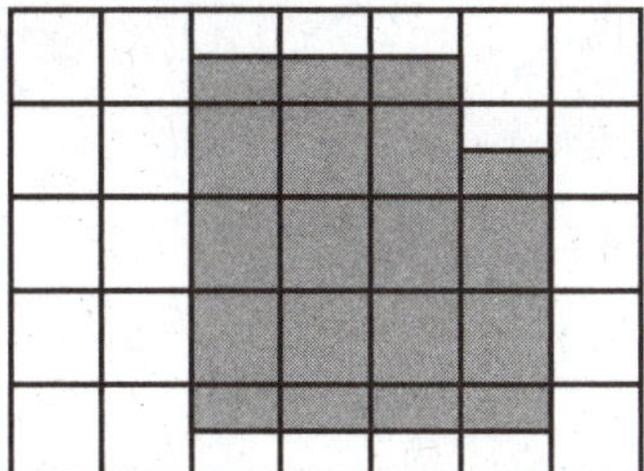

2. Find the area of the composite figure.

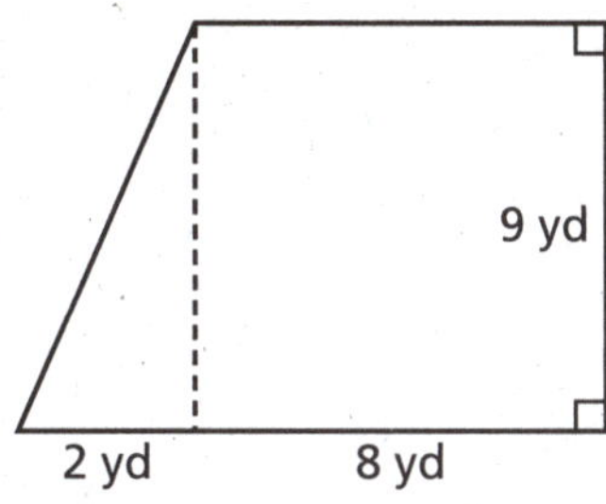

3. The Franklins want to wallpaper the wall of their daughters loft. How much wallpaper will they need?

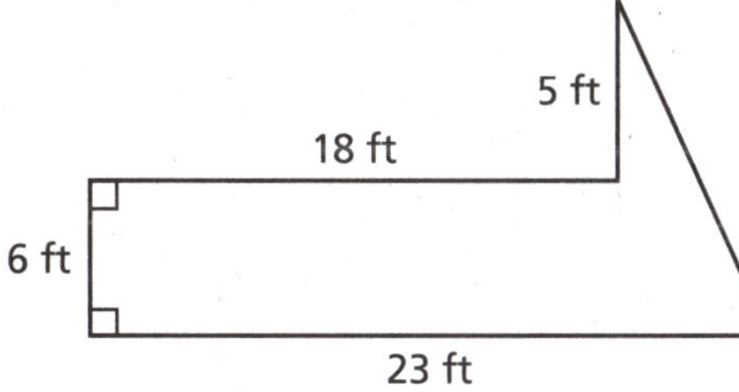

Holt Mathematics

Three-Dimensional Figures

LESSON
10-7

Lesson Objectives

Name three-dimensional figures

Vocabulary

polyhedron (p. 518) _______________________________

____

face (p. 518) _______________________________

____

edge (p. 518) _______________________________

____

vertex (p. 518) _______________________________

____

cube (p. 518) _______________________________

____

base (p. 518) _______________________________

____

Additional Examples

Example 1

Identify the number of faces, edges, and vertices on each three-dimensional figure.

A.

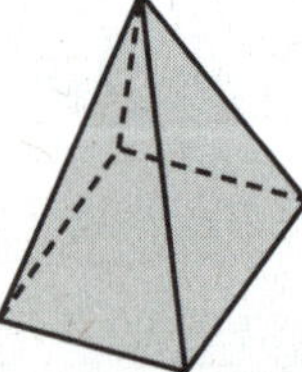

 faces; ☐ edges; ☐ vertices

B.

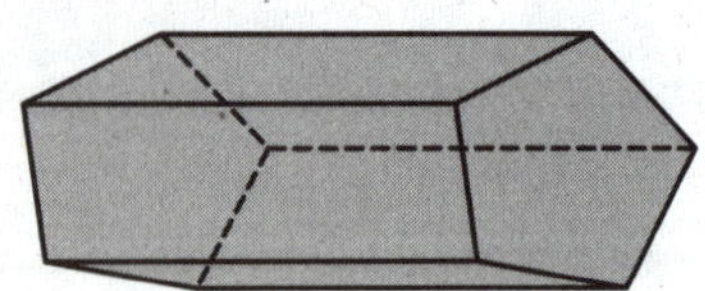

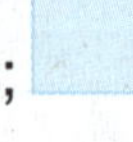 faces;  edges; ☐ vertices

Holt Mathematics

Example 2

Name the three-dimensional figure represented by each object.

A.

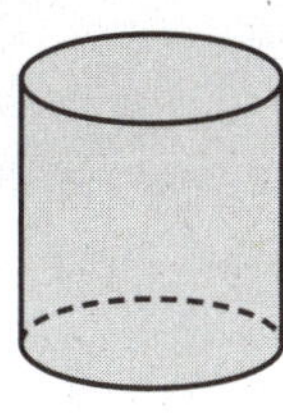

There is a ⬚ surface.

The figure is not a ⬚ .

There are two ⬚ , ⬚ bases.

The bases are ⬚ .

The figure represents a ⬚ .

B.

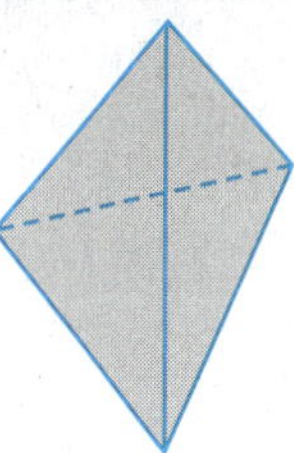

All the faces are ⬚ and are ⬚ .

The figure is a ⬚ .

There is one base and the other faces are ⬚ that meet at a point, so the figure is a ⬚ . The base is a ⬚ .

The figure is a ⬚ .

Check It Out!

1. **Identify the number of faces, edges, and vertices on the three-dimensional figure.**

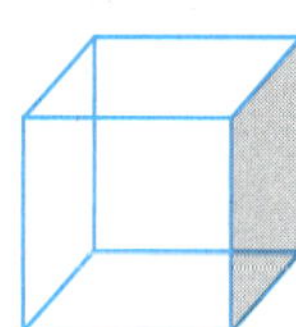

⬚

2. **Name the three-dimensional figure represented by the object.**

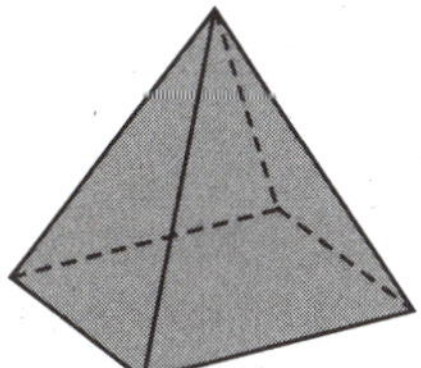

⬚

Holt Mathematics

Volume of Prisms

LESSON 10-8

Lesson Objectives

Find the volumes of rectangular prisms and triangular prisms

Vocabulary

volume (p. 524) _______________________________

____

Additional Examples

Example 1

Find the volume of the rectangular prism.

Step 1: Find the area of the base.

$B = \boxed{} \cdot \boxed{}$ The base is a $\boxed{}$.

$B = \boxed{}$ Multiply.

Step 2: Find the volume.

$V = Bh$ Write the formula.

$V = \boxed{} \cdot \boxed{}$ Substitute for B and h.

$V = \boxed{}$ in^3 Multiply.

The volume of the prism is $\boxed{}$ in^3.

Holt Mathematics

Example 2

Find the volume of the triangular prism.

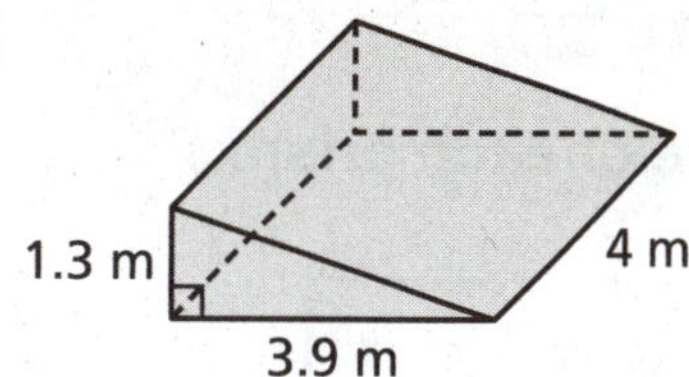

Step 1: Find the area of the base.

$B =$ ☐ $\cdot$ ☐ $\cdot$ ☐   The base is a ☐ .

$B =$ ☐   Multiply.

Step 2: Find the volume.

$V = Bh$ Write the formula.

$V = ($ ☐ $\cdot 4)$ Substitute for B and h.

$V =$ ☐ m³   Multiply.

Example 3

An artist wants to make glass paper-weights with the dimensions shown. He estimates that he will need less than 20 cubic centimeters of glass for each paperweight. Is his estimate reasonable? Explain.

Step 1: Find the area of the base.

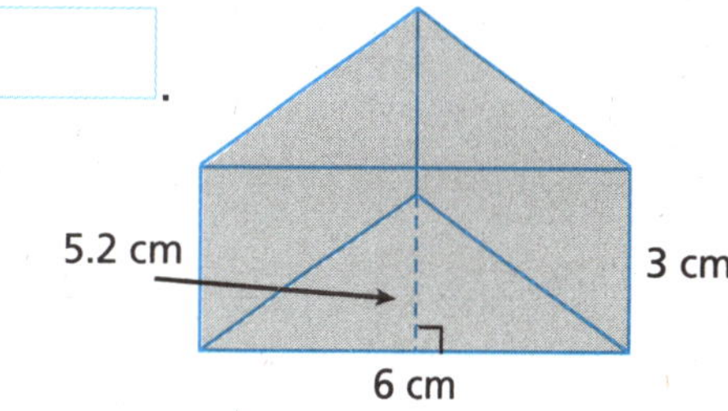

$B =$ ☐ $\cdot$ ☐ $\cdot$ ☐   The base is a ☐ .

$B =$ ☐   Multiply.

Step 2: Find the volume.

$V = Bh$ Write the formula.

$V =$ ☐ $\cdot$ ☐   Substitute for B and h.

$V =$ ☐ cm³   Multiply.

Each paperweight will require about ☐ cm³ of glass, so the estimate is ☐ reasonable.

Holt Mathematics

Check It Out!

Find the volume of each prism.

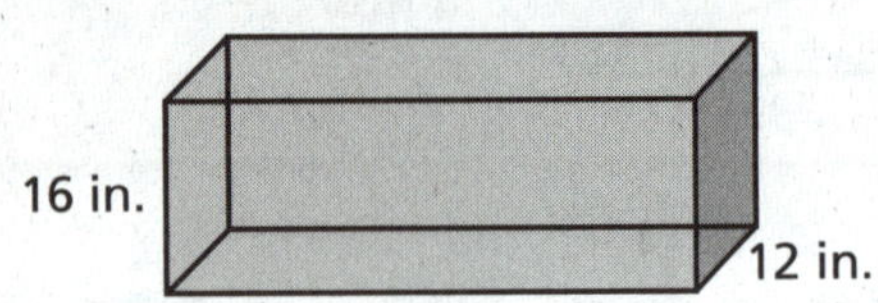

1.

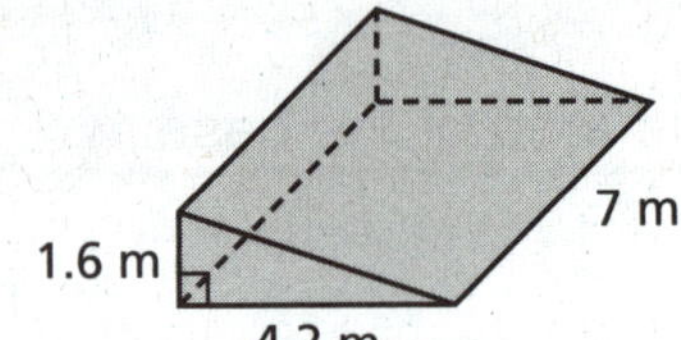

2.

3. An architect wants to make a model building with the dimensions shown. He estimates that he will need more than 60 cubic centimeters of paper for each building. Is his estimate reasonable? Explain.

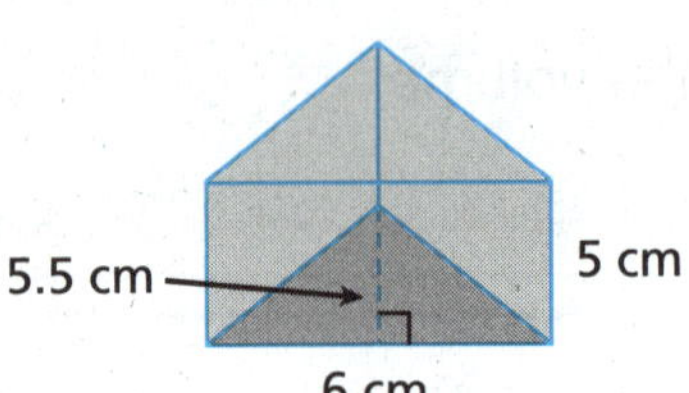

258

Holt Mathematics

LESSON 10-9
Volume of Cylinders

Lesson Objectives

Find volumes of cylinders

Additional Examples

Example 1

Find the volume V of the cylinder to the nearest cubic unit.

$r = 4$ ft; $h = 7$ ft

$V = \pi r^2 h$

$V = \boxed{} \times \boxed{}^2 \times \boxed{}$ Replace π with $\boxed{}$, r with $\boxed{}$,

and h with $\boxed{}$.

$V = \boxed{}$ Multiply.

The volume is about $\boxed{}$ ft³.

Example 2

Ali has a cylinder-shaped pencil holder with a 3-in. diameter and a height of 5 in. Estimate the volume of the cylinder to the nearest cubic inch.

Ali's pencil holder

3 in. ÷ 2 = 1.5 in.   Find the radius.

$V = \pi r^2 h$ Write the formula.

$V = \boxed{} \times \boxed{}^2 \times \boxed{}$ Replace π with $\boxed{}$, r with

$\boxed{}$, and h with $\boxed{}$.

$V = \boxed{}$ Multiply.

The volume of Ali's pencil holder is about $\boxed{}$ in³.

Holt Mathematics

Example 3

Find which cylinder has the greater volume.

Cylinder 1:

$V = \boxed{} \times \boxed{}^2 \times \boxed{}$

$V = \boxed{}$ cm³

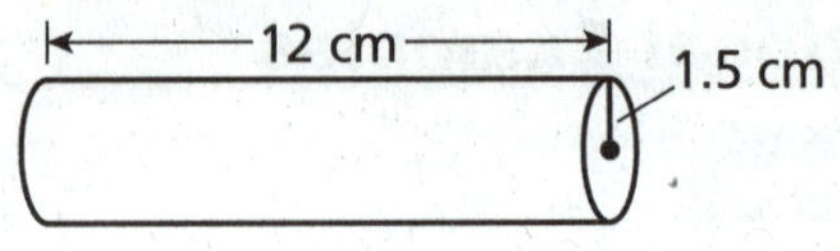

Cylinder 2:

$V = \boxed{} \times \boxed{}^2 \times \boxed{}$

$V = \boxed{}$ cm³

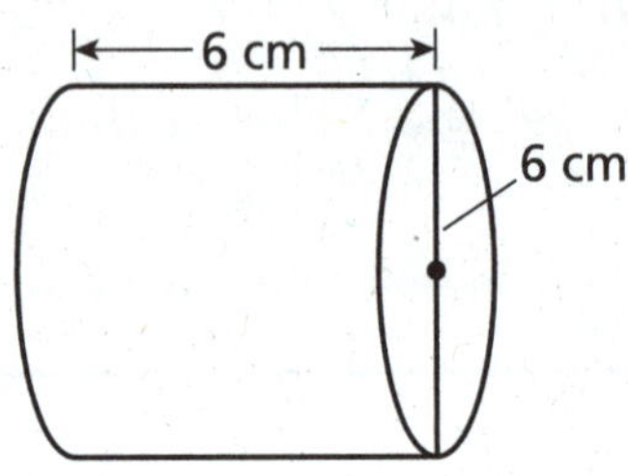

Cylinder 2 has the greater volume because $\boxed{}$ cm³ >

$\boxed{}$ cm³.

Check It Out!

1. Find the volume *V* of the cylinder to the nearest cubic unit.

$r = 6$ ft; $h = 5$ ft

2. Sara has a cylinder-shaped sunglasses case with a 3 in. diameter and a height of 6 in. Estimate the volume of the cylinder to the nearest cubic inch.

3. Find which cylinder has the greater volume.

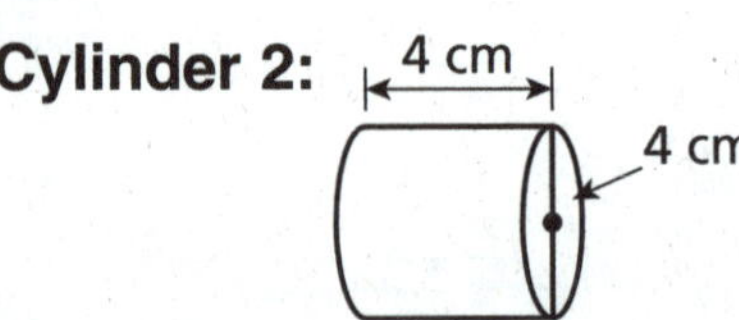

Holt Mathematics

LESSON 10-10

Surface Area

Lesson Objectives

Find the surface areas of prisms, pyramids, and cylinders

Vocabulary

surface area (p. 534) ____

____

net (p. 534) ____

____

Additional Examples

Example 1

Find the surface area *S* of the prism.

A. Method 1: Use a net.

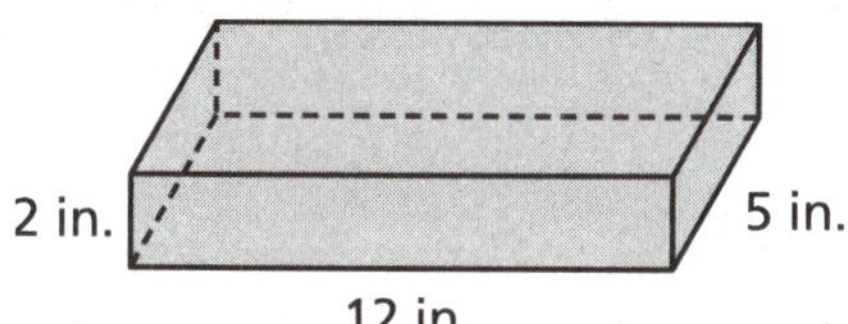 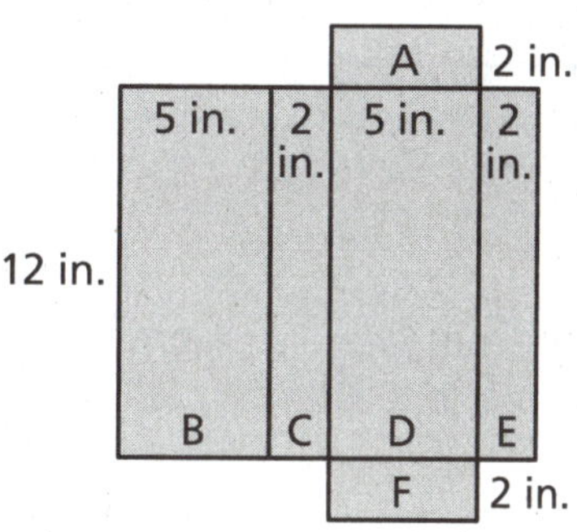

Draw a ☐ to help you see each ☐ of the prism.

Use the formula ☐ to find the area of each face.

A: $A = $ ☐ $\times$ ☐ $= $ ☐   D: $A = $ ☐ $\times$ ☐ $= $ ☐

B: $A = $ ☐ $\times$ ☐ $= $ ☐   E: $A = $ ☐ $\times$ ☐ $= $ ☐

C: $A = $ ☐ $\times$ ☐ $= $ ☐   F: $A = $ ☐ $\times$ ☐ $= $ ☐

☐ the areas of each face.

$S = $ ☐ $+$ ☐ $+$ ☐ $+$ ☐ $+$ ☐ $= $ ☐ in^2

The surface area is ☐ in^2.

Holt Mathematics

B. Method 2: Use a three-dimensional drawing.

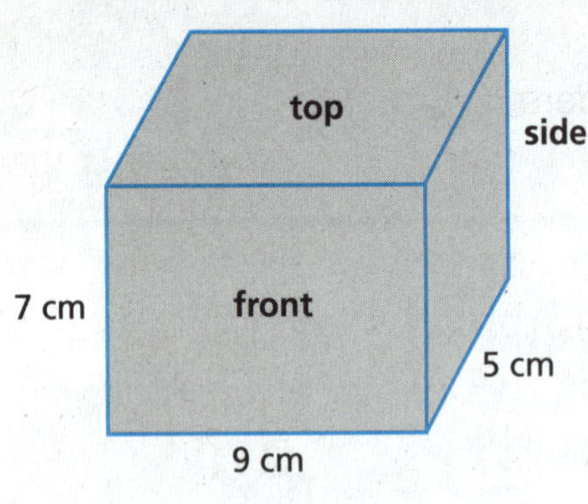

Find the area of the front, top, and side, and multiply each by 2 to include the opposite faces.

Front: ☐ • ☐ = ☐ → ☐ • 2 = ☐

Top: ☐ • ☐ = ☐ → ☐ • 2 = ☐

Side: ☐ • ☐ = ☐ → ☐ • 2 = ☐

$S =$ ☐ + ☐ + ☐ = ☐   ☐ the areas of each face.

The surface area is ☐ cm².

Example 2

Find the surface area S of the pyramid.

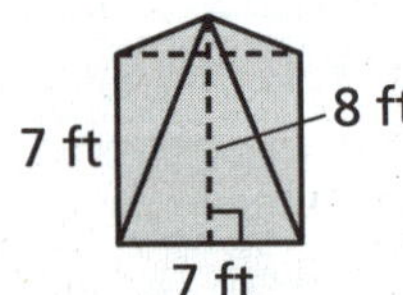

$S =$ area of ☐ + 4 × (area of ☐ face)

$$S = s^2 + 4 \times \left(\tfrac{1}{2}bh\right)$$

$$S = \boxed{}^2 + 4 \times \left(\tfrac{1}{2} \times 7 \times 8\right) \qquad \text{Substitute.}$$

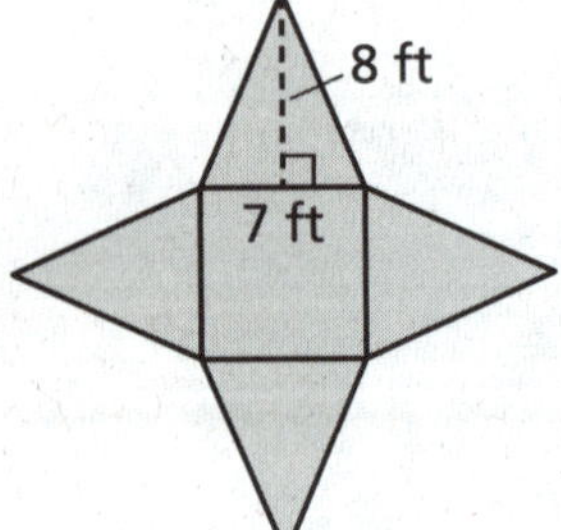

$$S = \boxed{} + 4 \times \boxed{}$$

$$S = \boxed{} + \boxed{}$$

$$S = \boxed{}$$

The surface area is ☐ ft².

Holt Mathematics

Example 3

Find the surface area *S* of the cylinder. Write your answer in terms of π.

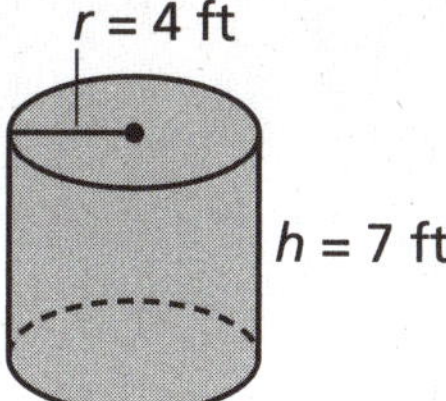

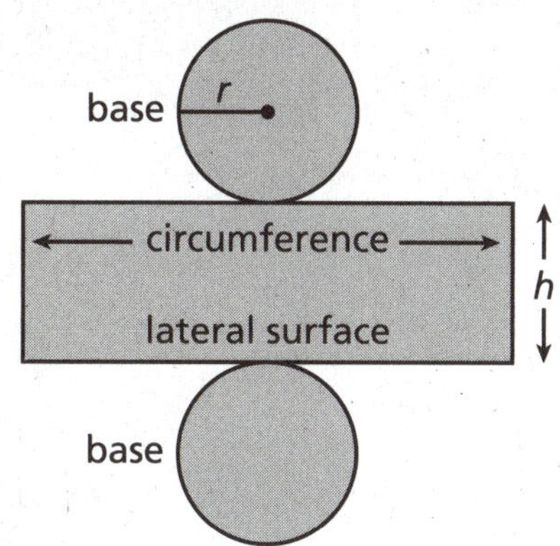

S = area of curved surface + (2 times area of each base)

$S = (h \times 2\pi r) + (2 \times \pi r^2)$

$S = (\boxed{} \times 2\pi \times \boxed{}) + (2 \times \pi \times \boxed{}^2)$ Substitute $\boxed{}$ for *h* and $\boxed{}$ for *r*.

$S = (\boxed{} \times 2\pi \times \boxed{}) + (2 \times \pi \times \boxed{})$ Simplify the power.

$S = \boxed{}\,\pi + \boxed{}\,\pi$ Multiply.

$S = (\boxed{} + \boxed{})\pi$ Use the Distributive Property.

$S = \boxed{}$

The surface area is about $\boxed{}$ ft^2.

Holt Mathematics

Check It Out!

1. Find the surface area
   S of the prism.

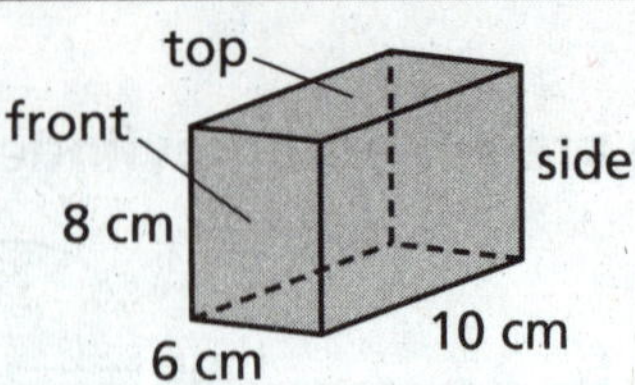

2. Find the surface area
   S of the pyramid.

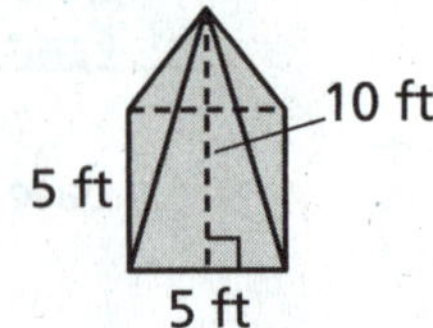

3. Find the surface area *S*
   of the cylinder. Write your
   answer in terms of π.

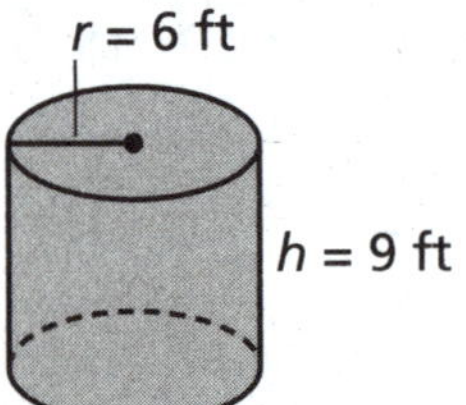

Holt Mathematics

Chapter Review

10-1 Perimeter

Find the perimeter of each figure.

1.
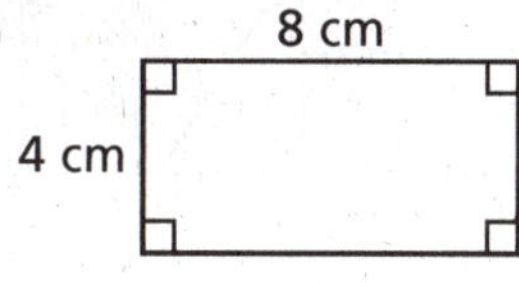
8 cm
4 cm

2.
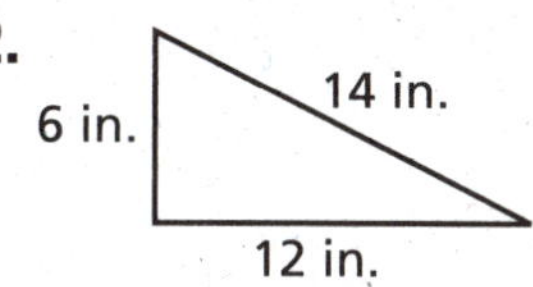
14 in.
6 in.
12 in.

Find the unknown measure.

3. What is the length of side b if the perimeter equals 50 ft?

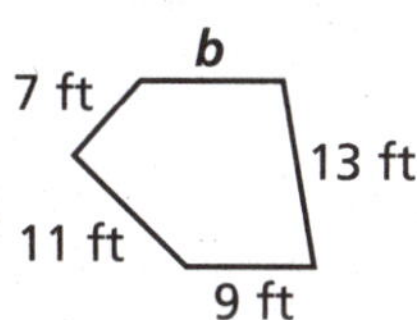
b
7 ft
13 ft
11 ft
9 ft

4. The width of a rectangle is 6 in. The perimeter of the rectangle is 30 in. What is the length of the rectangle?

10-2 Circles and Circumference

5. Point Q is the center of the circle. Name the circle, a diameter, and three radii.

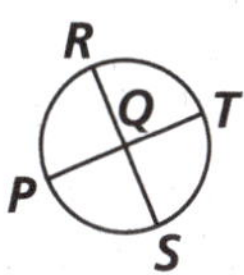
R
Q
T
P
S

6. A landscaping company needs to dig a circular hole for planting a tree. If the diameter of the circular hole is 3 ft, what is its circumference? (Find the circumference by rounding π to 3).

Find each missing value to the nearest hundredth. Use 3.14 for π.

7. $r = 5$ cm; $C =$ ______.

8. $d = 12$ in.; $C =$ ______.

Holt Mathematics

10-3 Area of Parallelograms

Find the area of each parallelogram.

9.

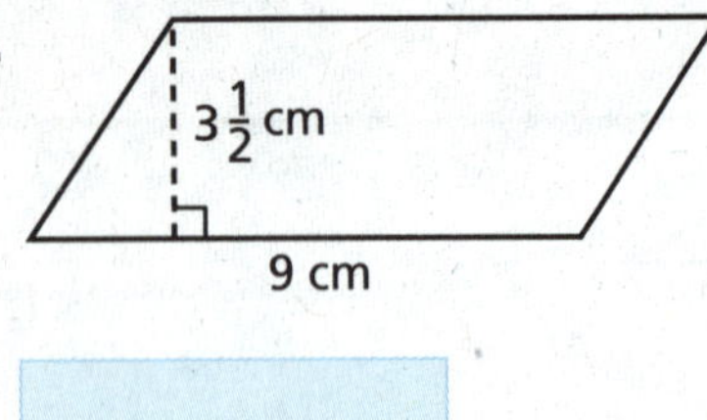

10.

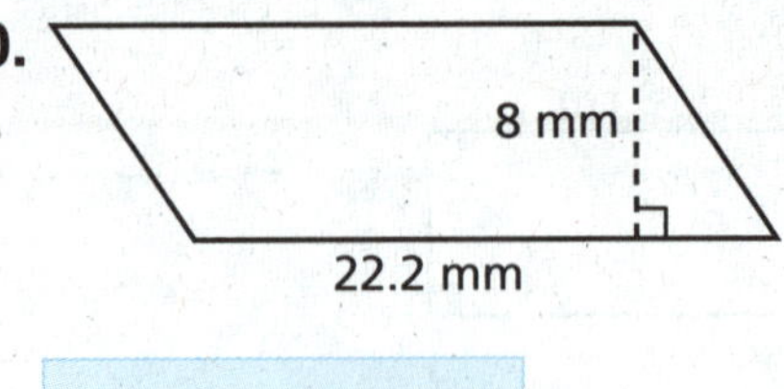

10-4 Area of Triangles and Trapezoids

Find the area of each triangle.

11.

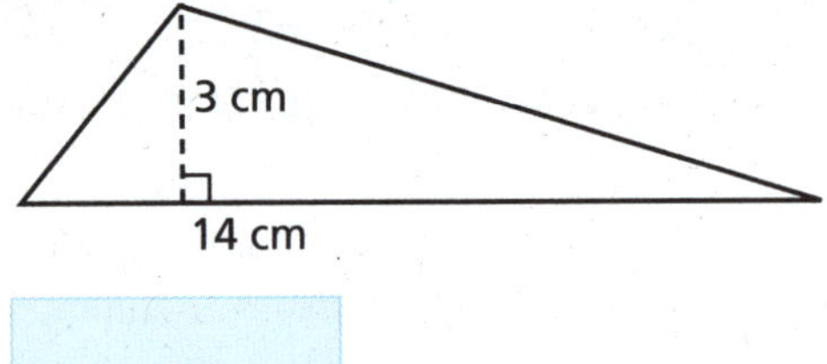

12.

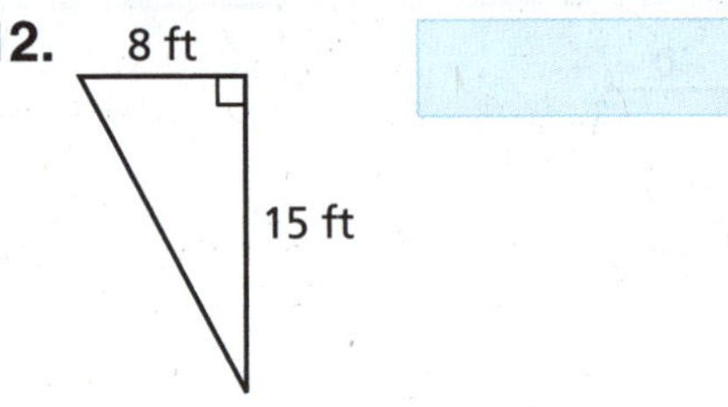

10-5 Area of Circles

Find the area of each circle to the nearest tenth. Use 3.14 for π.

13.

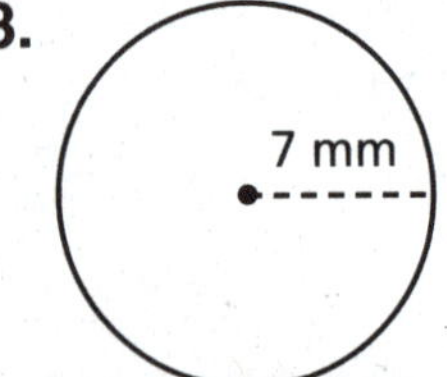

14.

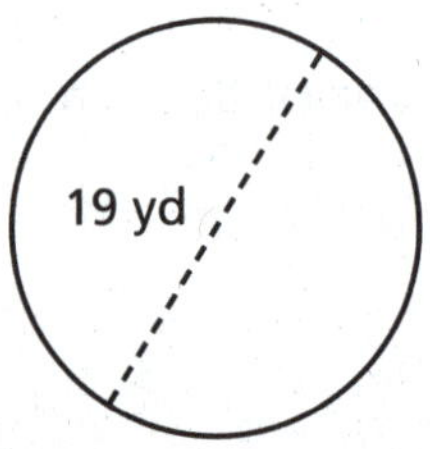

10-6 Area of Irregular and Composite Figures

Find the area of each figure. Use 3.14 for π.

15.

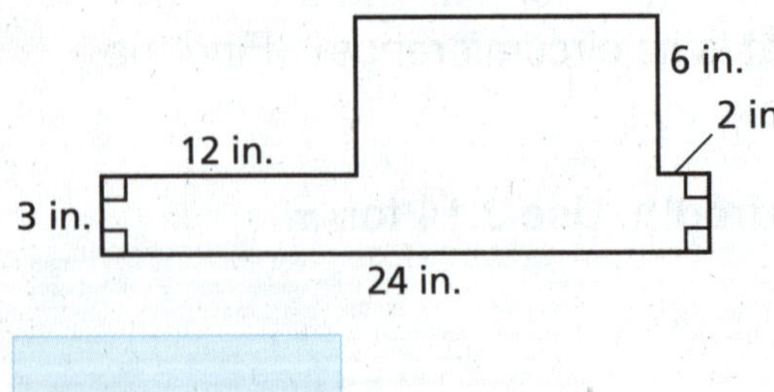

16.

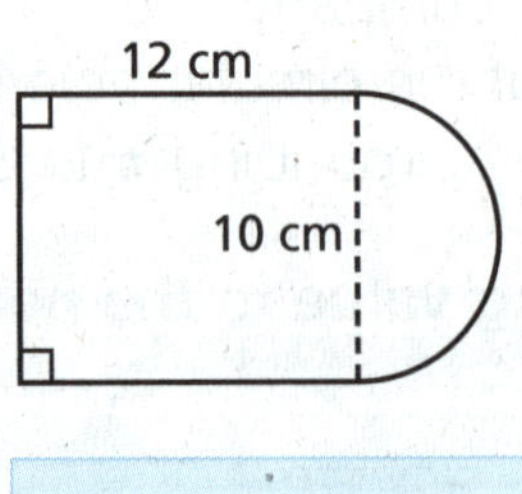

Holt Mathematics

10-7 Three-Dimensional Figures

Identify the number of faces, edges, and vertices in each three-dimensional figure. Then name the figure and tell whether it is a polyhedron.

17. 

18. 

10-8 Volume of Prisms

Find the volume of each figure.

19. 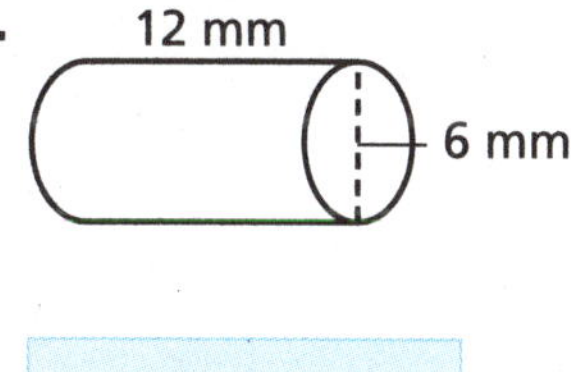

20. 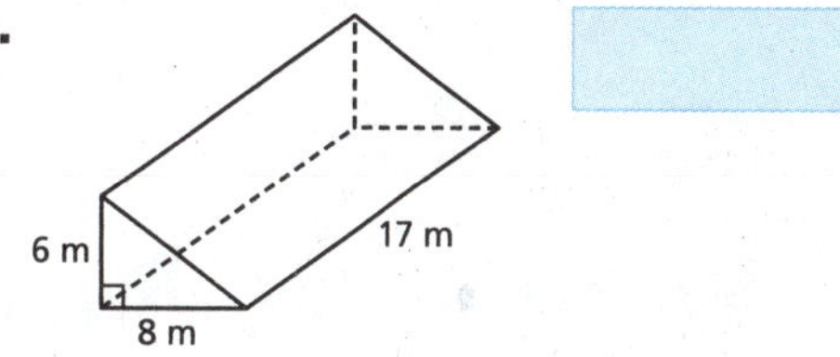

10-9 Volume of Cylinders

Find the volume of each cylinder to the nearest cubic unit. Use 3.14 for π.

21.

22. 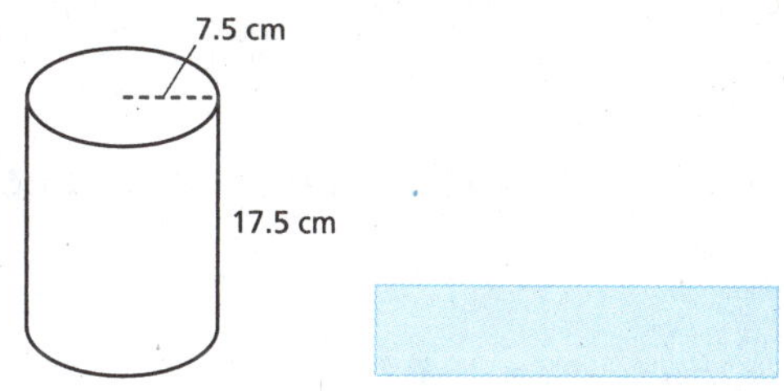

10-10 Surface Area

Find the surface area of each figure. Use 3.14 for π and round to the nearest hundredth.

23. 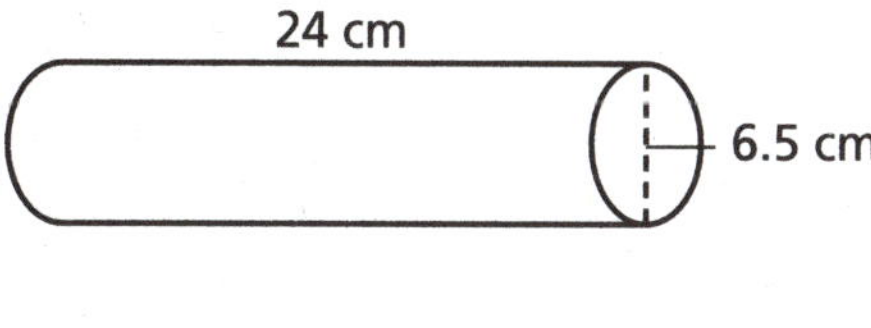

24. 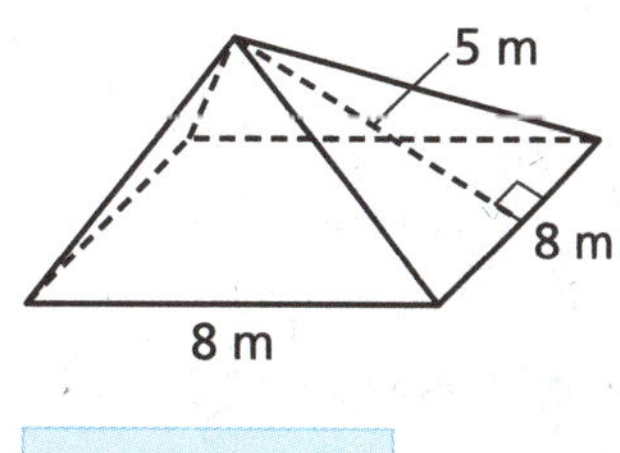

Holt Mathematics

Big Ideas

Answer these questions to summarize the important concepts from Chapter 10 in your own words.

1. Explain how to find the perimeter of a rectangle with length 19 inches and width 14 inches.

2. Explain how to find the area of a triangle with base 13 inches and height 12 inches.

3. Explain how to find the area of a circle with diameter 16 yards.

4. Explain how to find the area of a composite figure.

5. Explain how to find the volume of a cylinder with diameter 14 centimeters and height 18 centimeters.

For more review of Chapter 10:

- Complete the Chapter 10 Study Guide and Review on pages 542–544 of your textbook.

- Complete the Ready to Go On quizzes on pages 514 and 538 of your textbook.

Holt Mathematics

Solving Two-Step Equations

LESSON 11-1

Lesson Objectives

Solve two-step equations

Additional Examples

Example 1

Solve. Check your answer.

$$9c + 3 = 39$$

$$\underline{-} \quad \underline{-} \qquad \text{Subtract } \boxed{} \text{ from both sides.}$$

$$9c \quad = \boxed{}$$

$$\boxed{} = \boxed{} \qquad \text{Divide both sides by } \boxed{}.$$

$$c = \boxed{}$$

Example 2

Solve.

$$6 + \frac{y}{5} = 21$$

$$\underline{-} \qquad \underline{-} \qquad \text{Subtract } \boxed{} \text{ from both sides.}$$

$$\frac{y}{5} = \boxed{}$$

$$(\boxed{}) \frac{y}{5} = (\boxed{}) 15 \qquad \text{Multiply both sides by } \boxed{}.$$

$$y = \boxed{}$$

Holt Mathematics

Example 3

Jamie rented a canoe while she was on vacation. She paid a flat rental fee of $85.00 plus $7.50 each day. Her total cost was $130.00. For how many days did she rent the canoe?

Let d represent the number of days she rented the canoe.

$$7.5d + 85 = 130$$

$$-\boxed{} \quad -\boxed{} \qquad \text{Subtract } \boxed{} \text{ from both sides.}$$

$$7.5d = \boxed{}$$

$$\boxed{} = \boxed{} \qquad \text{Divide both sides by } \boxed{}.$$

$$d = \boxed{}$$

Jamie rented the canoe for $\boxed{}$ days.

Check It Out!

1. Solve.

$$-6m - 8 = -50$$

2. Solve.

$$8 + \frac{y}{2} = 48$$

3. Jack's father rented a car while they were on vacation. He paid a rental fee of $20.00 per day plus 20¢ a mile. He paid $25.00 for mileage and his total bill for renting the car was $165.00. For how many days did he rent the car?

Holt Mathematics

LESSON 11-2
Simplifying Algebraic Expressions

Lesson Objectives

Simplify algebraic expressions

Vocabulary

term (p. 558) _________________________________

____

coefficient (p. 558) _________________________________

____

Additional Examples

Example 1

Identify like terms in the list.

$$3t \quad 5w^2 \quad 7t \quad 9v \quad 4w^2 \quad 8v$$

Look for like [____________] with like [____________].

$3t \quad 5w^2 \quad 7t \quad 9v \quad 4w^2 \quad 8v$

Like terms: _________________________________

Example 2

Simplify. Justify your steps using the Commutative, Associative, and Distributive Properties when necessary.

A. $6t - 4t$ $6t$ and $4t$ are [____________] terms.

$6t - 4t$ [____________] the coefficients.

[____________]

B. $45x - 37y + 87$

In this expression, there are [____________] to combine.

271

Holt Mathematics

Example 3

Write an expression for the perimeter of the triangle. Then simplify the expression.

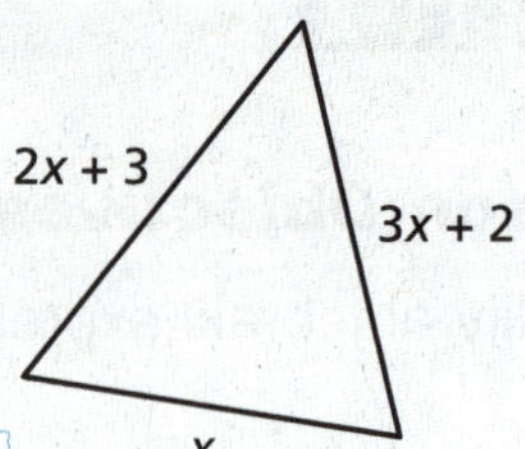

$2x + 3 + 3x + 2 + x$ Write an ______

using the side lengths.

(______ + ______ + ______) + (______ + ______)   Identify and ______

like terms.

______   ______ Property

Check It Out!

1. Identify like terms in the list.

$2x$ $4y^3$ $8x$ $5z$ $5y^3$ $8z$

2. Simplify. Justify your steps using the Commutative, Associative, and Distributive Properties when necessary.

$4x^2 + 5y + 3x^2 - 4y + 2x^2 + 5$

3. Write an expression for the perimeter of the triangle. Then simplify the expression.

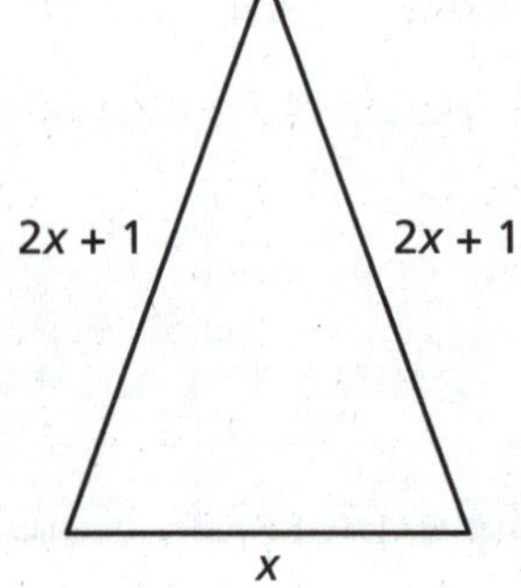

LESSON 11-3 Solving Multi-Step Equations

Lesson Objectives

Solve multi-step equations

Additional Examples

Example 1

Solve $12 - 7b + 10b = 18$.

$$12 - 7b + 10b = 18$$

$12 + \boxed{}\,b = 18$ Combine $\boxed{}$ terms.

$-\boxed{} \qquad -\boxed{}$ Subtract $\boxed{}$ from both sides.

$$3b = \boxed{}$$

$\dfrac{\boxed{}}{} = \boxed{}$ Divide both sides by $\boxed{}$.

$$b = \boxed{}$$

Example 2

Solve $5(y - 2) + 6 = 21$.

$$5(y - 2) + 6 = 21$$

$5(\boxed{}) - 5(\boxed{}) + 6 = 21$ Distribute $\boxed{}$ on the left side.

$5y - \boxed{} = 21$ Simplify.

$+\boxed{} \qquad +\boxed{}$ Add $\boxed{}$ to both sides.

$$5y = \boxed{}$$

$\dfrac{5y}{\boxed{}} = \dfrac{25}{\boxed{}}$ Divide both sides by $\boxed{}$.

$$y = \boxed{}$$

Holt Mathematics

Example 3

PROBLEM SOLVING APPLICATION

Troy has three times as many trading cards as Hillary. Subtracting 8 from the combined number of trading cards Troy and Hillary have gives the number of cards Sean has. If Sean owns 24 trading cards, how many trading cards does Hillary own?

1. **Understand the Problem**

   Rewrite the question as a statement.

   • Find the number of trading cards that ____________ owns.

   List the important information:

   • Troy has ____ times as many trading cards as Hillary has.

   • Subtracting 8 from the combined number of trading cards that

   ____________________ have gives the number of cards

   ____________ owns.

   • Sean owns ____ trading cards.

2. **Make a Plan**

   Let c represent the number of trading cards Hillary owns. Then $3c$

   represents the number ____________ owns.

   Troy's cards + Hillary's cards − 8 = Sean's cards

   ____________ + ____________ − 8 = ____________

   Solve the equation $3c + c - 8 = 24$ for c.

Holt Mathematics

3. Solve

$$3c + c - 8 = 24$$

$$4c - 8 = 24$$ Combine like terms.

$$+\boxed{} \quad +\boxed{}$$ Add $\boxed{}$ to both sides.

$$4c = \boxed{}$$

$$\frac{4c}{\boxed{}} = \frac{\boxed{}}{\boxed{}}$$ Divide both sides by $\boxed{}$.

$$c = \boxed{}$$

Hillary owns $\boxed{}$ cards.

4. Look Back

Make sure that your answer makes sense in the original problem. Hillary owns $\boxed{}$ cards. Troy owns $3(\boxed{}) = \boxed{}$ cards. Sean owns $\boxed{} + \boxed{} - 8 = 24$.

Check It Out!

1. Solve $14 - 8b + 12b = 62$.

2. Solve $3(x - 3) + 4 = 28$.

3. John is twice as old as Hiro. Subtracting 4 from the combined age of John and Hiro gives William's age. If William is 29, how old is Hiro?

Holt Mathematics

LESSON 11-4
Solving Equations with Variables on Both Sides

Lesson Objectives

Solve equations that have variables on both sides

Additional Examples

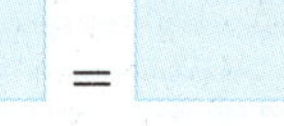

Group the terms with variables on one side of the equal sign, and simplify.

A. $60 - 4y = 8y$

$60 - 4y + \boxed{} = 8y + \boxed{}$ Add $\boxed{}$ to both sides.

$\boxed{} = \boxed{}$ Simplify.

B. $-5b + 72 = -2b$

$-5b + \boxed{} + 72 = -2b + \boxed{}$ Add $\boxed{}$ to both sides.

$\boxed{} = \boxed{}$ Simplify.

Example 2

Solve.

$7c = 2c + 55$

$7c - \boxed{} = 2c - \boxed{} + 55$ Subtract $\boxed{}$ from both sides.

$\boxed{} = \boxed{}$ Simplify.

$\boxed{} = \boxed{}$ Divide both sides by $\boxed{}$.

$c = \boxed{}$

Holt Mathematics

Example 3

Christine can buy a new snowboard for $136.50. She will still need to rent boots for $8.50 a day. She can rent a snowboard and boots for $18.25 a day. How many days would Christine need to rent both the snowboard and the boots to pay as much as she would if she buys the snowboard and rents only the boots for the season?

Let d represent the number of days.

$$18.25d = 136.5 + 8.5d$$

$18.25d - \boxed{} = 136.5 + 8.5d - \boxed{}$ Subtract $\boxed{}$ from both sides.

$\boxed{}\, d = \boxed{}$ Simplify.

$\dfrac{9.75d}{\boxed{}} = \dfrac{136.5}{\boxed{}}$ Divide both sides by $\boxed{}$.

$d = \boxed{}$

Christine would need to rent both the snowboard and the boots for

$\boxed{}$ days to pay as much as she would have if she had bought the snowboard and rented only the boots.

Check It Out!

1. Group the terms with variables on one side of the equal sign, and simplify.

$$-8b + 24 = -5b$$

2. Solve.

$$54 - 3q = 6q + 9$$

3. A local telephone company charges $40 per month for services plus a fee of $0.10 a minute for long distance calls. Another company charges $75.00 a month for unlimited service. How many minutes does it take for a person who subscribes to the first plan to pay as much as a person who subscribes to the unlimited plan?

277

Holt Mathematics

LESSON 11-5 Introduction to Inequalities

Lesson Objectives

Read and write inequalities and graph them on a number line

Vocabulary

inequality (p. 572) _______________________________________

____

algebraic inequality (p. 572) _______________________________

____

solution set (p. 572) _____________________________________

____

compound inequality (p. 572) _______________________________

____

Additional Examples

Example 1

Write an inequality for each situation.

A. There are at least 15 people in the waiting room.

"At least" means _______________ than or _______________ to.

B. The tram attendant will allow no more than 60 people on the tram.

"No more than" means _______________ than or _______________ to.

Holt Mathematics

Example 2

Graph each inequality.

$n < 3$

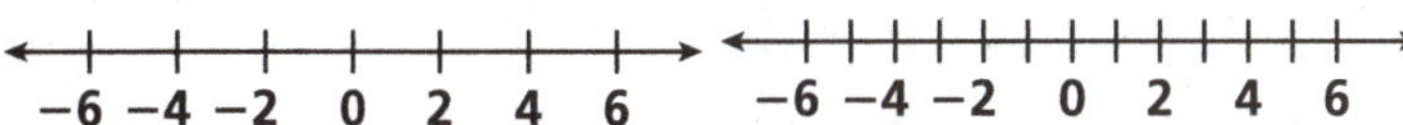

Draw an [ ] circle at 3. The solutions are values of n less than 3, so shade to the [ ] of 3.

Example 3

Graph each compound inequality.

$m \le -2$ or $m > 1$

Graph $m \le -2$. Graph $m > 1$.

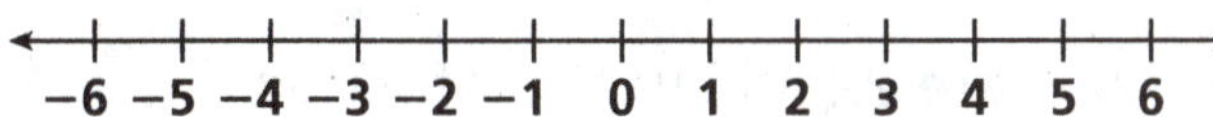

Include the solution shown by either graph.

Check It Out!

1. Write an inequality for the situation.

There are at most 10 gallons of gas in the tank.

2. Graph the inequality.

$p \le 2$

3. Graph the compound inequality.

$5 > g \ge -3$

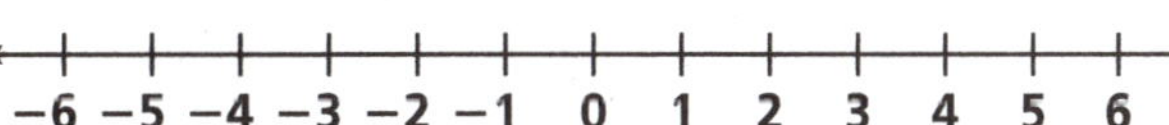

Holt Mathematics

LESSON 11-6 Solving Inequalities by Adding or Subtracting

Lesson Objectives

Solve one-step inequalities by adding or subtracting

Additional Examples

Example 1

Solve. Then graph each solution set on a number line.

A. $n - 7 \le 15$

$$n - 7 \le \qquad 15$$

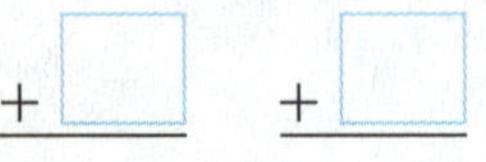

$+ \boxed{} \qquad + \boxed{} \qquad$ Add $\boxed{}$ to both sides.

$$n \qquad \le \qquad \boxed{}$$

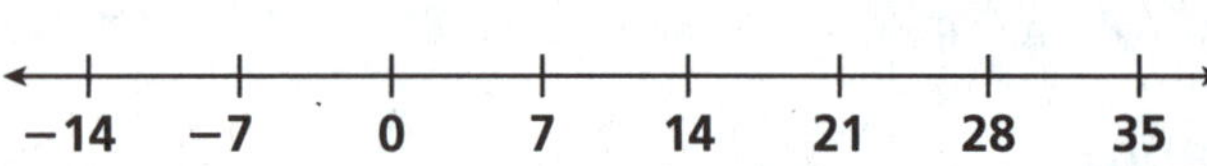

$$-14 \quad -7 \quad 0 \quad 7 \quad 14 \quad 21 \quad 28 \quad 35$$

Draw a $\boxed{}$ circle at 22. Solutions are 22 and values of n less

than 22, so shade the line to the $\boxed{}$ of 22.

Example 2

Solve. Check each answer.

A. $d + \quad 11 > \qquad 6$

$- \boxed{} \qquad - \boxed{} \qquad$ Subtract $\boxed{}$ from both sides.

$$d \qquad > \qquad \boxed{}$$

Check

$$d + 11 > 6$$

$$\boxed{} + 11 \overset{?}{>} 6 \qquad 0 \text{ is } \boxed{} \text{ than } -5. \text{ Substitute 0 for } d.$$

$$11 \overset{?}{>} 6 \checkmark$$

Holt Mathematics

Example 3

Edgar's August profit of $137 was at least $20 higher than his July profit. What was July's profit?

Let p represent the profit increase from July to August.

August profit	was at least	$20 higher than	July's profit

$$\boxed{} \quad \geq \quad \boxed{} \quad + \quad p$$

$$\underline{137 \geq 20 + p}$$

$$-\,\boxed{} \quad -\,\boxed{} \qquad \text{Subtract } \boxed{} \text{ from both sides.}$$

$$\boxed{} \geq p \qquad \text{Rewrite the inequality.}$$

$$p \leq \boxed{}$$

Edgar's profit in July was at most $\boxed{}$.

Check It Out!

1. Solve. Then graph the solution set on a number line.

$$b - 14 \geq -8$$

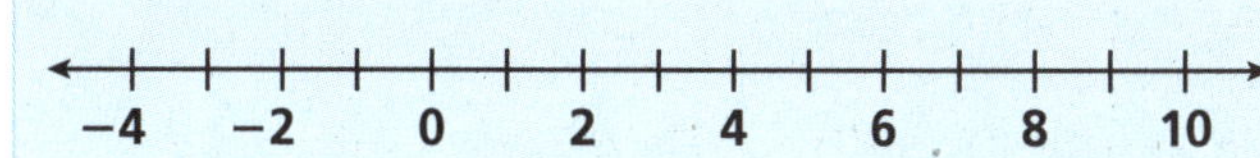

2. Solve. Check the answer.

$$a + 15 \leq 20$$

3. Rylan's March profit of $172 was at least $12 less than his February profit. What was February's profit?

Holt Mathematics

LESSON 11-7 Solving Inequalities by Multiplying or Dividing

Lesson Objectives

Solve one-step inequalities by multiplying or dividing

Additional Examples

Example 1

Solve.

$$\frac{t}{-4} > 0.3$$

$$\left(\boxed{}\right)\frac{t}{-4} \le \left(\boxed{}\right)0.3$$

Multiply both sides by $\boxed{}$ and $\boxed{}$ the inequality symbol.

$$t < \boxed{}$$

Check

$$\frac{t}{-4} > 0.3$$

$$\frac{\boxed{}}{-4} \overset{?}{>} 0.3$$

-2 is $\boxed{}$ than -1.2.
Substitute -2 for t.

$$0.5 > 0.3 \checkmark$$

Example 2

Solve. Check each answer.

$$5a \ge 23$$

$$\boxed{} \ge \boxed{}$$

Divide both sides by $\boxed{}$.

$$a \ge \boxed{} \quad \text{or} \quad \boxed{}$$

Check

$$5a \ge 23$$

$$5\left(\boxed{}\right) \overset{?}{\ge} 23 \qquad 5 \text{ is } \boxed{} \text{ than } 4\frac{3}{5}. \text{ Substitute 5 for } a.$$

$$25 \overset{?}{\ge} 23 \checkmark$$

Holt Mathematics

Example 3

It cost Josh \$85 to make candles for the craft fair. How many candles must he sell at \$4.00 each to make a profit?

Since profit is the amount earned ⬚ the amount spent, Josh

needs to earn ⬚ than \$85.

Let c represent the number of candles that must be sold.

$4c$ ⬚ 85

$\dfrac{4c}{⬚}$ ⬚ $\dfrac{85}{⬚}$ Divide both sides by ⬚.

c ⬚ ⬚

Josh cannot sell 0.25 candle, so he needs to sell at least ⬚ candles,

or more than ⬚ candles, to earn a profit.

Check It Out!

1. Solve.

$$\dfrac{r}{-3} > 0.9$$

2. Solve. Check your answer.

$$6b \geq 25$$

3. It cost the class \$15 to make cookies for the bake sale. How many cookies must they sell at 10¢ each to make a profit?

Holt Mathematics

LESSON 11-8

Solving Two-Step Inequalities

Lesson Objectives

Solve simple two-step inequalities

Additional Examples

Example 1

Solve. Then graph each solution set on a number line.

A. $\dfrac{y}{2} - 6 > 1$

$\underline{+\ \boxed{}\quad +\ \boxed{}}$ Add $\boxed{}$ to both sides.

$\dfrac{y}{2} > \boxed{}$

$(\boxed{})\dfrac{y}{2} > (\boxed{})7$ Multiply both sides by $\boxed{}$.

$y > \boxed{}$

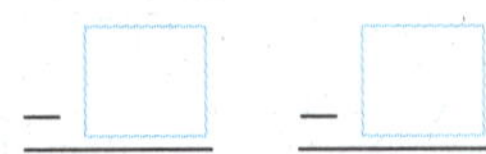

$$\begin{array}{ccccccc} -21 & -14 & -7 & 0 & 7 & 14 & 21 \end{array}$$

B. $5 \ge \dfrac{m}{-3} + 8$

$\underline{-\ \boxed{}\quad -\ \boxed{}}$ Subtract $\boxed{}$ from both sides.

$\boxed{} \ge \dfrac{m}{-3}$

$(-3)(-3) \le \dfrac{m}{-3}(-3)$ Multiply both sides by $\boxed{}$, and

$m \ge \boxed{}$ $\boxed{}$ the inequality symbol

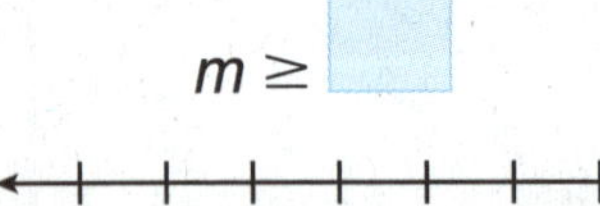

$$\begin{array}{ccccccc} -3 & 0 & 3 & 6 & 9 & 12 & 15 \end{array}$$

Holt Mathematics

Example 2

Sun-Li has \$30 to spend at the carnival. Admission is \$5, and each ride costs \$2. What is the greatest number of rides she can ride?

Let r represent the number of rides Sun-Li can ride.

$5 + 2r \le 30$

$-\boxed{} \quad -\boxed{}$ Subtract $\boxed{}$ from both sides.

$2r \le \boxed{}$

$\boxed{} \le \boxed{}$ Divide both sides by $\boxed{}$.

$r \le \boxed{}$, or $\boxed{}$

Sun-Li can ride only a whole number of rides, so the most she can ride

is $\boxed{}$.

Check It Out!

1. Solve. Then graph each solution set on a number line.

$-9x + 4 \le 31$

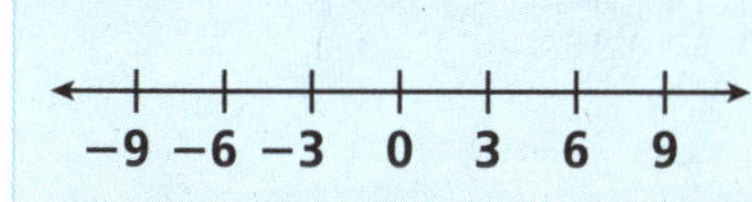

2. Brice has \$30 to take his brother and his friends to the movies. If each ticket costs \$4.00, and he must buy tickets for himself and his brother, what is the greatest number of friends he can invite?

Holt Mathematics

CHAPTER 11

Chapter Review

11-1 Solving Two-Step Equations

Solve. Check each answer.

1. $3x + 9 = 72$

2. $2q - 7 = 13$

3. $-4y + 11 = 75$

4. A salesperson earned a paycheck for $2,750. The paycheck was a $500 bonus plus a flat rate for three seminars attended. What was the salesperson's rate of pay for each seminar?

11-2 Simplifying Algebraic Expressions

Identify like terms in each list.

5. x y^2 x^4 $2y^2$ $\dfrac{x}{5}$ $4y$

6. 4 p^3 $7q$ $2q^2$ $9p^3$ 13

Simplify each expression.

7. $2e + 4f + 7e$

8. $b^2 + 2c + 9b^2 + 2$

11-3 Solving Multi-Step Equations

Solve.

9. $2y + 8 + 4y = 44$

10. $11c - 12 - 2c = 6$

11. $14 = -2x + 14 + x$

12. $3z + 4 - 6z = -20$

11-4 Solving Equations with Variables on Both Sides

Group the terms with variables on one side of the equal sign, and simplify.

13. $6x = 2x + 24$

14. $-4y + 10 = 6y$

15. $3c - 32 = -5c$

Solve.

16. $7x = 2x + 70$

17. $3p + 14 = -2p + 74$

Holt Mathematics

11-5 Inequalities

Write an inequality for each situation.

18. There are no more than 25 students in each class.

19. The height of that cliff is at least 500 feet.

Graph each compound inequality.

20. $x > 1$ or $x \leq -2$ **21.** $-2 \leq x < 3$ **22.** $4 < y \leq 7$

11-6 Solving Inequalities by Adding or Subtracting

Solve. Then graph each solution set on a number line.

23. $x + 1 < 10$ **24.** $y - 3 \geq -2$ **25.** $-12 < p - 8$

11-7 Solving Inequalities by Multiplying or Dividing

Solve.

26. $\dfrac{x}{6} < 2$ **27.** $\dfrac{y}{-2} \geq 1$ **28.** $-5y \geq 15$

29. JoAnne needs to raise $150. How many hours must she baby-sit at a rate of $4.50 per hour, in order to have enough money?

11-8 Solving Two-Step Inequalities

Solve. Then graph each solution set on a number line.

30. $3x + 3 \leq 30$ **31.** $\dfrac{y}{5} + 7 > 19$ **32.** $-15 \geq 3z + 6$

Holt Mathematics

Big Ideas

Answer these questions to summarize the important concepts from Chapter 11 in your own words.

1. Explain how to solve the equation $8x - 7 = 57$.

2. Explain how to solve the equation $4y + 9 - y = -3$.

3. Explain how to solve the equation $5z + 6 = -2z + 27$.

4. Explain how to solve the inequality $-8a \geq 32$.

5. Explain when to draw a closed circle or an open circle when graphing inequalities.

For more review of Chapter 11:

- Complete the Chapter 11 Study Guide and Review on pages 592–594 of your textbook.
- Complete the Ready to Go On quizzes on pages 570 and 588 of your textbook.

Holt Mathematics